AN ARCHAEOLOGY OF INTERACTION

AN ARCHAEOLOGY OF INTERACTION

Network Perspectives on Material Culture and Society

CARL KNAPPETT

OXFORD
UNIVERSITY PRESS

OXFORD

UNIVERSITY PRESS

Great Clarendon Street, Oxford OX2 6DP,

Oxford University Press is a department of the University of Oxford.
It furthers the University's objective of excellence in research, scholarship,
and education by publishing worldwide. Oxford is a registered trade mark of
Oxford University Press in the UK and in certain other countries

Published in the United States of America by Oxford University Press
198 Madison Avenue, New York, NY 10016, United States of America

British Library Cataloguing in Publication Data

Data available

Library of Congress Cataloging in Publication Data

Data available

ISBN 978-0-19-921545-4 (Hbk)
ISBN 978-0-19-870693-9 (Pbk)

Acknowledgements

I owe a deep debt of gratitude to Professor Jan Driessen and his wife, Florence Driessen-Gaignerot, for their warm hospitality while I was on sabbatical at Université Catholique de Louvain. I cannot thank them enough. My time in Leuven was also made very enjoyable thanks to the company and generosity of Tim and Delia Cunningham. Friday evening pizza with Ilse Schoep and Peter Tomkins was also a treat. The wonderful group of Ph.D students at Louvain-la-Neuve—Maud Devolder, Piraye Hacigüzeller, Simon Jusseret, Charlotte Langohr, and Quentin Letesson—were also incredibly welcoming and I much enjoyed the chats and chocolate. Hubert Fiasse was also generous with his time, particularly with computing matters. A good deal of this book was written in Leuven, and this would not have been possible without such fabulous support.

In Greece, where I conducted fieldwork that underwrites much of this volume, I have been immensely lucky to work in recent years with Colin Macdonald at Knossos, Irene Nikolakopoulou at Akrotiri, and Hugh Sackett, Sandy MacGillivray, and Tim Cunningham at Palaikastro.

Thanks also to many other scholars and students for their thoughts, discussion and feedback: Iro Mathioudaki, Jill Hilditch, Julien Zurbach, Wolf Niemeier, Ivonne Kaiser, Nicoletta Momigliano, Andy Bevan, Cyprian Broodbank, Todd Whitelaw, Elissa Faro, Alexandra Karetsou, Gerald Cadogan, and Jean-Claude Poursat. In the area of networks, I am immensely grateful to Ray Rivers and Tim Evans for their patience in working with an ignorant social scientist, and for their inquisitive interest in all matters concerning the prehistoric Aegean.

I cannot thank enough those who took the trouble to read earlier versions of this text and provide really invaluable feedback. Sara Angel, Andrew Bevan, Jan Driessen, Clive Gamble, Quentin Letesson, Chris Watts, thank you so much!

I am very grateful for help with images from Sean Goddard and Alexandra Makos; and to Elena Soboleva, who designed the cover.

This manuscript was completed at the University of Toronto, where I have found a very welcoming new home in the Department of Art. Thanks go to Elizabeth Legge, Gaby Sparks, Joanne Wainman, and Vicky Dingillo. In the Archaeology Centre I have enjoyed discussions with its director, Michael Chazan, and Ted Banning, Edward Swenson, Tim Harrison, and Danielle Macdonald, and with Dimitri Nakassis and Ben Akrigg from Classics.

Many thanks also to the OUP team, in particular to Dorothy McCarthy and Hilary O'Shea.

C.K.

Contents

List of figures

Part I

Interaction, Materiality, and Scale

1

Introduction:
An Archaeology of Interaction

INANIMATE INTERACTION

Every summer hundreds of archaeologists from around the world descend on Greece, joining the hundreds of archaeologists already working in the country all year round. Many devote weeks on end to the meticulous study of extensive collections of ancient objects. From monumental statues to miniscule seal-stones, from tiny scraps of sherds found on surface surveys to pristine personal accoutrements recovered from unlooted tombs: the variety of objects under study is spectacular. Some of these objects may seem quite prosaic, others more beguiling. Yet all somehow exert a powerful hold on those who study them, drawing them back over and over again for years and often decades of detailed study.

I confess to being one of these archaeologists. I study pottery—by now many thousands of pots and probably millions of fragments. Sometimes people wonder how this can continue to be attractive; I am not able to reply very convincingly. Perhaps I say something ambitious about the research questions being very important, but at heart I probably enjoy it. I am not sure how heartening it is to know that I am certainly not alone. I have senior colleagues who have been doing it for half-a-century and are still drawn back, encountering old and new finds alike with ill-concealed zeal.

How can this be? Somehow, objects get a hold of us. Yet we cannot quite admit it. On the other hand, it is considered the most natural thing in the world for us to be drawn into social interactions with other human beings. Although, as Ruth Finnegan puts it, in beginning her important book *Communicating: The Multiple Modes of Human Interconnection*, it is perhaps not all that obvious when we step back a few paces:

> Like other living creatures human beings interconnect with each other. When you come to think about it, this is actually something remarkable—that individual organisms are not isolated but have active and organised ways of connecting with

others outside themselves; that we can reach out to others beyond the covering envelopes of our own skins. (Finnegan 2002, 3)

Humans go to great lengths to make sure that they can interconnect in some systematic way, and we rarely stop and acknowledge how remarkable this is. What is even more remarkable, though, is not only that we *can* reach out to others, but that we find it difficult *not* to. Imagine the case of a person stranded alone on a desert island. Without anyone to talk to, what happens? If humans merely possess an ability to communicate, then presumably that ability is not exercised and the marooned individual in question can get along just fine. But if humans possess something more than a capacity, but rather an urgent desire to communicate and interconnect, then that desert-island scenario rapidly descends into a kind of isolationist torture. It is not difficult to sympathize with the Tom Hanks character in the film *Castaway* that presents just such a scenario. Starved of human interconnection, he makes a character of a washed up volleyball (named by him 'Wilson', the brand of volleyball), to which/whom he talks at some length, using Wilson as a sounding-board of sorts. Although fictional, this scenario nonetheless conveys the deep sense of need for interconnection that goes beyond a mere capacity.

But let's stop and think about this. Here the volleyball is presented as a kind of stopgap, making do as a proxy for interaction when no human is available. And for Wilson to function in interaction, the castaway character eventually feels a need to anthropomorphize him, painting him with a face (in his own blood). Perhaps most of us would do something similar in such an extreme situation. Yet the archaeologists studying objects in Greece do not quite find themselves in such conditions, though occasionally 'marooned' by a lack of Greek. Neither do they feel the need to anthropomorphize their objects, at least not so conspicuously. Nor, generally, do they interact with single objects, but rather with multiples. Each of these points needs addressing. But first let us look briefly at some of the evolutionary explanations that have been offered for *why* humans engage in social interactions at all.

WHY INTERACT? EVOLUTIONARY PERSPECTIVES

As Finnegan indicates, we are not the only animal species to interconnect (in ways that seem to go beyond the solely productive or reproductive). We can agree that some species are more 'social' than others: the social insects, for example, where interaction is complex (e.g. ants, termites, bees), and gestures such as the 'waggle dance' of the honeybee signal the direction of food sources. Dolphins, porpoises, and whales are also often cited as species that communicate using a range of clicking sounds, with the 'songs' of humpback whales being particularly complex (Finnegan 2002). The primates appear to be the most interactive and communicative, with vervets having three types of alarm call for different predators (Cheney and Seyfarth 1990), not to mention the fabled communicative skills of chimpanzees. Yet in each of these cases it would seem that there is a *capacity* for communication more than an urgent *desire*. Humans, then, are not only the *most* interactive, communicative species of all; they are perhaps driven to communicate like no other.

The enhanced human *capacity* for interaction and communication is usually attributed to language. This quite understandably creates approaches that are heavily biased towards the linguistic in understanding human interaction. However, evolutionary approaches aimed at establishing how and why human interaction evolved to the point it has reached today are trying to undo this privileging of language. Rather, the unique capacity for language is seen as a facet of a broader set of demands placed on early human groups in which intense social interaction was advantageous. This is known as the 'social brain' hypothesis (Dunbar and Shultz 2007). The argument is that the unusually large brains of early hominids are attributable to the computational demands of regulating numerous social relationships, rather than speech or pattern recognition. The evidence cited in support of this notion is that increasing brain size in early hominids is seen to correlate with increasing group size. Thus language becomes just another means of regulating intense social interactions, particularly pair-bonding, alongside other means such as grooming.

This functional, adaptive explanation places communication within the context of group dynamics; but this doesn't quite manage to cover the apparent drive to communicate even when the regulation of group dynamics is not an issue—as in the desert-island example. We'll come back to this. But we should, for now, certainly acknowledge the significance of embedding language in relation to gesture and other forms of communication and interaction, rather than picking it out as a unique motor for cognitive change. And it is not only in evolutionary anthropology and psychology that we see such embedding of language in other bodily practices. We can see it in sociology, such as in the work on communication by Ruth Finnegan mentioned above, and in applied linguistics, for example in the work of Charles Goodwin (1990; 1994; 2010). Goodwin examines a variety of intimate social interactions, such as conversations over the breakfast table, or exchanges between personnel on an archaeological excavation. What he brings to each of them is an awareness of the role not only of language but also of bodily gesture and material objects in together creating the particularities of each interaction.

It is not only his explicit use of archaeology as one of his case studies that should make Goodwin's work appealing to archaeologists, but also the foregrounding of objects as an active component in proximate social interactions. In some archaeological quarters the relevance of his work has been duly noted

(Malafouris and Renfrew 2010). A similar approach is pursued by Michael Schiffer, in what he dubs 'behavioral archaeology' (Schiffer and Miller 1999). This move means that we should not see ourselves as totally hamstrung by the inevitable lack of language in our objects of study (at least for the prehistorians among us). When we encounter particular combinations of artefacts in prehistoric contexts, we may still be able to reconstruct important aspects of ancient interactions, even at the micro-scale.

Goodwin's approach is interesting because its relationship to evolutionary perspectives is not hard to see, and we can imagine its application to non-human interaction too, particularly among primates. We will come back to some of these evolutionary and psychological concerns. However, now we need to consider other means for understanding the role of objects in human interactions. It turns out that archaeology has been more affected by approaches developed in ethnography and social anthropology.

MATERIAL CULTURE AND MATERIALITY

Over the last twenty years there has been a growing trend across many disciplines to give serious attention to materiality and material culture (see Hicks 2010 for an excellent recent review). The work of Danny Miller has been pivotal in much of this since the mid-1980s, providing an anthropological perspective that has been influential across sociology, archaeology, and human geography. From an initial ethnoarchaeological analysis of the role of artefacts as categories in an Indian village (Miller 1985), this work shifted towards areas traditionally tackled in sociology, that is, the industrialized West, with studies of mass consumption (1987), shopping (Miller 1998), and living-rooms in housing estates (Miller 1988; 2001). At the same time a current more firmly rooted in traditional ethnographies was also putting material culture back on the agenda (Keane 1997; Hoskins 1998; Ferme 2001).

With the work of Miller in particular, and others in the same tradition working together at University College London Anthropology (see e.g. Tilley 1999; Tilley *et al.* 2006; Buchli 2000; 2002), material culture has retaken its rightful position at the core of modern social life. Instead of being conceived as the backdrop against which human agents play out their lives (interconnectedly), very much secondary and passive in contradistinction to the primary and active humans, artefacts become key props through which sociocultural practices are enacted. The baton has been taken up in sociology (e.g. Molotch 2003; Dant 2005; Woodward 2007), archaeology (e.g. Hahn 2005; Knappett 2005; Boivin 2008), and neither should we forget the traditional focus on material culture in American 'folklore' studies (Deetz 1977; Glassie 1975; 1999).

Meanwhile, Miller has contributed to a subtle shifting of the goalposts; while 'material culture' as a term is still very much in commission (e.g. Tilley *et al.* 2006), some of the debate has reoriented around the term 'materiality' (Miller 2005; Meskell 2005). This has provoked a certain amount of debate, with some authors finding the term an unedifying neologism (Ingold 2007*a*). Though the debate is perhaps not helped by the reluctance of some to define the term (Miller 2005; 2007), it can perhaps be most easily glossed as the processes of human life that are irreducibly both social and material (Tilley 2007). Despite misgivings in some quarters, the term does seem to have the advantage of finding ready linkages with related research currents, in such varied fields as human geography, sociology, literary theory, art history, and design. These find further discussion in subsequent chapters. Suffice it to say here that, taken together, they form a bundle of innovative perspectives on material culture that hold much promise for enriching our understanding of what it means to be human in a material world.

FROM OBJECTS TO ASSEMBLAGES

Inevitably, though, this new horizon of approaches is hazy. There is not as much interaction between these different strands as there might be. Some blind-spots also are evident, at least when judged from the perspective that I seek to develop here. One such oversight is the emphasis on individual artefacts at the expense of a consideration of whole assemblages. To consider human interactions with artefacts one at a time can certainly make for a convincing story, as the *Castaway* example well shows, and as do numerous studies of the biographies of things (e.g. Hoskins 1998). However, such accounts of human interactions with individual objects do not quite apply to instances where *assemblages* are concerned, as with the archaeologists in Greece with whom we began. What is different about the ways in which *multiples* of objects get a hold on us? Somehow, approaches that do broach the terrain of multiples are not very convincing. Archaeologists, for example, cope with multiples by ordering them into typologies, defining artefactual categories that are related to one another hierarchically. These typologies can come across as absurdly asocial, as if the categories interact independently of any human presence. How else might we deal with multiples?

An approach is needed that foregrounds the relations between objects and people more effectively. I argue in this book that a powerful way to do this is through *network* thinking. This is where Actor-Network Theory (ANT) comes into play, as a wide-ranging approach that puts things on an equal footing with people in socio-material interactions (e.g. Callon 1986; Law 1992; Hetherington 1997; Thrift 2005; Latour 2005). ANT maintains that both people and things can be 'actants' in social relations, and a series of case studies has demonstrated this to great effect, looking at artefacts ranging from the low-tech, everyday end of the technological spectrum, such as speed-bumps and hotel keys, to aircraft technology and metro systems. Yet while the 'actor' component of ANT has received elaboration, the 'network' side has been more of a sleeping partner. Though there are networks in ANT, these networks are little more than a heuristic for encouraging relational thinking. Networks are extremely useful heuristic devices, and this is a significant step. However, we can convert network thinking into network analysis by thinking explicitly in terms of nodes and links, and the different topologies that networks may have and how they affect human patterns of interconnection. Network models are, I argue, powerful means for explicitly assessing connectivity between different kinds of entity, human and non-human.

FROM NETWORK THINKING TO NETWORK ANALYSIS

A particular concern I have in this volume is to take some of this theoretical work on network connectivity and wed it to more methodical approaches to space, so that we can understand the role of distributed materiality in human interconnectedness much more fully.

Fortunately, I am not starting from scratch. A burgeoning domain of interdisciplinary work exists on network modelling. Network analysis has been used for decades in sociology, but has not really been connected with ANT, for example, or indeed with any number of other interactionist approaches. It has certainly had very little impact upon archaeology, as we shall see in the following chapters. This tradition of social network analysis has received a huge boost in the last decade from the burst of activity in network theory, primarily in the physical and biological sciences, but increasingly engaging with the social sciences. I propose to draw on some of these exciting developments in exploring human interactions, although many of these models have as yet paid scant attention to themes of materiality (an important exception being Lane's 'agent-artefact space'—Lane, Pumain, and van der Leeuw 2009).

Yet these forms of network analysis, though they have certain advantages over ANT, have generally only looked at one kind of entity—usually humans *or* objects. They lack the key advantage of ANT: the commitment to treating the interactions of humans and objects symmetrically. This may be why not very much overlap seems to exist between Social Network Analysis (SNA) and ANT. But network analysis actually is capable of conveying this, even if only rarely used in this way. By combining SNA with ANT we can bring together people and things both methodologically and theoretically.

NETWORKS, SPACE, AND SCALE

Thus, from ANT we have an effective means for thinking through the distributed nature of socio-technologies and materiality. It is network thinking that can achieve a thorough decentring of human agency and the elaboration of an *enactive* approach: one proposing that humans and non-humans bring each other into being, each enacting the other, thereby locating agency between them (Law and Mol 2008). And from SNA we acquire an explicit methodology for characterizing connections. Though this has not been bi-modal, on the whole, dealing with objects and people together, it can be readily adapted so as to combine the two.

Networks offer something else. They allow us to think more explicitly about different dimensions of space, social and physical. As conceived in both ANT and SNA, network thinking and network analysis respectively provide means for thinking about social space. For ANT, technological practices are critical in the co-creation of social space, and this has been an important part of the 'spatial turn' in human geography (e.g. Soja 1996; Thrift 2005; 2006; DeSilvey 2006; 2007; Wilford 2008). Yet, however strong these approaches have been in 'spatializing' materiality, and in considering the different topological possibilities for space, the conception of space has been largely socio-technical, and only minimally 'physical' (though note Soja's concern for bringing the two together in his notion of 'thirdspace'). For archaeologists, being less caught up in these theoretical currents has had certain advantages. In archaeological thinking there is still a definite connection between 'network' and physical space, with most archaeologists probably thinking of regional distribution maps covered in 'nodes'. Although a path that may not have been much used in geography, the network as a basic method does still allow us to think through both social and physical space.

When we think about space, whether social and/or physical, we inevitably encounter the question of scale too. The spatial turn in geography and related disciplines certainly contemplates scales as well as topologies (e.g. Callon and Law 2004, 3; Thrift 2006, 139). The multi-scalar character of human existence is of central concern, as conveyed in the following quote from Edward Soja:

> Territoriality and place-making are, like synekism, different aspects of a larger, more embracing spatiality, part of what may be the most fundamental spatial attributes of human life: that we all live our lives in a multi-scale hierarchy of nodal regions that ranges from the space of the human body to the unevenly developed world of the global. There is nothing on the face of the earth (at least) that is not spatial, that is not part of socially constructed human spatiality. (Blake 2002, 154)

Yet there are different responses to the multi-scale problem. One solution is to find ways of exploring multiple scales simultaneously, without artificially subdividing the continuity of lived experience into analytical categories. This is encapsulated in the term 'glocalization', which describes the ability of individuals increasingly to operate across different scales, from the local to the global (Wellman 2001; Swyngedouw 2004). An alternative solution, however, is to recognize these trans-scale continuities and to find means of ensuring that these are respected while also using categories such as micro-, meso-, and macro-scale to facilitate analysis. This is the path taken here. And it is the concept of the network that allows for the articulation of these scales, as networks can exist at any scale, from neural networks to global networks. I therefore argue that network approaches facilitate the articulation of different scales of interaction that has so far proven elusive in archaeological method and theory (and indeed in the social sciences generally).

So to summarize, networks offer us a number of important methodological advantages. First, they force us to consider *relations* between entities. This makes them good for thinking about assemblages and their interactions. Secondly, they are inherently spatial, with the flexibility to be both social and physical. Thirdly, networks are a strong method for articulating scales. Fourthly, networks can incorporate both people and objects. And last but not least, more recent network analysis incorporates a temporal dimension that means networks can begin dynamically to unravel the complexities of how spatial patterns are generated by processes over time. These last two points are particularly advantageous as far as archaeology is concerned.

These five qualities of networks lend them analytical power. But these qualities have further implications, not just for analysis but for human experience. The combination of people and objects across scales is arguably a more general social phenomenon. Although there is a tendency to think about people–object interactions at the micro-scale, as with the *Castaway* case, or the archaeologist with his or her Greek pots, objects act at many scales. As objects proliferate, some inevitably spill out beyond the confines of proximate social interaction, becoming physically absent albeit potentially cognitively present. The capacity for an object to act as a kind of marker of a non-present space (and time) gives materiality a very potent role, *enabling* humans to exist across scales. This is a key part of the argument in this book, and owes a debt to arguments developed by Clive Gamble, oriented around the idea of the 'release from proximity'. We can now examine these arguments, focused largely on early prehistory.

BACK TO EVOLUTION

Perhaps ironically, the strictures of the Palaeolithic have encouraged some clear thinking when it comes to thinking about scale. Clive Gamble (1998; 1999; 2007) has developed a network perspective on the different scales of human interaction in our evolutionary past, and raises many questions that I will be reprising, albeit with much later material, through the course of this book. One of the primary questions he tackles is that unique facet of human interaction— the ability to transcend the face-to-face and to interact across distances, both spatial and temporal. This is what has been dubbed the 'release from proximity', a term coined in evolutionary anthropology/psychology (Quiatt and Reynolds 1993, 141). Gamble develops this idea further by arguing that it is material culture that in large part facilitates this release from the limitations of face-to-face interaction (Gamble 1998; 1999, 40–1; 2007). He is concerned with identifying the processes in human evolution that encouraged this develop-ment, creating the uniquely human capacity to think and act across spatial and temporal scales (see also Read and van der Leeuw 2008, 1966).

Gamble exemplifies this in reaching across wide regions and across many millennia in his work on the Palaeolithic societies of Europe (Gamble 1999). Indeed, as a discipline archaeology habitually works across many scales, both through space and time. Yet this scale-shifting tends to be implicit and intui-tive—we might discuss household distribution patterns in one breath, before moving on to regional distribution patterns in the next, without much thought as to how the one relates to the other. This reluctance to explicitly demarcate our scales of analysis may be due to their association with the early system-atizing outlook of processual archaeology, with David Clarke spelling out at some length distinct analytical scales, from the micro- to the macro- (Clarke 1972). Explicit consideration of scale seems still to remain rather rare, with occasional exception (e.g. Lock and Molyneaux 2006). Explicit or not, archae-ologists ought to think through the hows and whys of human interconnected-ness across considerable time-depth, and between extensive spatial regions. More significantly still, archaeology has to find ways to articulate many differ-ent scales, from the micro-scale of human interaction (e.g. daily, face-to-face) through to the macro-scale of the *longue durée* and the inter-regional interac-tions among assemblages of humans and things.

Much work needs to be done, following Gamble's lead, in exploring *how* we as humans act and interact across different scales—with materiality as a key factor in this process. But there is the equally enthralling question of *why* we should interact beyond the face-to-face. Some scholars have been content to tackle the how of human communication without speculating as to the why (Finnegan 2002). Gamble (2007) begins to address the question in terms of identity, and Dunbar in terms of coping with size of social groups (1996). Yet the question of the why of human interaction—in all its networked, multi-scalar materialized complexity—has not been posed with sufficient regularity or clarity. This brings us back to the distinction made earlier in this chapter between capacity and desire: it is not only that humans have particular capacities for interconnecting; they seem driven to do so almost regardless of any functional advantage that may or may not be conferred. This could certainly fit in broad terms with Gamble's notion of identity being a crucial goal of interconnectedness. We can even think back to the start of the chapter and how archaeologists feel compelled to return to their assemblages of study year after year. A large part of the reason is not the objects themselves, but how their study makes the archaeologist part of a wider social community. Ongoing participation in this distributed socio-material community becomes a fundamental dynamic in the archaeologist's identity.

OBJECTS AND NETWORKS: THE BLINDSIDE

At the same time, however, the archaeologist is not entirely in control. The artefacts do exercise their own pull. Perhaps the archaeologist does not fully understand why he or she keeps on coming back. Humans abdicate some degree of control over their drive to interconnect as soon as they involve material culture. Things establish themselves in ways that are not entirely comprehensible, and they exert a powerful hold on human social and cognitive dynamics. This seemingly paradoxical assertion is starting to receive fuller exploration in fields such as 'thing theory' (see the following chapters), with scholars asking what pictures and objects 'want' of us (Mitchell 2005; Gosden 2005).

When this logic is extended across broader scales, the implication is that the socio-material networks humans establish in the release from proximity are far from stable and under their control. If neat object categories are resisted, then neat network interactions are probably resisted too. There are gaps and empty spaces in networks between the nodes and links. The network is just one topology that cannot address all the variability and mess out there in the world. Hence scholars have argued for other topologies, such as 'meshworks' (Ingold 2007*b*) or 'gels' (Sheller 2004). Such topologies might unfold at different scales and see quite different material arrangements. Yet while these are sometimes proposed as alternatives to networks, I think we need to try to imagine the coexistence of different topologies. In the same way that an artefact can be simultaneously obedient and recalcitrant, both fitting into the archaeologist's schemes while also resisting them in some details, so can the wider socio-physical spaces exhibit both properties. I argue in the latter part of the book that it is more fruitful to work with this tension rather than denying it.

SUMMARY AND BOOK STRUCTURE

Beyond Gamble's groundbreaking work, mostly in connection with early human societies, there is actually very little systematic scholarly attention given to the role of material culture in human interaction (see also the critique in Schiffer and Miller 1999). There may exist any number of theories about human interaction that rely on linguistic models, but these seem destined to be partial and incomplete given the ubiquity of material culture in human societies. It may seem odd that across the width and breadth of the social sciences there is such a lack of dynamic interactionist perspectives that incorporate materiality; but there are perhaps some deep-seated structural reasons why this is so, which will be addressed in Chapter 2.

In Chapter 3 the focus turns to network approaches and how they might provide the basis for a more satisfactory interactionist perspective. Network approaches in different disciplines, such as anthropology and geography, are briefly reviewed, as is the relative lack of network methods in archaeology. I provide a synopsis of some of the key characteristics of networks and how they can be utilized in archaeology.

Moving from Part I of the book (Chapters 1–3) to Part II (Chapters 4–6), the focus shifts to a multi-scale analysis of materiality. Chapters 4 to 6 cover micro-, meso-, and macro-scale interactions respectively. In each chapter I use archaeological case studies from a particular time and place: the Bronze Age of Crete, often called 'Minoan' Crete after the mythical King Minos. This choice is partly because it is my own area of specialization, but also because it presents an interesting case of the conjunction of material and social differentiation across different scales. In particular, we see the enactment of new forms of connectivity between agents and artefacts, in practices of production, distribution, and consumption, and these are strongly implicated in the rise of 'palatial' society, with centralized elite buildings having strong economic, social, and political influence over large towns and territories.

The capacity for achieving political control over social practices across multiple scales derives, I argue, from a new approach to relations with the artefact world that may stretch far back in time to the beginnings of the Neolithic (cf. Gamble 2007), but which ratchets up in the Bronze Age; it is an approach that might be dubbed, ironically enough, 'network thinking', such that relationships between agents and artefacts are increasingly objectified and systematized (see also Read 2010, on the shift from experiential to classificatory means for understanding kin relations). This process creates assemblages that can 'occupy' space and time more explicitly, creating a more structured 'agent-artefact space' (Lane, Pumain, and van der Leeuw 2009). This in turn can then form the basis for subsequent ratcheted changes, since such an objectified assemblage space makes it easier to institutionalize innovations.

This pertains to what has been dubbed 'the innovation innovation' (Read, Lane, and van der Leeuw 2009). What this book does is cautiously identify some of the early stages in the development of the kind of network thinking that this study itself uses as an analytical tool.

Then, in Part III (Chapters 7–9), I move from questions of *how* humans interact to ask *why* they interact. Finnegan chooses to ask only how and not why. Gamble implies that human interaction is directed, over the very long term, towards constructing *identity*. There is not a single answer, so I explore three alternatives (not mutually exclusive). In Chapter 7 I consider how networks of objects function, and the benefits they bring. Chapter 8 considers the flipside of this—the costs of object networks—particularly in terms of the opacity of things that they fail to capture. In Chapter 9 the focus falls on time, and the ways in which the exercise of 'biographical care' can help to ensure a balance in the flicker between objects and things, and perhaps ultimately contribute to long-term resilience in human interactions.

In each chapter I keep on coming back to archaeology for my case studies. Why? Archaeology does not have a monopoly on the need to 'activate' material culture, but it is strongly felt in a discipline that comes up against a vast range and quantity of material culture and little else to mark past social interconnectedness. We desperately need a much broader suite of ideas—achieved by drawing upon various disciplines—about the nature of human interaction with material culture, and the role of artefacts in scaffolding interactions. Furthermore, archaeology confronts a wide range of past societies, from 'simple' to 'complex', at a global scale. Any interactionist perspective developed from an archaeological perspective has to take into account a wide range of parameters, and thus has a reasonable chance of having some applicability to the social sciences more broadly. Thus, an 'archaeology' of interaction is not meant to be limited to archaeology, but to encompass the contribution that archaeology can make to an understanding of social interactions across a range of scales.

I hope, then, that this volume can provide some new viewpoints on the interactive capacities and drives that are such decisive features of the human condition. And if it can help explain why I cannot resist those ancient Greek vases and sherds that exercise their hold on me year after year, so much the better!

2

Interaction, Space, and Scale

Archaeology, as with all the social sciences, inevitably deals with human interactions. Different approaches may, however, be more or less explicit in their conceptualization of relationships; and they may favour certain forms, or operate at specific scales. Bearing in mind the great range of possible interactions in human societies, it is hardly surprising that no unified approach has emerged. This chapter cannot hope to provide a comprehensive account of approaches to interaction in archaeology and the social sciences. It seeks merely to outline some broad trends, examining in particular why network approaches have only received very partial exposure in some areas. This will set the ground for an assessment of network approaches in the following chapter.

NEW GEOGRAPHY, NEW ARCHAEOLOGY: INTERACTIONS IN SPACE

There are many different kinds and levels of interaction. But ask a group of archaeologists what 'interaction' means to them and the chances are they will think of a distribution map, showing the distribution of settlements or artefact types across a region.[1] A typical example is shown in Figure 2.1, taken from the work of O. G. S. Crawford, the first editor of the journal *Antiquity*. The pattern of the distribution would then be taken to represent some human process of interaction: a certain distribution pattern of artefact types might suggest exchange interactions, while another might suggest the sharing of ideas between neighbours (also a form of interaction). A particular settlement pattern might be indicative of a settlement hierarchy, again implying certain interaction processes between communities. Thus a basic archaeological

---

[1] 'The distribution map lies behind some of the most central themes in archaeology such as trade, diffusion and culture' (Hodder and Orton 1976; 1).

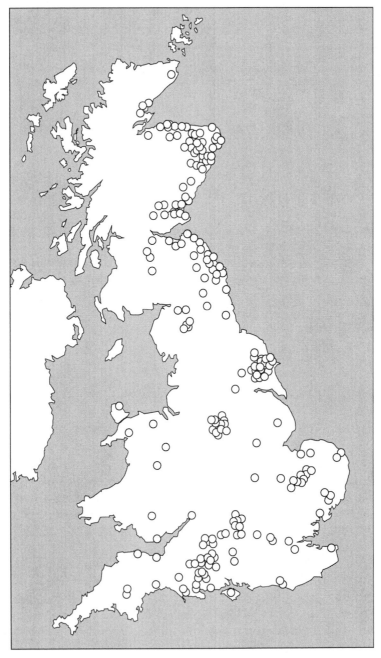

Figure 2.1. An archaeological distribution map, for Early Bronze Age Beakers

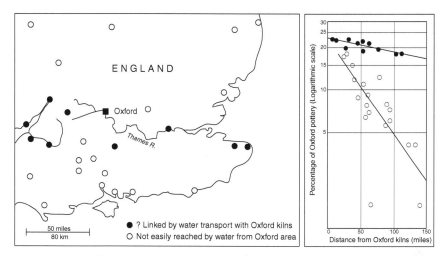

Figure 2.2. Hodder's work on Roman pottery distribution in southern Britain

understanding of interaction could be said to have two characteristics: it takes place within an absolute physical space, without altering the nature of that space, and it occurs at the macro-scale.

Distribution maps were a feature of the discipline from its early days (Crawford 1912; 1922; Willey 1953; Green and Haselgrove 1978, xxii). However, it was only with the New Archaeology of the 1960s and early 1970s that the *processes* underlying these patterns were systematically sought.[2] And it was the New Geography that was the greatest influence in this regard, with David Clarke drawing explicitly on the work of Chorley and Haggett, for example.[3] Their work aimed to interpret spatial patterns through techniques such as locational analysis, Thiessen polygons, point pattern analysis, and central place theory. This largely Cambridge-based move was continued in the mid-1970s by both Hodder and Renfrew, the former working on distributions of Roman pottery in southern Britain (see Figure 2.2), the latter on obsidian distribution in the Aegean.[4]

Yet these forms of spatial analysis in archaeology rarely used networks (even though today one can still encounter archaeologists talking about 'networks' when in fact all they have in front of them are distribution maps). This might seem odd, given the strong links between New Archaeology and New Geography, and the fact that network techniques were certainly in prominent

[2] Johnson 1977.

[3] Clarke 1968; 1972; 1977; Chorley and Haggett 1967; see review in Green and Haselgrove 1978.

[4] Hodder 1974*a*; *b*; 1978; Hodder and Orton 1976; Renfrew 1969; 1975; see also Kohl 1975, for an American perspective. Also Hammond 1972 and Flannery 1972 on settlement interactions, discussed in Smith 2003, 123–4.

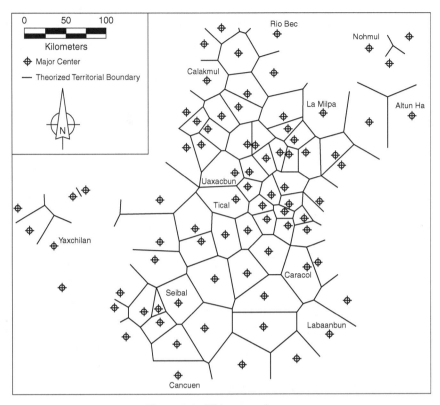

Figure 2.3. Thiessen polygons

use in the latter. What might explain this reticence towards networks in early processual archaeology, even at the regional scale?[5] It seems that one reason may be that archaeologists would rather not conceive of geographical connections as links but rather in terms of interaction 'zones' (see Smith 2005; Jennings 2006). If we look at the use of distribution maps of settlements (e.g. Willey 1953), one might imagine it to be a natural step to view the interactions between settlements in network terms. However, this does not seem to be what happens. A different conception of space is applied, one that seeks to define zones around sites, with interactions between sites occurring at the boundaries between these zones. We can see this, for example, in the approach of Hammond (1972) to interaction among Classic Maya settlements: he applies a Thiessen polygon lattice, as seen in Figure 2.3 (see discussion in Smith 2003, 123–4; and note the exception to this, in Flannery 1972, who *does* draw direct lines between sites—see Figure 2.4).

---

[5] Though see Irwin-Williams 1977 for an early exception.

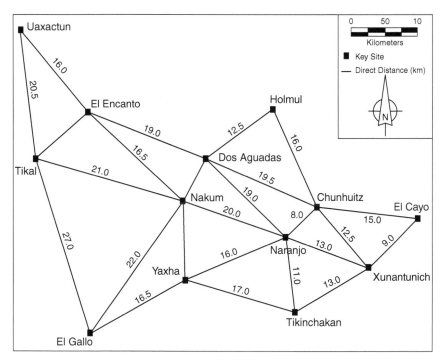

Figure 2.4. Nearest neighbour array

The reluctance of archaeologists to use networks, even in the availability of network ideas in closely related disciplines (see also work of Barnes 1972 in social anthropology), is intriguing. Yet somehow network thinking never really crossed these disciplinary lines except for the occasional small-scale, cross-border raid. One exception, for example, is Dickens's use of simple graph theory to analyse domestic architectural space, in effect an early form of space syntax (Dickens 1977; note his only bibliography is a key work in geography on networks, Haggett and Chorley 1969). An early paper on space syntax by Hillier and colleagues (from architecture/urban planning) also appears in an edited collection the year after, accompanied by a trenchant critique from the anthropologist Edmund Leach (Hillier *et al.* 1978; Leach 1978). Yet, according to one review (Wheatley and Gillings 2002), this very limited use of basic network ideas has barely extended any further since. It is argued that 'the use of networks has tended to be restricted to the analysis of domestic spaces, as exemplified by Hillier and Hanson's "Social Logic of Space" approach (Hillier and Hanson 1984)' (Wheatley and Gillings 2002, 135). Despite these early forays, it is indeed surprising that there has in the meantime been only sporadic application in archaeology (exceptions are Foster 1989; Banning 1996; Cutting 2003; Brusasco 2004; Letesson 2007), given the successful development of space syntax in architecture and urban planning (see Hillier 1996; 2005; Batty 2004). But Wheatley and Gillings do not go much further; their book *Spatial Technology and Archaeology* has barely two pages devoted to network ideas, and states that 'archaeologists have shown a very limited interest in networks as a medium for formal analysis of spatial relationships' (2002, 135).

Certainly, one might have expected a new phase of network analysis in archaeology in concert with the rapid growth in Geographical Information Systems (GIS). Indeed, another more recent review of GIS in archaeology (Conolly and Lake 2006) has a whole chapter on networks. Nonetheless, they too begin by expressing their surprise that network analysis has not seen more use in the field, particularly as 'the bulk of archaeological data is ultimately point based' (Conolly and Lake 2006, 234). They go on to distinguish between 'pure', 'flow', and 'transportation' networks, as well as discussing different means for analysing them (e.g. path length, clustering coefficients). Conolly and Lake are very much aware of the different scales at which analysis of network *structure* has been conducted in archaeology, providing examples at the regional scale, and of individual buildings (for example, space syntax, mentioned above, as well as measures of intervisibility). They also move beyond network structure to consider what might be called network *function* (see Newman 2006), though they talk in terms of 'location on networks' and 'routing on networks' (Conolly and Lake 2006, 248–52). The former concerns the relationship between network location and the allocation of resources in the network (and hence dubbed location-allocation models); the more central nodes in network terms may also be the ones that are more intensively used (Bell and Church 1985; Gorenflo and Bell 1991; Mackie 2001). As for 'routing on networks', this has found almost no use in archaeological GIS, but includes questions such as the 'travelling salesman problem', that is, how to find the most efficient path through a network with a particular function in mind (though see Chapter 6 below for an account of recent developments in this domain). Conolly and Lake also cover 'least-cost path analysis', which is used as a means of predicting routes.

It is not as if archaeologists never use the term 'network'. It is such a common and adaptable word that its use is perhaps inevitable, implicit, and intuitive. Every archaeologist has probably written loosely of 'social networks', 'trade networks', or 'interaction networks'. Yet more formal analysis of networks—the definition of which is no more than 'a set of items . . . with connections between them' (Newman 2003*a*, 168)—has barely featured in archaeological method and theory, as both Wheatley and Gillings (2002) and Conolly and Lake (2006) underline.[6] Both of these overviews recognize the use

---

[6] Some of the work of Gamble (1998; 1999) being a notable exception.

of graphs to understand 'space syntax' at the micro-level, though only Conolly and Lake see fit to tackle the application of network ideas to questions of regional interactions. Yet, they give the impression that the use of network ideas has been just as sporadic at the macro-scale as it has at the micro-level. If we look, though, at the study of island interactions we can see how network thinking has been used quite frequently, and in particular one area of graph theory known as Proximal Point Analysis (e.g. Hage and Harary 1991; Broodbank 2000). One should cite here the work of a number of island archaeologists working on colonization patterns in Oceania (e.g. Terrell 1977; Hunt 1988; Irwin 1992; Kirch 1997). This approach to regional interaction can in very general terms be traced back to Malinowski's ethnographic work on the Kula ring (Malinowski 1922), itself reworked using graph theory by Hage and Harary (1991; 1996). Although Harary was a leading mathematician in graph theory, generally the techniques employed are simple. Mention might also be made of Jack Davis's work on the centrality of Delos among Ionian city states in the Aegean, an early and somewhat isolated example of such work in the Mediterranean (Davis 1982). This was followed in the Aegean, though not explicitly, by the work of Broodbank on the Early Bronze Age Cyclades (Broodbank 1993; 2000).[7] He used proximal point analysis to assess the probable location of central sites in the Cycladic archipelago, to considerable effect.[8]

While Conolly and Lake do make the significant step of tackling regional network analysis, their examples are focused on GIS applications (naturally, in a 'manual' covering GIS in archaeology). But when one considers some of the examples cited above, which use network thinking but without GIS, then it emerges that there is a wider use of network ideas than they anticipate. Furthermore, they do not have the opportunity to assess the interaction between the different scales at which network analysis is conducted in archaeology, from households at one extreme, at the micro-scale, up to supra-regional networks at the other. While it should be possible in theory to link them up, they are not currently interconnected, and the continuing blind-spot archaeologists in general have for networks means these different scales are unlikely to be joined up in the near future.

A more substantive concern is that archaeologists are wedded to a geometric, Euclidean conception of space when thinking about connections (with Conolly and Lake 2006 as a notable exception). While having the twin advantages of being both rigorous and process-oriented, the approach

---

[7] Although Patton, in his book *Islands in Time* (1996), has a chapter titled 'Networks of interaction in Mediterranean island prehistory', his networks are distribution maps, i.e. the nodes are depicted but not the links.

[8] For land- and river-based examples of network analysis, see Peregrine's work on Cahokia (1991), and Jenkins on Inka road networks (2001).

'sublimates' space, making it into a homogenous container in which interaction occurs (Smith 2003, 30–77). Ironically, a fuller exploration of network methods may have led to the realization that networks are very capable of representing connections in *relational* space too, as is apparent in much social network analysis.[9] However, a more potent use of network ideas was never realized, as the reaction against the limitations of geometric spatial analysis led to a rejection of the formal study of relations altogether. In archaeology, this rather belatedly followed the spatial turn in geography.

INTERACTION IN GEOGRAPHY: THE SPATIAL TURN

The critique in geography of geometric approaches to space was not long in coming. Having published in 1969 one of the key texts on spatial analysis, David Harvey changed tack dramatically just a few years later with a move towards a more relational approach (Harvey 1969; 1973; Blake 2002, 143). This soon developed into a substantial and sustained critique of geometric approaches in geography (e.g. Olsson 1974; Harvey 1996; Thrift 1996; Hetherington 1997). The relational or 'topological' perspective that emerged, in which it is maintained that human practices create space rather than simply occurring within its confines, now dominates the field (e.g. Law 2002; Murdoch 2005; Massey 2005; Thrift 2006). Nonetheless, some see in this rise to prominence the problematic emergence of a 'bicameral' view of space, a split between geometric and relational perspectives (Soja 1996; Blake 2002, 141). Soja has advocated instead the development of a mediated perspective sitting between these two, what he calls 'thirdspace'.

It is interesting that this seismic shift in geography—away from physical interactions towards social ones—somehow escaped the attention of archaeology. It is as if the geography landlords pulled the rug out from underneath the feet of their archaeology tenants just as they were settling in. This is commented on very perceptively at the time by Green and Haselgrove (1978), in the introduction to an edited volume resulting from a conference, held in Cambridge in 1977, designed expressly to examine the interfaces between archaeology, geography, and anthropology. These authors are indeed aware of the major developments afoot in geography:

> a number of geographers have felt the need to break away from deterministic modes of analysis by reducing the degree of emphasis placed on the geometric outcomes of the spatial 'game' and instead focusing on the structures of thought

---

[9] Note again the exception of Gamble (1998; 1999), one of the few archaeologists to draw upon the domain of social network analysis.

and action which govern the behaviour of the individual actor in this game. In their opinion, spatial analysis has become a prisoner of its mode of reasoning founded in Cartesian logic, in which the ambiguity of human actions was negated in favour of the certainty of spatial form (Olsson 1974) . . . (Green and Haselgrove 1978, xi)

They go on to say that geography is in an incoherent state (in the mid-1970s), geographers 'united only in a common, often frantic, search for a social theory of spatial form' (1978, xii). Among these they cite Harvey 1973, which of course eventually emerges as a key work in the 'spatial turn' (Blake 2004). They also pick out three approaches of particular influence and promise: Marxism, structuralism, and phenomenology. Yet they are quite aware that this attack on positivist methodology is occurring unbeknownst to most archaeologists, citing Clarke (1977) as an example of the 'current enthusiasm for spatial analysis among archaeologists' (Green and Haselgrove 1978, xiii).[10]

Thus the geographical understanding of human interaction underwent a fundamental shift away from geometric towards relational approaches. This has been mirrored in archaeology, but with a considerable delay, more on which below in the section 'Post-processual approaches'.

INTERACTION IN SOCIAL ANTHROPOLOGY

Within the brief confines of this overview it is naturally impossible to do justice to the complexities of interactionist approaches in such a vast field as geography, or indeed anthropology for that matter. But in very broad terms it seems fair to say that if, in geography, interactionist approaches had initially given attention to physical space and the macro-scale, the same does not hold true for social anthropology, which has more generally concerned itself with relational space and the micro- to meso-scales. In other words, the focus has been on social relations at the proximate and community levels, as seen in the foundational ethnographic studies on such matters as kinship and exchange relations. This can be traced back to Durkheim, who was concerned with the integrative function of social relations and their particular structural properties (Maryanski and Turner 1991; also Orser 2005). While the functionalism of Durkheim was left behind, the structuralist tendencies were further developed, in two strands, British and French structuralism respectively (Maryanski and Turner 1991).

---

[10] Also note Blake's (2004) review of this process in geography and archaeology (and cf. Earle and Preucel 1987), and her use of the term 'spatial turn' to describe it.

On the one hand, British structuralism is represented principally in the work of Radcliffe-Brown (1940), dubbed 'structural functionalism', although arguably the structuralist side was more to the fore than the functionalist (Maryanski and Turner 1991). On the other, French structuralism finds a connection through Marcel Mauss to Lévi-Strauss. Yet while the former stays true to Durkheim's notion of 'social facts', the idea that the primary social categories are those of interrelatedness in groups ('it was because men were grouped, and thought of themselves in the form of groups, that in their ideas they grouped other things', Durkheim and Mauss 1903, 82–4), the latter turns this idea on its head to argue that innate mental classifications precede social ones (Maryanski and Turner 1991). It is French structuralism that has had the broader intellectual impact, perhaps through the Lévi-Straussian connection with linguistic analysis.

Yet, for present purposes, it is the British school of structural analysis that is more relevant, as it maintained a commitment to a view of the social world as composed of positions and relations, requiring Durkheimian analysis in terms of their nature, number, and mode of combination (Maryanski and Turner 1991, 113). This subsequently developed into a tradition of structural analysis using network methods (Barnes 1954; 1972; Bott 1971 [orig. pub. 1957]; Lesser 1961; Mitchell 1974). J. A. Barnes used network ideas in his study of a Norwegian island parish (1954). Elizabeth Bott conducted an in-depth ethnographic analysis of twenty families in London in the 1950s to see the effects of different kinds of network connections on family life. James Clyde Mitchell worked on social networks in Central African towns. However, as we shall see in the following chapter, these groundbreaking ethnographic contributions have been largely overlooked in the current renaissance of network analysis.

Furthermore, this British tradition of network analysis seems to have had little discernible impact on New Archaeology, even though it was blossoming at about the same time and even earlier. For example, Barnes's 1972 *Social Networks* was published the same year as Clarke's *Models in Archaeology*.[11] In its commitment to a positivistic analysis of structure, at least, this tradition might well have suited processual archaeology. But the New Archaeology, in its British guise, appears to have had its eye on geography rather than social anthropology. This could be because the anthropological perspective on interaction was not particularly geometric and thus did not sit easily with the focus on regional distribution patterns and processes. Instead, the emphasis in their network analysis was on interaction as a social rather than physical phenomenon, and thus was based upon a 'topological' rather than 'geometric' understanding of space. This tradition of social network analysis has

---

[11] One exception is Hodder and Orton 1976, who briefly cite Barnes.

continued, and has recently undergone something of a boom; but it continues to have surprisingly little effect in archaeology (see Chapter 3).

POST-PROCESSUAL APPROACHES

Indeed, it could be argued that anglophone archaeological theory picked up on the French rather than the British strain of structuralism. Particularly when coupled subsequently with Saussurean semiotics, French structuralism and post-structuralism had a profound impact on archaeological theory in the 1980s and 1990s (e.g. Hodder 1982; Shanks and Tilley 1987; Bapty and Yates 1990; Tilley 1990). This influence came into archaeology through social theory and philosophy more than through anthropology, via Ricoeur, Barthes, Derrida, and Foucault, among others. These developments were not, however, particularly focused on new conceptualizations of space. One exception can be found in Thomas (1993), who uses both social theory and geography in a paper entitled 'The Hermeneutics of Megalithic Space'. He also draws upon Heidegger, a move that is crucial in opening up archaeological approaches to space and landscape to the influence of phenomenology (see also Thomas 2004).

Hence the critique of spatial absolutism that occurred in geography did eventually hit archaeology too, but with the customary time-delay (cf. Green and Haselgrove 1978; Earle and Preucel 1987; Blake 2004). Relational perspectives on space as 'place' came to the fore through this opening up towards phenomenology, instigated by Thomas and Tilley (Thomas 1993; Tilley 1994; also Gosden 1994; see review by Brück 2005, and also Johnson 2006, 125–30). However, it seems that this theoretical shift in the conception of space was facilitated, perhaps unconsciously, by a downsizing in *scale*, from that of the region to the individual site or, particularly, monument. British Neolithic monuments, especially, emerge as places (Brück 2005, 62). The focus of post-processual approaches is very much on interactions at the micro-scale; furthermore, these interactions are conceived relationally (topological) rather than absolutely (geometric). This has meant that there are now more dynamic accounts of the construction of place, but they are concentrated at one scale. The effects of the post-processual critique have not been felt at the macro-scale, where regional interactions continue to be 'mapped' geometrically.[12] There is thus a polarization of topology and geometry that goes hand in hand with a split between the micro-scale and the macro-scale respectively. Archaeologists, it seems, have become very selective about the kinds of interactions in

---

[12] Note that in the New Archaeology Clarke's approach was explicitly multi-scale, describing micro-, semi-micro-, and macro-levels (Clarke 1977).

which they are interested. Moreover, in those cases where different scales are considered, they are done so either from the top-down or the bottom-up, two scenarios which will be assessed in turn.

TRAVERSING SCALES: TOP-DOWN

Some archaeologists are of the opinion that both processual and post-processual approaches are too focused on a limited scale, that of the local (Kristiansen and Larsson 2005, 30). These authors argue that such problems in dealing with interaction across scales are remedied by a world-systems perspective, that can 'account for the interaction between local, regional and global or macro-historical changes in later prehistory' (ibid. 6). Yet while their intentions are extremely positive, and their realization of a lack of articulation between scales in archaeological theory is significant, their novel theoretical construct falls short.

First, their focus on *institutions* as the building-blocks of society overlooks a more basic scale of interaction at the micro-level, that of person-to-person (see Chapter 4). Secondly, they conceive the relationship between institutions and material culture hierarchically, such that institutions find themselves materialized in artefacts (and in this they follow DeMarrais, Castillo, and Earle 1996). This denies the 'enactive' role of material culture, a perspective increasingly to the fore in material culture studies (see Knappett and Malafouris 2008; Law and Mol 2008). Thirdly, their theoretical strategy for understanding interaction sees a kind of bricolage of Hodder's early ethnoarchaeological work on micro-level interactions and the role of material culture therein (Hodder 1982), with Sherratt's (e.g. 1997) macro-level work 'on the diffusion of economic and ritual practices and their implications for local transformations during the Neolithic of Europe' (Kristiansen and Larsson 2005, 25). These bottom-up and top-down approaches are lashed together in the hope that they will meet somewhere in the middle, ably fortified by a bit of strapping from Renfrew, in the form of his work with Cherry on peer-polity interaction (Renfrew and Cherry 1986).

Kristiansen and Larsson are not the only archaeologists to develop such a perspective. 'World-systems theory', or 'world-systems analysis', as Kardulias and Hall (2008) call it, is an approach that a number of scholars have sought to develop from the original formulation by Wallerstein. And though these authors quite justifiably point out that world-systems analysis has been subject to misconceptions, and remains a robust approach to regional analysis, problems nonetheless remain. It has not shown itself capable of reaching down to levels below that of the institution, and so seems incapable of multi-scalar analysis of the sort envisaged here. Furthermore, it disappoints in the rather vague way in which it depicts space. Boundaries need to be drawn between centre, semi-periphery, and periphery areas, but this is not always a straightforward process. When core–periphery models are applied to the ancient Mediterranean of the Archaic and Classical periods, for example, sometimes 'the core' is reckoned to be just Greece, sometimes the entire Mediterranean (Arafat and Morgan 1994, 131).[13] As these authors state, there are problems with either definition. We see here the manifestation of a broader problem: the tendency to conceive of geometric space in terms of areas. It is the same logic, essentially, as that used in locational analysis and in the drawing of Thiessen polygons. In the case of world-systems analysis, one space (the core) rubs against another space (the periphery, with or without a semi-periphery).[14] Thus, although world-systems analysis does make spatial relationships central to its understanding of political power (Smith 2003, 100–1), space is nonetheless constructed in absolute, geometric terms as a kind of container. What it does do, however, is acknowledge the existence of different kinds of container (that is, core space and peripheral space), so space is not homogeneous. In this it does add an extra level of sophistication when compared with much of the New Archaeology.

Despite its ambitious claims, doubts therefore remain concerning the capacity of world-systems theory/analysis, and related interactionist approaches such as those of Sherratt, or Kristiansen and Larsson, to traverse scales effectively. Some hope is offered, however, in a recent contribution from Stein (2002), who critiques the dominance of world-systems theory as the main approach for tackling interregional interaction (see also Stein 2005). Rather than assuming that the interregional level determines lower organizational levels, Stein seeks an interregional approach that does attend to different scales, and which allows for interaction to be generated from the bottom-up as well as top-down. Studies of regional interaction, he argues, need not only to be multi-scalar (here also citing Lightfoot, Martinez, and Schiff 1998), but also to recognize the heterogeneity of complex societies. Stein's perspective is very promising in its attempt to do justice to a range of scales, though there is certainly scope for further methodological development concerning the actual interlinking of micro-, meso-, and macro-scales. He does mention 'networks' of interaction on occasion (Stein 2002, 906), but in little more than colloquial usage, principally to break up the notion of set core and peripheries (networks can cross-cut them). Nonetheless, in this book I shall recommend a more

---

[13] There are, however, those who believe world-systems approaches nonetheless have much to offer when it comes to studying the ancient Mediterranean, e.g. Sherratt 1995; Sherratt and Sherratt 1991; 1998.

[14] This conceptualization of space as interacting areas is also seen in similar work on the Aegean Bronze Age by Berg (1999). Note that although she talks of 'networks', her areas of interaction do not depict either links or nodes (as one might expect of a 'network').

explicit development of network thinking to accomplish such multi-scalar analyses.

While Stein successfully critiques the failings of world-systems theory in relation to analytical scales, he addresses himself rather less to the spatial assumptions inherent in the approach. The baton is taken up by Jennings (2006), who argues that even those who have critiqued world-systems theory have done so without challenging the 'underlying architecture', which is that of a radial model (Jennings 2006, 347).[15] He suggests that there are three deficiencies in the radial model: the neglect of regionalism, the accentuation of core–periphery relations and the assumption of certain structural links. These points do hit the mark, and it seems clear that interregional interactions are wed to a geometric conception of space; nonetheless, we still need explicit methods to challenge these embedded assumptions more successfully. A much clearer thinking through of the huge possible range of spatial arrangements is demanded.

TRAVERSING SCALES: BOTTOM-UP

Other approaches that are alert to the problem of multiple scales begin from the bottom and work up. Yet they are potentially faced with the inverse problem of top-down approaches: of never quite managing to be convincing when it comes to the analytical scales furthest from their starting-point. One such micro-scale perspective is known as *symbolic interactionism*, a term coined by Herbert Blumer in the 1960s, and derived from American pragmatism (G. H. Mead). Erving Goffman is also often, and debatably, labelled a symbolic interactionist; he nonetheless developed a micro-sociology focused on face-to-face interaction (Goffman 1959; 1967). This is continued in the work of the 'everyday life' or '*quotidien*' perspective of scholars such as Certeau (1984), Lefebvre (1991), and Bachelard (1964).[16] A very general criticism is that approaches of this kind are unable to deal with social-structure and macro-sociological issues.

But perhaps it is simply that these works did not overly concern themselves with traversing analytical scales. Other more recent 'bottom-up' approaches in both anthropology and archaeology do appear to be more alert to the need to move across scales. One example, here selected because of its explicit debt to the work of Certeau mentioned above, is Marianne Ferme's study of violence and the everyday in Sierra Leone (Ferme 2001). She explicitly seeks to link

---

[15] See also M. Smith 2005.

[16] For extended discussion of the relationship between the '*quotidien*' and Surrealism, see Sheringham 2006.

different scales in her analysis of the cultural idiom of ambiguity: 'I analyze how strategies of concealment permeate multiple levels of discursive and spatial practice, from the realm of regional politics to the more mundane realms of domesticity and productive activities' (ibid. 1).

Yet Ferme does tend to work from the bottom up, beginning with everyday practices such as weaving cloth, hair-plaiting, net hunting and fishing, cooking, using clay and oil on the body, and even the techniques for getting rid of bedbugs. It is as if it is impossible to gain purchase on the broader social canvas other than through these vignettes of daily life: 'Thus through these small things—the 'narrow gate' of a bed, or the paths taken by a cooking pot—one can more easily follow the intersection between women's social roles in the context of kinship, marriage, age, and other identifications, and their actual choices and strategies. In this sense, as Bachelard suggests, the detail opens up a whole world' (ibid. 156).

The idea that the whole is rarely present, but is rather viewed through fragments, that may in some instances come together, can also be found in other recent ethnographic work. Although it does not cite the work of Ferme, a recent contribution by Empson (2007) on relations between objects and things in Mongolia has much in common in its treatment of present parts and absent wholes. Empson aims to illuminate the character of kinship in Mongolia through a micro-scale analysis of household chests: how they are located in the house, and what is found on, around, and inside them. On and around the chest there are, for example, photographs of kin members and embroideries sewn by daughters-in-law. Things inside the chest remain concealed and are never revealed to guests. They include parts of the body of close family members, such as pieces of umbilical cords and children's hair (ibid. 123). Children may eventually leave home, but this painful separation is already anticipated: by keeping back a part of the body whole, relations are in some sense continued. However, there is an intensity to this connection through shared blood that demands some detachment (ibid. 124), and containment in the chest serves this end. This metonymic process, whereby complex, shifting family relations are stabilized and given place through hidden fragments, is thus very important in the maintenance of kin networks.

Both Ferme and Empson, in different ways, use ideas of metonymy, with parts standing for wholes, to 'scale up' from the micro- to the macro-scale. They conceive of the micro-scale as a fragment or portion of the macro-scale. However, this scale-hopping means negotiating some substantial gaps: while convincing at the level of the everyday, neither work is quite so convincing on a larger scale (just as a world-systems perspective does not manage to filter down successfully to the micro-scale). One problem they face is the lack of a methodology that is squarely aimed at coping with these shifts in scale. It is merely stated that the part and the whole are connected. I will come back to this issue in the section below on 'interaction and artefacts', showing that there are some methodological possibilities here.

The examples from Ferme and Empson are both ethnographic; but what of bottom-up approaches in archaeology? Perhaps the most explicit example comes in some of the work of Clive Gamble, focusing on Palaeolithic societies (Gamble 1998; 1999). While he does not make any reference to the '*quotidien*' perspective used by Ferme, he does cite Goffman's interactionism, drawing also on Hinde's work on human and animal interaction (1976). Gamble identifies a general failing in studies of the Palaeolithic to access social organization, in large part, he argues, because of an overriding tendency in archaeology to define social organization in terms of groups and institutions. In order to have any chance of getting at sociality in the Palaeolithic, a more bottom-up approach is required that focuses first on individuals and their interactions. It is interesting how Gamble subsequently turns to two quite separate fields in order to garner further insights on the nature of these 'low-level' social interactions: social network analysis on the one hand (e.g. Mitchell 1974; Milardo 1992), and studies of primate behaviour on the other (Quiatt and Reynolds 1993; Rodseth *et al.* 1991). In more recent work he has further bolstered his interactions with primatologists in understanding early human face-to-face interaction in a long-term study with Robin Dunbar and John Gowlett (Dunbar, Gamble, and Gowlett 2010; Aiello and Dunbar 1993; Dunbar 1996). Yet the concern with 'scaling up' remains, with the need to understand the ways in which in human societies there is a 'release from proximity' (Gamble 1998, 431), and Gamble sees network analysis as the means to understand this. He describes four different levels of networks, from the intimate to the effective to the extended to the global, each sustained by different kinds of resources—emotional, material, and symbolic (ibid. 432). This carefully constructed, bottom-up approach is innovative in a number of ways, but here we might pick out one feature: the argument that the larger-scale networks are sustained by 'symbolic' resources, by which Gamble means material culture. This sees much fuller development in subsequent work (Gamble 2007), and we shall return to this key component below.

MULTI-SCALE AND MULTI-TOPOLOGY

We have now considered both top-down and bottom-up approaches to the problem of articulating scales. However, there is another way of looking at scale, emergent in human geography and sociology, and that is to deny the separate existence of distinct scales altogether. Rather than trying to define a priori the local and the global, the proximate and the distant, our efforts might be better spent, it is argued, examining the processes whereby both the local and the global are actively created (Callon and Law 2004, 3). These same authors cite the work of Kwa (2002), who differentiates between two social-science paradigms for approaching complex wholes: the romantic and the baroque.[17] The romantic seeks order and clarity: the world can be analysed and made sense of, with things falling into hierarchical categories. The baroque starts with the assumption that no such order exists, that entities are heterogeneous, shifting, and indissoluble. In the romantic view, therefore, we would be justified in separating distinct scales of analysis and experience, but not in the baroque view.

There does seem to be a growing recognition in the above-mentioned disciplines of the need to attend to the different topologies that organize (or disorganize) human life across multiple scales (e.g. Massey, Allen, and Pile 1998; Soja 2002; Callon and Law 2004; Hetherington 2004; Thrift 2006). This goes further than the spatial turn described earlier, in which the shift was from absolute, physical conceptions of space to more relational, active views of space as a social construct. Network approaches can be both physical and relational, and yet these have been deemed in some quarters to be too rigid, with Mimi Sheller, for example, stating: 'Rather than mathematically precise network analytical approaches to describing social worlds, I argue that a "messier" imagery of liquid social dynamics will enable a better understanding of the complexity of these mobile social interactions' (Sheller 2004, 41). However, even though networks have come to be associated with rigidity and passivity, as Latour bemoans (Latour 1999, 15; cf. also Callon and Law 2004, 8), this absolutely need not be the case. Yes, there do need to be nodes and links, and this does inevitably set limits; but networks can very readily be dynamically emergent, as will be discussed in the following chapter. Still, Sheller is seeking some kind of topology that can do justice to the incredible 'processes of mobilization of people, objects, and information enabled by the new communicational technologies' (Sheller 2004, 46). She sees more 'fluid' topologies as a possible answer, citing, among others, Harrison White and his idea of a 'gel' (White 1992). Sheller is particularly interested in how this more fluid topology acts to dissolve the micro–macro division, with 'this messy gel of sociality occurring at different scales and scopes' (Sheller 2004, 47).

As Sheller notes, a number of scholars previously have shown a concern for fluid metaphors of one kind or another. Deleuze and Guattari (1988) describe space as either 'striated', like a network, or 'smooth', more fluid or gel-like. Lee and Brown (1994) pick up on this distinction and criticize ANT for only dealing with the striated space of networks and not at all with smooth space (see also discussion in Knappett 2005, ch. 4). Mol and Law also stress that the network is just one topological form, and that we need to find ways of doing justice to 'fluid

---

[17] Their meanings as used by Kwa do not relate clearly to common usage in art and literature.

space', an overlooked social topology (Mol and Law 1994). Ingold (2007*a*, *b*) has also recently critiqued the network as too limiting, and has started to suggest the 'meshwork' as an alternative topology that captures the movement and flow of human experience (this I will return to in Chapter 3).

Yet these various calls for the recognition of fluid social topologies do not appear to be accompanied by a set of methodologies. If we return to the difference drawn above between romantic and baroque paradigms for tacking complex wholes (Kwa 2002), then it is as if the romantic has methods while the baroque does not; or even that the baroque is anti-method. Or perhaps it is just early days. Callon and Law (2004), for example, feel their way towards a possible opening; in asking: 'how, then, should we think about this baroque world?' They acknowledge that 'social science is not particularly well equipped to handle this question' (ibid. 7).

What I argue here is that methodologies are needed to tackle the socio-material world, no matter how messy that world might be (contra Law 2004). In so doing we must try to recognize, however, that the methods we use only capture some portion, some fragment of reality, of the elusive whole. We must remain cognizant of the particular processes of attention we bring to bear on our subject matter, so we can try—perhaps a futile effort—to retain the sense of what kinds of fragments we are producing. If we can do this then we may gain some purchase on what is not captured. For example, if we decide that networks give us a toolkit for studying socio-material interactions across different scales, this does not mean that we can only conceptualize everything that we study in network terms. In many instances a network model will fail to describe or offer satisfactory explanations of a given scenario; in such cases we must imagine the other spaces, smooth or fluid, escaping our attention, in between the lines and nodes of the network.

Why networks? This question is to be fully addressed in the chapter that follows. But here one important point does need to be made, in light of the comments from Sheller and others that have been briefly discussed above. Networks have come to be associated, in the fields of human geography and sociology at least, with rigidity and passivity (Latour 1999, 15). This characteriza-tion may have been justified as recently as ten years ago; and certainly, much of the work in social network analysis up to this point had employed rather static network models (see discussion in Turner and Maryanski 1991, 557–8). How-ever, the world of network theory has since been completely transformed, thanks in large part to initiatives in the physical and biological sciences (see next chapter for references). In brief, the new world of network theory involves some very dynamic models that are far from being rigid and passive, and which in fact can describe bottom-up, emergent, 'chaotic' processes that are not all that far from the 'baroque' paradigm outlined above Kwa (2002). These dynamic network models are increasingly finding their way into the social sciences, but there are still limitations. One of these is the general tendency to model connections between either humans or non-humans, but not both together; another is the tendency to pitch these network ideas at a single scale, without working across social scales. We shall see examples of this in the next chapter. Yet networks *do* have the potential to absorb both of these concerns.

INTERACTION AND ARTEFACTS

Callon and Law (2004) struggle to see ways of tackling many different scales simultaneously. This is ironic, given that they are leading proponents of Actor-Network Theory (e.g. Callon 1986; Law 1992; Latour 2005), and the argument to be developed in the following chapter that networks provide solutions for traversing scales. Yet despite its name, Actor-Network Theory (ANT) is oddly reticent when it comes to networks, using the network concept rather loosely. In fact its real strength has been its focus on the constitution of technology and the active role of 'non-humans' therein. Rather than assuming, as in many sociological studies, the intrinsic primacy of humans over non-humans, ANT has sought to create a level playing-field by treating these two categories symmetrically in social formations. This profoundly relational approach states that no such 'pure' entity as human or non-human exists, as the two co-construct one another. Take the example of the plough. The blacksmith who made the plough is like a shadow hovering over the shoulder of the plough-man; hence technologies are critical in 'folding together places, actors, or actants separated by time and space' (Callon and Law 2004, 6). The 'symmetrical anthropology' of ANT, though initially developed in socio-anthropology, has now a wide following in social theory (e.g. in human geography: see Murdoch 1998; 2005) though is not without its critics (Ingold 2008). Indeed, Callon and Law themselves see limitations, recognizing that vocabularies for describing the conjunction of the human and the non-human are poorly developed in the social sciences. They consider that the best hope for progress in this regard probably lies in semiotics of one form or another (Callon and Law 2004, 7).

I agree on both counts—on the lack of vocabularies and the promise of semiotics—but think that the situation is currently more advanced than these authors admit. Concerning the role of semiotics, ANT is generally somewhat vague on this, taking semiotics to mean little more than relationality; but if a specifically Peircean semiotics is invoked (which it rarely is in ANT), then considerable advances can be made in studying socio-technical linkages across scales (more on this in Chapter 5; and see also Preucel 2006). And as for the role of technology in 'folding together', this is also much further along in its study; I would suggest that the move that Callon and Law and others in human geography seem keen to make would actually be greatly facilitated by adopting perspectives currently under development in archaeology and related fields. For example, 'material engagement' is a perspective that puts artefacts centre stage, with the emphasis on the active role of artefacts and the environment in 'distributed cognition' (e.g. Renfrew 2004; Malafouris 2004; Malafouris and Renfrew 2010).[18] Furthermore, studies of 'materiality' also underline the centrality of artefacts to social interactions (e.g. Tilley 2004; Miller 2005; Meskell 2005). ANT has itself been something of an inspiration to some scholars in this field, a connection brought out explicitly in a recent call for a 'symmetrical archaeology' (Webmoor and Witmore 2005; Watts 2007; Shanks 2007; Olsen 2007; Coudart 2007, 138).

However, the same lack of methodology for traversing scales could be said to apply to all of the above, despite the important foregrounding of materials and technologies in human interaction. That said, some recent work in archaeology has been working within these traditions while also developing some means of grappling with the scale-traversing properties of artefacts in more concrete fashion. John Chapman, for example, has developed an approach that seeks to understand processes of deliberate fragmentation observed in the archaeological record.[19] We might remind ourselves that in this concern with fragments, or parts of wholes, there are resonances with the work of Empson (2007) mentioned above. He argues that fragments of whole artefacts could have been used metonymically, with the part (pot fragment, for example) standing for the whole (the complete pot). As parts can be separated and moved they may be effectively utilized in the social practice of 'enchainment', such that interaction networks may be maintained across space and time through such traces (as indeed in the case of Empson 2007). It is through enchainment that Chapman sees the possibility of distributed personhood (on which, see e.g. Strathern 1988). Parts can also be accumulated, however, and Chapman sees a tension at work between enchainment and accumulation. Gamble has developed these ideas still further, connecting the social practices of accumulation and enchainment more explicitly with the human body, which he sees as the basic metaphor from which 'symbolic force' springs (Gamble 2007). He argues that human corporeality is conceptualized metaphorically in terms of 'containers' (the trunk) and 'instruments' (the limbs), and that these bodily categories have proxies in material culture. He adds further refinements to Chapman, drawing on Knappett (2006) to suggest that accumulation is often a layering process, and also criticizing Chapman's tendency to use fragmentation and enchainment interchangeably (Gamble 2007, 137).

---

[18] This perspective owes much to ideas in cognitive science and philosophy that work from the micro-scale and the level of the body, for example Hutchins 1995, Clark 1997, Kirsh 1995, Goodwin 1994. More on this will follow in Chapter 4. See also Knappett 2005.

[19] Chapman 2000; Chapman and Gaydarska 2006.

Like both Ferme and Empson in their ethnographic studies, these archaeo-logical approaches are bottom-up, and in Gamble's case in particular stem from the micro-scale of the human body. Yet the concepts of accumulation and enchainment[20] add an extra dimension. They provide an explicit means for shifting scale from the micro to the macro, from part to whole. However, Gamble remains alert to the dangers of adopting a limited perspective on society: 'This may seem to put too much emphasis on the individual as the starting point for any social project, and to ignore pre-existing institutions and structures' (Gamble 2007, 129). He then goes on to suggest that network models might allow for either top-down or bottom-up approaches, but does not pursue this further (note also his earlier work using network ideas—Gamble 1998, 1999). What I shall argue in the following chapter is precisely this: network models can indeed allow for a shifting of scales, and can work from both the top-down and the bottom-up. This is not to say, of course, as already discussed, that networks are the only social topologies; but they do provide an explicit methodology, and they do have the capacity to incorporate humans and non-humans. Furthermore, they may also go some way towards identifying the 'baroque' of Kwa, or the 'gel' of Harrison White and Mimi Sheller.

DISCUSSION

Thus there are now perspectives emerging that pay attention to material culture, and which see the need to traverse scales. Some—for example, those of Chapman and Gamble—have sought to develop methodological means to achieve this end, but these are nevertheless hampered, I would argue, by an inability to move both up and down scales. This is to some extent solved by the fuller application of network techniques for modelling and interpreting inter-actions (see Chapter 3). However, they are also limited by the very deep-rooted split between geometric (absolute) and topological (relational) space. The post-processual corrective to the processual over-reliance on concepts of geometric space has simply served to replace one incomplete conception of space with another: a swing from the physical to the relational. This is a problem that goes beyond archaeology; in geography and social theory too, symbolic interactionism, the '*quotidien*', and Actor-Network Theory are all highly relational approaches that do not do much justice to the spatial patterning of social phenomena (or, arguably, to the macro-scale). While the work of such influential scholars as Bachelard, Certeau, Lefebvre, Latour, Law,

---

[20] Or layering and networking—see Knappett 2006.

Thrift, and Soja has been very significant in showing how social practices construct space, it has perhaps been excessively anti-geometric and has thus left little room for understanding the *interaction* of the absolute and the relational (see Smith 2003; Hillier 2005; Knappett, Evans, and Rivers 2008). This is surely where the real interest and challenge lies: understanding how these two articulate or co-construct each other. However, we should not underestimate the depth of this division, as it is redolent of the deep-rooted differences that keep on emerging between processual and post-processual archaeologies, or more starkly still, between 'an unbridled science on the one hand, and a disabling relativism on the other' (Johnson 2006, 131).

Yet I do not think it is an impossible gulf to bridge. I have tried to show, by going back to the development of spatial analysis in archaeology in the late 1960s and 1970s, that it was not so much the fact that processualism focused on spatial analysis that has led to this impasse, but rather the particular ways in which it did so that are more to blame. The techniques used were, arguably, just too tied to geometric conceptions of space, such as Thiessen polygons. Had other techniques been used—like networks—then this polarization of the geometric and the topological might never have played out in the way it ultimately did. Why? Because networks do allow for both geometric and topological understandings in the analysis of spatial relations.[21] Networks also permit analysis between scales; thus far in archaeology space is tackled at limited scales (despite the best intentions of Clarke); one might even go so far as a caricature that paints processual and post-processual archaeologies as different scalar approaches to the past.

In the chapter that follows I propose network concepts and methods as means of remedying this problem of traversing multiple scales. I will also look into the peculiar archaeological aversion to network techniques (with some exceptions of course), and ask why most early spatial analysis seemed more focused on areas—such as polygons—rather than nodes and links (with the exception of Flannery, for example).

---

[21] *Contra* Gamble's claim that networks are spatial containers too (2007, 101).

3

Networks Between Disciplines

There seems to be no limit to the problems that can be tackled with the help of networks, and it is tempting to think that some new analytical panacea has been discovered. But the very heterogeneity of applications should make us cautious. Perhaps 'networks' is just another fashionable word.

(Barnes 1972, 1)

INTRODUCTION

The above remarks from J. A. Barnes, a social anthropologist, were made nearly forty years ago. There have evidently been false dawns before for the rise of network analysis. Therefore, in advocating the development of network approaches in this and subsequent chapters a certain degree of caution is called for. What is different now from the early 1970s, and why should we feel more optimistic? In the previous chapter reviewing interactionist approaches in the social sciences, we saw some of the disciplinary fault-lines that have prevented the emergence of satisfactory approaches to human interaction. If we continue to allow such fault-lines to fracture research, then we cannot expect to fare much better than forty years ago. In terms of network analysis, for example, there is the irony that 'network ideas are remarkably poorly networked among themselves' (Knox, Savage, and Harvey 2006, 114). There is no better case in point that that of J. A. Barnes himself, barely cited in much of the new flurry of activity in network science.

Thus, for new network approaches to be successful in archaeology they have to be as profoundly transdisciplinary as we can possibly make them. Otherwise they run the risk of once again dissipating (Knox, Savage, and Harvey 2006, 114), only to re-emerge in another form. By drawing upon the strengths of various network perspectives, I argue in this chapter that for archaeology it is possible and desirable to move towards a rigorous development and application of network approaches, as this would bring three main advantages. First, the nodes and links of a network can be placed in actual physical space, or alternatively can be positioned purely in relational terms. Thus networks can be used to understand both geometric and topological interactions, and thereby can help overcome the 'bicameral' approach (see Blake 2002) that renders them so separate. Secondly, nodes and links can exist at many different scales: a node can be used to depict an individual human, or an entire community, and a link a single face-to-face interaction or a whole bundle of connections between regions. This quality means that networks allow us to grapple with interactions across different scales, and to examine the articulation of these scales; the difficulties in traversing analytical scales that were identified in Chapter 2 can be substantially remedied (if not entirely solved) through a network approach. Thirdly, networks can be heterogeneous, composed of different classes of node and with various kinds of link: this means we can use networks to make the all-important step of combining both people and things in social networks.[1] While network approaches do hold these distinct advantages, there are also inevitably some limitations to which we should remain alert. One of these is that network analysis risks being excessively structural, creating static descriptions of social relations. This problem is addressed through the course of this chapter, in which I argue that networks can be both descriptive and explanatory when the interaction of structure and function is considered. First, however, we should address some of the basic characteristics of networks.

WHAT IS A NETWORK?

One reason that networks seem to be constantly reinvented, with prior work conveniently overlooked, is that the basic definition is hardly that technical. As Bott realized decades ago, 'network' can function as a metaphor for connectedness, and can be used 'in a very loose sense to mean virtually any kind of social entity' (Bott 1971, 319). Even when defined more specifically, a network can be simply characterised as 'a set of items ... with connections between them' (Newman 2003a, 168). The 'items' can be almost anything, such as neurons, cells, organisms, people, or cities. They are described in network terms as 'nodes' or 'vertices'. The connections between them are described in

---

[1] In an earlier work I suggested that networks are a dynamic means of conceptualizing the distributed nature of agency and cognition, such that both people and things might be implicated (Knappett 2005, 64–84). Given the paucity of network thinking within archaeology, I adopted an interdisciplinary perspective, briefly examining the genesis of network ideas, their application in biology, cognitive science, and sociology, and reviewing new 'sociophysical' approaches, such as Watts (2003) and Barabási (2002). The current chapter builds on this earlier work, but has different aims.

network terms as 'links' or 'edges'. These may also be varied in character, from physical structures such as roads or railways, to relational ties of friendship or kinship. Borgatti *et al.* (2009) usefully distinguish between four basic types of links: similarities, social relations, interactions, and flows. Networks may be composed of just a handful of nodes connected by short links, or millions of nodes connected by distant links.

Networks are also known as 'graphs' in the mathematics literature. 'Graph theory' underlies much of the analysis of network structures. It is interesting to go back more than 250 years to the birth of graph theory, usually attributed to Leonhard Euler's famous answer to the Bridges of Königsberg problem in 1736 (see Euler 1953; Harary 1960). The residents of Königsberg were curious to know if it was possible to take a walk around their town crossing each of its seven bridges only once and return to their starting-point. No one was able to figure this out, until Euler, a Swiss mathematician, decided to tackle the problem by breaking up the continuous line of the walk. He did this by differentiating the different areas of land as nodes, and representing each bridge connection as a link (see Figure 3.1). He was able to deduce that 'a connected graph can be traversed by a complete closed line sequence if and only if every point is even' (Harary 1960, 123). That is to say, every node must have an even number of links to/from it. In the Bridges of Königsberg example, every node has an odd number of links, and so the problem is unsolvable.

Thus the continuous lines of 'lived experience' (walks through the city of Königsberg, in this case) can be broken up and analysed as a graph composed of nodes and links (or vertices and edges). In this way, underlying patterns can be discerned that might otherwise be imperceptible from within the lived process itself. There is an important differentiation here between experience

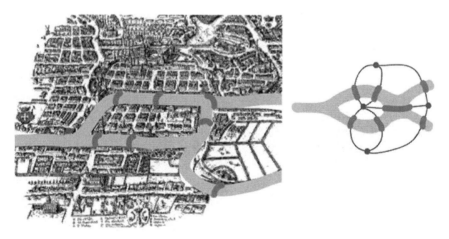

Figure 3.1. The Bridges of Königsberg

and analysis. Ingold (2007*b*) has recently argued that the world is not a set of points, but a mass of intersecting lines. This is stated as part of a critique of the concept of the network, which Ingold would like to substitute with the term 'meshwork' (ibid. 80–2) as more representative of the fundamental human process of 'wayfaring'. This distinction Ingold makes itself intersects nicely with the Bridges of Königsberg problem. I would not disagree with Ingold's point that life is a series of intersecting lines, as is amply demonstrated in the Königsberg example: one can very well see the life of the town's residents being composed of unbreakable paths. They would surely not have experienced their walks in terms of nodes and links. And yet this did not mean they were able to find a solution to their question either. This only arrived through an analysis that did dissect their experience and cut it up into discrete chunks (of nodes on the one hand and links on the other). In my view there is no need to oppose meshworks (arrays of intersecting lines) and networks; they can be considered as experiential and analytical dimensions respectively. Moreover, the analytical purchase achieved by thinking in network terms need not be confined to the modern scientific process—past peoples may also have conceived of interactions as networks, albeit within a different conceptual framework. This we will revisit in Chapter 7.

If we try to contextualize Euler's breakthrough in the mid-eighteenth century, we must begin by acknowledging that Euler was not the only scholar to engage with network ideas at the time, contrary to the impression that might be gained from the brief historical synopses provided in current network science reviews (e.g. Newman, Barabási, and Watts 2006). Parrochia (2005) maps out a rather more complex 'prehistory' of networks (see also Parrochia 1993; Musso 2003; Knappett 2005, 64–6). Through the sixteenth and seventeenth centuries the network (*réseau*) was conceived as a mesh of interwoven fibres. This is the sense in which the term was employed by Descartes in the late seventeenth century, though later in the eighteenth century a more dynamic view of the mesh emerged, with Diderot conceiving it more like a spider's web (Parrochia 2005, 11–12). However, as Parrochia points out, until the eighteenth century the conception of the network is such that there is no sense that anything 'flows' along its fibres. Parrochia traces developments in network ideas through the eighteenth century, with crystallography and geometry, for example, seeing networks in more spatial terms. This trend continues through the nineteenth century and eventually finds florescence in the regional analysis of the geographer Christaller in the 1930s (ibid. 13). Still, there is little sense of what is circulating in these spatial networks, whether at the molecular or regional scale (ibid.). Ideas of flow in networks emerged in a different domain, in the context of biological treatments of the workings of the body: Harvey's early seventeenth-century work on the circulation of the blood was key in this respect (ibid. 14). Such ideas of flow and circulation were carried through into ways of thinking about transport networks, particularly with the emergence of the railways through the course of the nineteenth century. Thus there existed a whole range of ideas concerning networks, some physical and geometric, others more organic, within which Euler's work was situated. While many of these, however, were philosophical, as with Descartes and Diderot for example, Euler's insights were methodological in nature, relatively 'neutral' in ideological terms (ibid. 16). Yet the promise of Euler's methods, later to be known as graph theory, did not see much further growth until the twentieth century.

Network thinking has been coming and going for many decades, making a strong appearance in one discipline, before fading away and emerging anew in another. From Moreno's sociometry in the 1930s, to Barnes, Bott, and colleagues in British social anthropology in the 1950s, to the development of spatial analysis in geography in the 1960s (Haggett and Chorley 1969), there is a history of work that should not allow us to labour under the pretence that network thinking constitutes a radical new departure for the social sciences (Knox, Savage, and Harvey 2006; Borgatti *et al.* 2009). Indeed, one might argue that, despite the constantly shifting centre of gravity, there has been a continuous thread, taken up in the 1970s by sociology (Borgatti *et al.* 2009), where it has morphed into 'social network analysis', or SNA (e.g. Wasserman and Faust 1994; Scott 2000; Carrington, Scott, and Wasserman 2005; see also White and Johansen 2005 in anthropology). This has probably become the most sustained and formalized study of networks, with SNA holding its own conferences and running a dedicated journal, *Social Networks*. In the mid-1990s network analysis was described by some commentators as 'one of the most promising currents in sociological research . . . its practitioners include some of the most highly respected figures in the profession' (Emirbayer and Goodwin 1994, 1412). This was also the year when the leading text in the field was published (Wasserman and Faust 1994).

NODES, LINKS, AND NETWORK STRUCTURES

What insights into social networks, then, have been offered by social networks analysis? Let us look briefly at some of the concepts that are commonly used to distinguish systematically between different kinds of *nodes*, *links*, and network *structures*. Let us begin with a straightforward network in which both links and nodes are all of the same kind (Figure 3.2).

There can still be variation, in that some nodes may feasibly have more links than others. So in Figure 3.2 some of the nodes have just one link, some have two, and some have three. The number of links to/from a node is known as its *degree*—the more links a node has, the higher that node's degree. A node with many links may also be described as possessing high *degree centrality*. Yet,

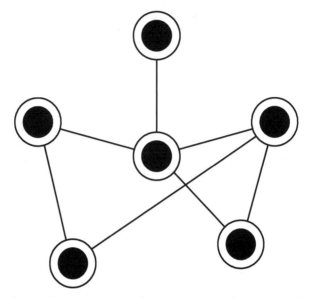

Figure 3.2. Network with links and nodes all of same kind

having a lot of links, or high degree, does not necessarily make a node well connected in terms of the network as a whole. A node may have many links, but they may all be localized. Some nodes may have fewer links, but those links may be key bridges *between* subgroups in the network. We can see this in Figure 3.3.

Such nodes may then be described as having high *betweenness centrality.*[2] While one might expect degree and betweenness centrality to overlap in many cases, they need not. As Radicchi *et al.* state (2004, 2658), 'it is clear that, when a graph is made of tightly bound clusters, loosely interconnected, all shortest paths between nodes in different clusters have to go through the few inter-cluster connections, which therefore have a large betweenness value'. But these edges need not be those in the network with the greatest degree centrality. Note that we have been describing links as if they are a property of nodes; but by the same token we may reverse the equation and say that nodes are properties of links. Links too can be seen as variable, connecting different numbers of nodes, with varying directionality and strength.

Regardless of whether one privileges nodes or links, the question of cluster-ing is critical. It raises the matter of overall network structure. Social networks are neither entirely regular, like a crystal lattice, with all nodes of the same

---

[2] There are other measures of centrality, such as eigenvector centrality and closeness centrality.

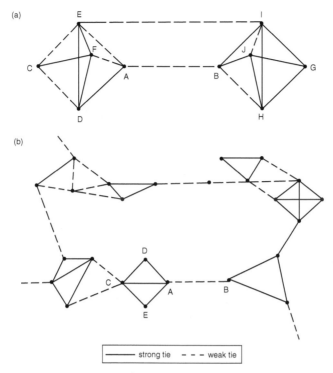

Figure 3.3. Some nodes act as bridges between subgroups

character and all links of equal length, weight, and directionality; nor are they entirely irregular and random. They combine elements of each—they may be regular in parts and irregular in others. It is highly unlikely in a social network for nodes to be uniformly distributed or equally connected (as we have noted above with the varying centrality of different nodes). Indeed, we so easily take it for granted that social networks are made up of tightly bound clusters with loose interconnections that we overlook the ins and outs of how such networks might actually be identified. Since the 1950s and 1960s, when serious work on social networks really began, this intermediate status of social networks (between the regular and the random) has been very effectively recognized and indeed demonstrated, not least in the groundbreaking work of Stanley Milgram on 'small world' networks and that of Mark Granovetter on the strength of 'weak ties' in social networks (Milgram 1967; Granovetter 1973).

One might also in the context mention the seminal study by Zachary (1977) on friendship networks in a karate club, the data seeing much re-analysis since. New techniques and approaches continue to be developed for the identification of subgroups in social networks though, rather confusingly, various terms are used to describe them, such as 'cliques', 'clusters', 'blocks',

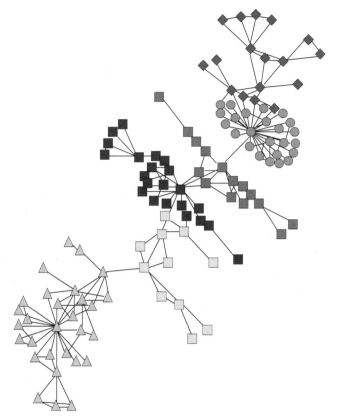

Figure 3.4. Network showing communities in collaboration networks

or 'communities'. If we take just one of these terms, 'communities' are 'subsets of vertices within which vertex–vertex connections are dense, but between which connections are less dense' (Girvan and Newman 2002, 7821). The orthodox method for defining communities is through hierarchical clustering.[3] Moody and White (2003) develop an alternative method ('cohesive blocking') that is a variant of 'blockmodelling', itself based on ideas of structural or regular equivalence (White, Boorman, and Brieger 1976; Emirbayer and Goodwin 1994, 1422; Doreian, Batagelj, and Ferligoj 2005; Wolfe 2006). Essentially this involves reducing the nodes in a network to see how many can be lost before the network's (or community's) cohesiveness is affected. An alternative approach is to reduce the number of links rather than nodes, removing in particular those links with highest betweenness first and

---

[3] From an archaeological angle, one might note that this technique involves the creation of dendrograms, of the type frequently used to find subgroups in complex multivariate datasets, such as those generated in chemical analysis (e.g. Neutron Activation Analysis).

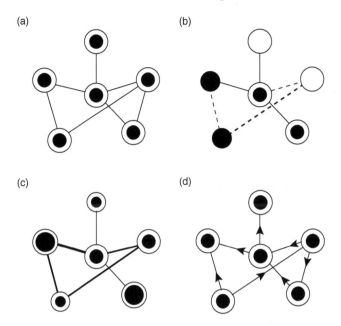

Figure 3.5. Different kinds of networks with variations in nodes and/or links

continuing until community structure is revealed as the network breaks apart (Figure 3.4; Girvan and Newman 2002; Watts 2004, 253–4).

Thus far we have assumed that all nodes (vertices) and links (edges) are of the same kind. However, as Newman notes, 'in most kinds of networks there are at least a few different types of vertices', (Newman 2003a, 190–1). This is shown in Figure 3.5, for example in (b) and (c), where the nodes and links are of different character, represented graphically by varying line thickness or node size.

Newman gives as an example a food web, in which plants, herbivores, and carnivores may be the different kinds of vertex (node). The kinds of connections in such networks will also depend substantially on the types of vertex: herbivores will connect frequently to plants, and herbivores to carnivores. Yet there will be hardly any connections in the network between plants and carnivores, or herbivores to other herbivores—this kind of selective linking Newman describes as 'assortative mixing' or 'homophily' (Newman 2003a, 191). However, he defines these forms of selectivity as 'like seeking like'. In particular, he works on the tendency of vertices of high degree to seek out others also of high degree (Newman 2002).[4] Thus, following his own

---

[4] This notion of 'like seeking like' can be connected with the concept of the *gravity model*, to be discussed in Chapter 6.

definitions, the selective linking between a carnivore and herbivore would appear to be instead an example of disassortative mixing (it is hardly like seeking like). While some definitions of assortative/disassortative mixing focus only on vertex degree, Newman (2003b), in another publication, is somewhat broader, suggesting the terminology can simply refer to the selectivity of vertices for other vertices that are like or unlike them *in some way*. Newman argues that social networks are different from many other kinds of network in that they invariably display assortative mixing or homophily (Newman 2003a, 193; Newman and Park 2003). Certainly homophily seems to be a significant feature in social networks: or as McPherson, Smith-Lovin, and Cook put it, 'similarity breeds connection' (2001, 415). This phenomenon might also be associated in many networks with the existence of separate communities or 'cliques' (see above).

UNIPARTITE AND BIPARTITE NETWORKS

Coming back to the question of diversity in networks, as indicated in Figure 3.5, we can actually go further with this, distinguishing between nodes in terms of their size, let us say, while maintaining that the nodes are all qualitatively the same. Let us assume that all our nodes are archaeologists. They may vary in age, nationality, or other characteristics, and we may choose to denote this in a network in some way. This is the kind of network that we most commonly see depicted, and is called a 'one-mode' or 'unipartite' network. Thus one might depict a network of relations among archaeologists, on the basis of having worked together on an excavation project. And one might see that cliques or communities occur according to regional specialization, university affiliation, or languages spoken. Let us say though, that the nodes in a network are not archaeologists, but the excavations on which they work. Again, one might differentiate between large and small, between different countries, between research and rescue, and so on. The links between them might be drawn according to the staff running them.

However, it is also possible to have networks in which the nodes are not all of the same quality. So in terms of the above examples, we would combine both archaeologists and excavations on a single network. As these are two quite different kinds of entity, they would be graphically differentiated in the network, which would thus be labelled a 'two-mode' or 'bipartite' network. Moreover, bipartite networks are also often 'affiliation networks', in that one would not link excavations directly to one another but only indirectly via their participants (Wasserman and Faust 1994; Faust 1997; 2005; Newman 2003a, 204). This is best shown in Figure 3.6.

The bipartite networks shown in the upper part of this figure are often collapsed into unipartite ones, shown in the lower part of the figure. When this

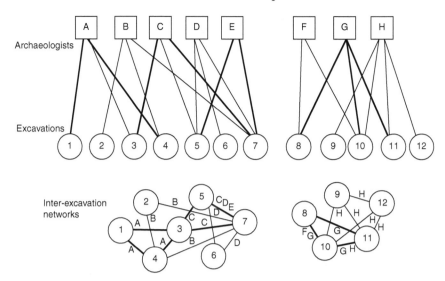

Figure 3.6. Hypothetical affiliation network of archaeologists and excavations

happens, one set of nodes essentially becomes the link. Below we will come back to this interesting feature inherent in many social networks, as it proves to have particular use for thinking through the connections between humans and artefacts in socio-material networks.

While social network analysis (SNA) has evidently achieved a great deal in revealing the above-mentioned features of social networks and developing methods for their study, it also necessarily has its limitations and weaknesses. Ironic as it may sound, SNA is not particularly well 'networked', with limited visibility in other disciplines (in the case in archaeology, at least). Although a 2005 review in SNA suggested that 'interest in social network analysis has grown massively in recent years' (Wasserman, Scott, and Carrington 2005, 1), the impetus for this came not from SNA alone but rather from advances in physics, notably with the identification of the mathematical properties of 'small world' (Watts and Strogatz 1998; Watts 1999; 2003) and 'scale-free' networks (Barabási 2002). The key paper of Watts and Strogatz (1998) was able to show mathematically how the properties of small-world networks— that is, the combination of clustering and short path lengths (which means moving from one node to any other node in the work can be done in a small number of steps)—could be achieved by introducing just a relatively small number of random connections (through a process of 'rewiring') in an otherwise regular clustered network. This work kick-started a whole slew of studies on the mathematical and physical properties of various kinds of biological, economic, and social networks (a small selection includes Watts 1999; 2002; 2003; Barabási and Albert 1999; Barabási 2002; Newman 2003*a*;

2006; Evans 2004; Newman, Barabási, and Watts 2006). These identify a wide range of network features, such as preferential attachment, assortative mixing, scale invariance, and power laws. Some idea of the scale of this new work is given by a simple search of the www.arxiv.org website, an archive of e-prints. A search for 'social network' in the abstracts of the physics section alone produces hits for 646 papers, and searching the titles of papers alone generates 182 hits (accessed 22 February 2011).

It is unfortunate, however, that much of this output fails to recognize the considerable efforts made in social network analysis over the past decades to understand the characteristics of social networks, albeit without the same range of powerful mathematical tools at their disposal. This criticism is levelled at the complex networks literature in a recent overview of SNA (Carrington, Scott, and Wasserman 2005), though this had already been anticipated to some extent in a conciliatory article by Watts (2004), paying due credit to the contributions made by social network analysts (principally in sociology). The relationship between SNA and the new complexity science is a developing one, and there is still a risk that previous incarnations of network studies, such as in social anthropology, may be overlooked. One obstacle to creating an effective dialogue is that network analysis continues to be 'a loose federation of approaches' (e.g. Burt 1980) rather than a predictive social theory (Emirbayer and Goodwin 1994, 1414).

Nevertheless, the hard sciences and the social sciences are in closer contact than ever (Watts 2004; Newman 2003; Newman, Barabási, and Watts 2006; Lane, Pumain, and van der Leeuw 2009), though this relationship requires a lot of work if it is to continue to open doors between disparate disciplines. As Emirbayer and Goodwin pointed out already more than fifteen years ago, 'there has been an unfortunate lack of interest in situating network analysis within the broader traditions of sociological theory, much less in undertaking a systematic inquiry into its underlying strengths and weaknesses' (1994, 1412). These authors offer such an inquiry, revealing some key points for consideration; and we might further point to more very useful work in this direction (Knox, Savage, and Harvey 2006; Borgatti *et al.* 2009; Butts 2009). Such efforts will certainly be important if we wish to introduce network approaches systematically into archaeology.

STRUCTURE, AGENCY, AND FUNCTION IN NETWORKS

Yet what many network approaches do share, however sophisticated either sociologically or mathematically, is a fundamentally structuralist bias, which means they will almost inevitably encounter problems in their handling of agency.[5] While the prognosis offered by Emirbayer and Goodwin is fairly bleak, network approaches *can* show some sensitivity to agency despite their inevitable structuralizing tendencies. Part of the problem is that networks are often taken as given in sociological analyses, with insufficient attention devoted to their growth and dynamics (see Watts 2004). Yet if we pay attention to the coming together of different kinds of agents, human and non-human, at the micro-scale, then we put ourselves in a much better position to achieve a satisfactory articulation of structure and agency. This is what I hope to demonstrate in Chapter 4, and it is certainly an important step to take if archaeologists, and other social scientists for that matter, are to be at all convinced by network analysis, given the emphasis placed on agency in much recent archaeological theory.[6] A second problem, not to be under-estimated, is that network analysis may have proven itself as a powerful means of *describing* social interaction, but has been less convincing in *explaining* interaction or accounting for *change*. This again relates to the unfortunate tendency to treat networks as fixed entities. If patterns of change are sought, it is often through comparing a sequence of static snapshots. This limitation also requires addressing if archaeology is to take network thinking on board. How might we think of networks in dynamic ways, as structures that can shift over time? Again, this is entirely feasible, as I intend to show in subsequent chapters.

One way in which networks can seem static is when their function or purpose is not foregrounded. Network structures not only allow certain functions, they are shaped by them too. We perhaps need to be clearer about networks as *cause* and *effect* in relation to particular activities, and in so doing allow ourselves to capture their dynamic qualities. For example, numerous studies have used network models to understand the spread of epidemics; one such study examines the role of social networks in the obesity epidemic in the United States (Christakis and Fowler 2007; 2009). The spread of obesity is an effect rather than a cause of the structure of these social networks. Network techniques are also employed to analyse communication networks: mobile-phone networks appear to have a structure characterized by strong local clusters bridged by weak ties, and this feature lends itself to searchability (Onnela *et al.* 2007). However, as these authors clearly state, 'the purpose of the mobile phone is information transfer between two individuals' (ibid.

---

[5] Though Emirbayer and Goodwin (1994, 1425–6) do differentiate between three forms of structural bias—structuralist determinism, structuralist instrumentalism, and structuralist constructionism—and acknowledge that the last of these does go some way towards incorporating both culture and agency (e.g. Padgett and Ansell 1993), they nonetheless conclude that even this falls short.

[6] The role of Agent-Based Modelling in the growth of bottom-up network approaches in archaeology should also be borne in mind here.

7334), so the overall network structure must be an effect, albeit one that offers functionality. Although in this and many other studies (e.g. Newman 2003a) a neat demarcation is maintained between structure and function in networks, this is largely because in such studies the functionality of the network observed is clearly an effect rather than a cause of network structure. What *does* cause the network structure is in many cases either overlooked or conveniently sidestepped. This is a charge that can even be laid at the door of the famous 'strength of weak ties' notion proposed by Granovetter (1973): weak ties may have the effect of increasing network 'searchability', but is that the reason they exist? Or does some other functional dynamic account for them? In reviewing some of the different network approaches that exist in the social sciences, we can see that this kind of question has not often been posed; this may be one reason why network analysis is seen as descriptive, static, and structuralist. Nonetheless, this is not an intrinsic failing of networks per se, but rather of the ways in which network analysis has been performed. There are ways to compensate for some of these faults, rendering network approaches the most powerful tools at our disposal for tackling social interaction across multiple scales.

Networks do not simply fall from the sky fully formed. They emerge and grow from somewhere, and generally occur for a reason. Recent reviews of network analysis have been at pains to underline this. Newman looks at models of network growth, before turning his attention to the processes taking place on networks (for example, the spread of information in social networks) (2003a, 212). Watts too is concerned with dynamics, acknowledging that 'the relationship between network structure and dynamical consequences is anything but straightforward' (Watts 2004, 256). He sees that structure and dynamics must surely be interrelated, but so far their interaction has barely been grasped, except in relatively simple cases to do with infection or information transmission. This reprises the point made above, in relation to distinguishing between the structure and function of the networks of obesity epidemics (Christakis and Fowler 2007; 2009) and mobile communications (Onnela *et al.* 2007).

Issues of network growth and evolution are now being tackled though, and promise to be a developing area into the future (see recent papers such as Palla, Barabási, and Vicsek 2007; Blondel *et al.* 2008; Toivonen *et al.* 2009).

NEW NETWORK APPROACHES IN ARCHAEOLOGY

Despite certain limitations and blind-spots, then, network analysis in the physical and social sciences goes from strength to strength. This flurry of activity has not had a pronounced effect on archaeology as yet. Nonetheless, some signs of its impact are apparent, with a rise in uses of network thinking in archaeology in the last five years or so, across a range of contexts. For example, Soren Sindbaek has been explicitly drawing upon advances in network science in developing new approaches for explaining the dynamics of Viking networks (Sindbaek 2006; 2007). He demonstrates how the particular topologies of long-distance exchange generated 'hubs' in specific locales. Turning from the Vikings to the Romans, Shawn Graham combines insights from network science with agent-based modelling to explore the network dynamics of the 'Antonine itineraries', a series of routes across the Roman empire.[7] My own work with Ray Rivers and Tim Evans has brought statistical physics together with network techniques to model some of the dynamics of exchange inter-actions in the Aegean Bronze Age (Knappett, Evans, and Rivers 2008; Evans, Knappett, and Rivers 2009; see Chapter 6). And stretching still further back in time, and moving further east, Fiona Coward employs network thinking in her investigations into Epipalaeolithic and early Neolithic networks in the Near East (Coward 2008; 2010; Coward and Gamble 2008). And in another, completely different context, in Mesoamerica, Jessica Munson and Martha Macri use network science to think through the regional socio-political dy-namics of the Classic Maya. Other current approaches to network analysis in archaeology draw more upon social network analysis (SNA), again across a wide range of settings, from Bronze Age Scandinavia (Johansen, Laursen, and Holst 2004), to the Kofun period in Japan (Mizoguchi 2009), to the Sepik Coast of Papua New Guinea (Terrell 2010).

Yet whatever the vein of influence from network science or SNA, or indeed the particular regional or temporal focus, almost all uses of networks in archaeology keep to the tried and tested terrain of analysing regional interac-tions in geometric space.[8] When we do see the use of relational network thinking, it is in museum studies rather than archaeology per se; furthermore it is non-geometric, and does not use the full potential of network methodol-ogies (Larson, Petch, and Zeitlyn 2007). Very few, if any, examples can be found that conjoin the relational and the geometric.[9] What are the problems that might result from this polarization? If some social network studies overlook the function of network structure, is it in part due to the very absence of physical space in the way they are modelled? Is it that social networks develop particular structures—such as strong local clustering with longer distance 'weak' ties—precisely because of spatial (and temporal) constraints? Indeed, in this regard it is interesting to note that many of the investigations of

---

[7] See http://electricarchaeologist.wordpress.com/agent-models/simulations/. Also on networks and itineraries see Isaksen 2008.

[8] The same is true at other scales of analysis: as with the use of space syntax analysis at the proximate scale (see Chapter 2).

[9] One recent example of an archaeological study that does seek to combine the two is Brughmans 2010.

epidemiological and communication networks, for example, depict these networks in topological rather than geometric terms. That is to say, they are almost exclusively concerned with the relational properties of the network rather than with any absolute physical properties it may or may not possess. For example, the mobile-communication network involves users who are in particular geographical locales at specific times when they make their calls. This general observation is made also by Gastner and Newman (2006), pointing out that very few of the new network approaches have paid any attention whatsoever to geographical space. They show that geographical networks whose nodes do reside in a particular geometric space behave very differently to relational networks. So we may be able to turn the archaeological focus on geometric space into a positive rather than a negative.

A second unacknowledged advantage to network approaches in archaeology is that the field evidently has as one of its principal aims the reconstruction of long-term social and cultural change. Hence there are datasets that would allow for the study of the evolution and growth of social networks over time, though the data would definitely require adaptation before being amenable to network analysis. And thirdly, archaeology can, in theory at least, incorporate artefacts into its network thinking. Social network analysis, on the other hand, tends to forget artefacts and technologies, or at best render them as secondary protagonists; they are the background for social action. In network terms, the nodes are always human actors and their links are social ones. But not only is it a mistake to completely submerge physical space in favour of relations, it is also problematic not to involve artefacts (or 'non-humans': Law and Mol 2008; Jones and Cloke 2008). It is particular sets of practices—more often than not technological in some regard—that enable physical space to be 'created' in some form or other. As we shall see in Chapter 6, the archipelago environment of the southern Aegean may have a 'given' physical configuration, but it is particular maritime technologies that render that shape 'human'; and rowing versus sail technologies make for two very different archipelagos.

This recognition of the active and participatory role of non-human protagonists in social networks may turn out to be a necessary step in understanding the structure and function of networks more fully. Social—or perhaps more accurately socio-material—networks take shape because there are certain dynamics creating those structures. These dynamics must surely include the need or desire to sustain relations over space and time; and there may be many reasons to do so, from maintaining connections to ensure reproductive viability in small groups, to the need to obtain rare raw materials such as metal ores from distant sources. Artefacts and technologies are absolutely key in enabling human groups to achieve this across vastly increasing scales; this will be a central part of the argument in Chapters 5 and 6 in particular.

This point may not have been taken on board in most of the new 'network science', but it has certainly been a fundamental driving-force behind

Actor-Network Theory (see also Chapters 1 and 2). Generally when we consider the balance of agency between people and things the primacy is always ascribed to the human, with the non-human having at best 'secondary' agency (e.g. Gell 1998). Actor-Network Theory (ANT), also known as symmetrical anthropology, challenges the assumed ontological primacy of humans by adopting an analytical impartiality (Ashmore, Wooffitt, and Harding 1994, 735). This decentring of the human subject allows for artefacts to be brought to the fore if necessary rather than always assumed as the background, little more than the passive stage for human action. This process has been particularly useful in science studies within sociology and anthropology, the domain of the principal protagonists of ANT (e.g. Callon 1986; Law 1992; Latour 2005). Though this influential paradigm has been rather slow to take on in archaeology, perhaps surprisingly given the discipline's inevitable artefactual emphasis, this imbalance is belatedly rectified in a series of publications on 'symmetrical archaeology' (Webmoor and Witmore 2005; Knappett 2005; 2008; Olsen 2007, Shanks 2007, Witmore 2007; Watts 2007).[10] While the 'network' component of ANT has been somewhat underdetermined, with infrequent explicit discussion of the network properties of human–non-human assemblages (see Knappett 2008), the ANT approach is nonetheless consistent with the more formal network approaches. This we can demonstrate by returning to a particular kind of network we have mentioned above—the affiliation network.

AFFILIATION NETWORKS OF ACTORS AND ARTEFACTS

Earlier in this chapter I discussed the affiliation network as a form of bipartite network, that is to say, with two kinds of node. In our example, the two modes of node were archaeologists and their excavation projects. The modes do not have to be 'actors' and 'events' though. They might just as well be 'actors' and 'artefacts'. Though not explicitly recognized as such, this is what we see in depictions of an 'inter-artefactual network', such as the one employed by Neich in showing the stylistic relationships between Maori meeting houses (Neich 1996; discussed also in Gell 1998). Such a network is of particular archaeological interest because it has been taken up recently by archaeologists (Gosden 2005, fig. 1; Jones 2007, 81). This network is shown in Figure 3.7.

Each of the vertices represents a Maori meeting house, and the edges stand for stylistic connections between them. As a unipartite network this would

---

[10] Though ANT is not without its critics—see Ingold 2008.

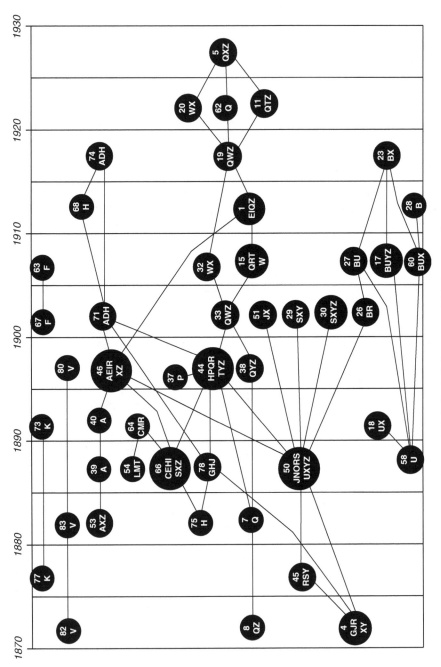

Figure 3.7. Stylistic links among Maori meeting houses

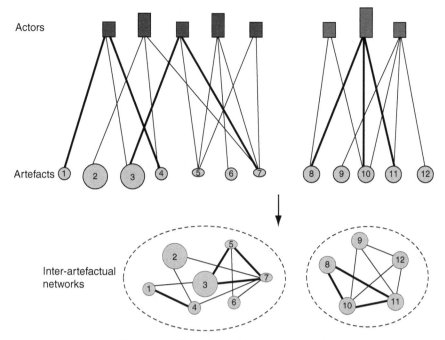

Figure 3.8. Hypothetical bipartite network

appear to suggest that meeting houses interact directly among themselves, which is of course unlikely. What we have to remember is that these vertices are in fact inhabited by human individuals or groups: they are what connect the various houses. This would be far clearer if the unipartite network shown here was reformatted as a bipartite network showing both the artefacts and the actors as vertices with edges between actors and artefacts, but not directly among actors or among artefacts (Figure 3.8). What the network can then show is the affiliations among actors towards a particular artefact, or indeed vice versa.

A key difference exists, however, between the hypothetical network of archaeologists–excavations mentioned earlier and the Maori meeting-house network shown here. In the former case the network of affiliation is imagined as a snapshot of relations in time. It does not have a temporal unfolding, although one could include time as a dimension, given that archaeologists move from one project to another, and projects tend to come to an end. In the latter case, though, of the Maori meeting houses, time is an integral part of the network. As can be seen in the network diagram, links can only exist as protentions or retentions, moving forward or backward in time. There are no 'vertical' connections linking coeval houses, even though such connections do exist, in that certain stylistic features (represented by letters 'A' etc.) are

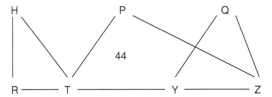

Figure 3.9. Maori meeting house as a network of stylistic traits

shared by houses in any given period. For example, in the period immediately after 1900 houses 51, 29, and 30 all share feature 'X', but no line is drawn indicating this link. This raises the further complication that each house in the network diagram is a multidimensional artefact, composed of numerous stylistic features. Each house could itself be represented as a small network diagram, with connections between its features, as in Figure 3.9.

This mini-network among the stylistic components of the individual Maori house is depicted as a unipartite network—the humans that are in the interstices, in the links, are not shown. This is projected from an unknown bipartite affiliation network combining both human and non-human protagonists. In other words, 'H' does not directly link to 'R', but only via a human actor (or actors) who participated in the construction and transmission of both features.

Why is this important? Network ideas of this kind, deriving from Gell's notions of 'oeuvre' and 'inter-artefactual domain', are finding some purchase in archaeology (Gosden 2005; Jones 2007). Yet their network qualities have not really been explored. The network diagram of Maori meeting houses used by Gell hides a great deal of complexity, with the 'artefacts' being multidimensional. The same holds true for the network of protentions and retentions Gell uses to describe the oeuvre of Marcel Duchamp in terms of retentions and protentions: each 'work' is multidimensional in a similar fashion. If we are to tackle archaeological artefacts in similar fashion, as Jones does, then we need to be aware of the information that a node represents (this is not apparent in Jones 2007, 83, fig. 5, for example). By the same token, attention must also be paid to the character of the connections, which also can be decidedly variable. It is relevant here that the direction of influence for Jones's use of 'networks' comes from Gell and Actor-Network Theory, neither of which are particularly clear on the variable character of nodes and links; by feeding different streams of network thinking into one another, for example with the inclusion of social network analysis, a fuller appreciation of the complexities of networks might be more forthcoming.

This discussion of bipartite/unipartite networks allows us to see the different textures that might reside in links (which can vary in directionality and weight too). A key feature of a bipartite or affiliation network is that the focus is on the position of actors in relation to one another, as defined through a third party, in this case an artefact. This seems to be consistent with what Emirbayer and Goodwin (1994, 1422) call 'positional analysis', one of two strategies generally employed by network analysts. This strategy focuses on finding structural equivalences in the network and thus is adept at identifying 'cliques' or 'blocks'. The other strategy is termed 'relational analysis' by Emirbayer and Goodwin (ibid. 1419), and this does tackle the direct ties between actors, assessing their strength, density, directionality, and so on. While it is thus stronger than positional analysis in characterizing the links between actors, it is weaker in terms of analysing the structural position of the actors within the network as a whole. They cite the work of Padgett and Ansell (1993) on the rise of the Medici in fifteenth-century Florence as a classic example of positional analysis.[11]

Another way of seeing relational and positional analysis is as micro- and macro-scale perspectives respectively. The former risks being too narrow, though does pay suitably close attention to agency, while the latter has the advantage of structural overview though it risks ignoring agency. A combination of these two strategies and scales of analysis would seem to be the ideal (and ultimately this is what Emirbayer and Goodwin advocate, in as many words). And yet with either approach there is an equal danger of merely describing network characteristics (which is already a lot more than is usually achieved in archaeology) rather than *explaining* them.

IN SUMMARY

Network analysis brings with it numerous advantages. It is a relational rather than 'categorical' approach (Emirbayer and Goodwin 1994, 1414; Emirbayer 1997), which fits well with our overall desire, as outlined in Chapter 1, to create a strong focus on interactions, thereby enabling more dynamic and fluid accounts of human socio-material assemblages. Secondly, network analysis considers both individual and group levels, making it possible 'to bridge the "micro–macro gap"—the theoretical gulf between microsociology, which examines the interaction of individuals, and macrosociology, which studies the interaction of groups or institutions' (Emirbayer and Goodwin 1994, 1418; see also Watts 2004, 265). Thirdly, it can integrate social and physical space, or in other words topology and geometry (even if many approaches tend to favour one or the other). And fourthly, networks can have heterogeneous nodes and links, which means in principle we can include both people and things

---

[11] There is new work in the domain of bipartite networks—see Guillaume and Latapy 2006; Guimera, Sales-Pardo, and Amaral 2007.

in networks, and indeed connections of various weights, directions, and distances.

This does not mean, though, that it is without its problems. The literature on network analysis hardly adds up to a unified social theory. On the one hand is the sociological literature, well established for some decades, but not immediately comprehensible to all sociologists, let alone other social scientists. The use of terms that are not immediately suggestive, such as 'degree', 'betweenness', or 'assortative mixing' does not do anything to encourage take-up. On the other hand is the physics or 'sociophysics' literature, which has done a good job of developing a popular profile in a short period of time (e.g. Buchanan 2002), but which has not done enough to integrate with sociology and has not had very long to bed down. Moreover, the level of the mathematics involved can very quickly surpass the abilities of even the more numerate archaeologists. Perhaps most problematic, though, is its tendency to be overly structuralist and descriptive, producing an unhelpful separation of network structure from function.

Nevertheless, we can gain much from these various network ideas if we show a little patience and ingenuity. For example, we can actually mobilize archaeological strengths—the focus on geometric space, long-term patterns, and material culture—to leverage still further use from network ideas.

If over the course of the following chapters we are to conduct an enquiry into the 'prehistory' of networks, then we certainly need to be thinking about the advantages that distributed interconnectedness might have offered to human groups. This takes us back to the question raised in Chapter 1: why do humans interconnect in ways that go far beyond the simplest possible forms, and why do they do so over considerable distances, time-depths, and using artefacts? We should think of networks, and forms of interconnectedness in general, as solutions to problems.

Part II

Networks in Practice:
From Micro to Macro

4

Micro-networks: Proximate Interactions

SOCIAL INTERACTIONISM

When we think about micro-scale human interactions, what probably come to mind are those face-to-face dealings that define everyday sociality. We might imagine a conversation, perhaps a ritualized one of 'good morning, how are you', in which no particular information is exchanged; though such interactions may easily continue into some exchange of information concerning the wellbeing of friends, or the like. Within sociology so-called 'interactionist' perspectives have developed around the analysis of such social settings, with the work of Goffman particularly central, in which he develops a dramaturgical approach to everyday interactions (Goffman 1959; 1967; Turner 1991, 447–71). While Goffman does place language and gesture centre stage, with his idea of 'framing' there is also some attention given to the material setting as backdrop (Goffman 1974). This approach to interaction is essentially continued in more recent sociological treatments of communication, albeit with a fuller recognition of the uses of the various senses in communication, and the emergent rather than codified nature of much interaction; Finnegan has called communication a 'multiple, relative and emergent process' (2002, 28).

This seems perfectly sensible at first glance: to privilege the social face-to-face exchanges in micro-scale interaction, while not overlooking completely the role of the surroundings in influencing interaction to some secondary degree. It is interesting that another important strand of research that has focused on the micro-scale of human interaction, with more of an ethnographic and anthropological flavour, also seems to owe a debt to the work of Goffman. While generally recognized as one of the most influential figures in putting material culture back on the map within social anthropology, Daniel Miller, at least in his early work, certainly uses Goffman's work, particularly in his first monograph *Artefacts as Categories* (Miller 1985; see also 1987, 101). Miller stresses the importance of certain categories of traditional pottery in framing ritual activities in the Indian village he studied. Arguably this interactionist influence has continued to shape his research, in which material culture may be the initial spur, while repeatedly falling into the background and becoming a 'frame' for the social interactions which are his primary concern.[1] Miller has covered many kinds of modern Western material culture, such as kitchen design and use on housing estates in London (Miller 1988; see also 2001), clothing (Küchler and Miller 2005) and mobile phones (Horst and Miller 2006). These ethnographies of everyday things have inspired a whole host of studies; in relation solely to everyday domestic space, one might cite the work of Riggins (1994) examining the layout of everyday objects in domestic sitting-rooms; the study by Chevalier comparing the use of domestic and garden space in suburban England and France (Chevalier 1998); or that of Daniels on Japanese household space (Daniels 2001). This body of work tends to feature material culture as an integral part of micro-scale human interactions, with particular artefacts seen as props through which social relations and identities are constructed and maintained. One might also consider the recent volume by Shove *et al.* (2007), and indeed many of the contributions to the journal *Home Cultures*.

However, these kinds of approaches have come under some criticism for not paying sufficient attention to the materials that they purport to place centre stage (Ingold 2007*a*). Many studies of 'materiality' do seem to be far more focused on the social rather than the material qualities in micro-scale interactions, though in fairness 'materiality' as a term is meant to signify the conjoined material and social character of these interactions (Tilley 2007; Knappett 2007). Nonetheless, there is a significant tradition of focusing much more on material qualities (and this runs the parallel risk of being insufficiently social), and we may trace this back through Ingold to ecological psychology, as envisaged by J. J. Gibson (Gibson 1979).

MATERIAL INTERACTIONISM

Gibson conceived of human perception in terms of movement within an environment. In moving through an environment, an agent inevitably encounters various kinds of entity, which are not necessarily understood primarily as natural or cultural artefacts, or via any other kind of representation that has been socially conditioned.[2] Rather, the agent interacts with surfaces, surfaces constituting the interface between substances and the media they

---

[1] Note also his use of ideas from Hall (1966) on proxemics—see Miller 1987, 100.

[2] It is perfectly possible for these other entities to be humans, though not interacted with socially as such: an example is crowd interactions, especially when under stress. See the work of Helbing (e.g. Helbing, Johansson, and Al-Abideen 2007) modelling crowd dynamics, in which human interactions are so much more physical than social that they can be successfully modelled using notions from particle physics.

inhabit (leaves on a tree moving in the air, a wet pebble on a beach). This triple distinction between substances, media, and surfaces is key in Gibson's approach (see Ingold 2004; 2007a), and they combine in certain ways that may or may not afford action to an agent. Hence Gibson talks of the 'affordances' of things. This notion of affordances is evidently highly relational: it depends on the action repertoire of the agent. A door may afford opening to many adults, but it will not afford opening to a child who cannot reach the handle. As Costall (2006) underlines, for example, it is important to remember the scale of the body in simple actions such as climbing stairs. Staircases afford action in relation to bodies, which can of course differ in their capabilities.

The scale of the body, and the ensuing action repertoire, is crucial to keep in mind. But there is also the 'scale' of the environment to take into consideration here too. If perception relies much more on touch than we generally recognize (Noë 2004), and if it is also geared towards movement and action, we need to think in terms of what is proximate, within reach. The proximate also includes other senses, such as smell and hearing. But together they form a nested sense of the body's reach (and of course material culture can be perceived with different senses). This should help us define the micro-scale in terms of what the body, as a sensorimotor organism, is capable of atuning itself to. The notion of proxemics may be useful here, providing a communicative and spatial dimension (Hall 1966; 1968; Moore 1996).

The work of Gibson certainly provides a strong framework for studying the interaction of an individual human with an environment, but has received valid criticism for its rather asocial character (Reed 1988, 1991; Costall 1995). Scholars since influenced by Gibson, such as Costall and Ingold, have sought to adapt his approach accordingly; while others have taken the work into new areas, such as cognitive science. Donald Norman, for example, working out of a cognitive science department, though also firmly situated in a design setting, talks a lot about affordances in his discussions of the psychology/design of everyday things (Norman 1988). The same may be said of David Kirsh, working out of the same San Diego department, in his work on the distributed cognition in playing the computer-game Tetris (Kirsh and Maglio 1995) and organizing kitchen space (Kirsh 1995), or Ed Hutchins on navigation as a distributed cognitive practice (Hutchins 1995). Other significant work situating cognition in bodily practice, thereby challenging the Cartesian privileging of mind over matter, can be found also in cognitive philosophy (Clark 1997), cognitive linguistics science and technology studies (Suchman 2006, 1st edn. 1987), and human–computer interaction (HCI) research (Harper, Taylor and Molloy 2008). This body of work is certainly fundamental in the growing emphasis on distributed approaches in cognitive archaeology (Malafouris 2004; Renfrew 2004; Knappett 2005; Malafouris and Renfrew 2010). Although in much of the above the angle is predominantly cognitive, it is nonetheless profoundly interactionist and focused on the micro-scale of human action. Nonetheless, it could still be accused of being a good deal less socially oriented than the work of Miller and colleagues, while having the advantage of giving more serious attention to the material properties of things and how humans interact with them.

PRAXEOLOGY: ALSO MATERIAL INTERACTIONISM?

Another approach that may have more scope for reaching out into the social domain is the praxeology of Jean-Pierre Warnier (2001; 2006; 2007). He underlines the importance of starting not with the body per se, but the body in action; he notes that attempts to create an anthropology of 'the body' itself have led to an epistemological dead end (Warnier 2006, 186). While this might be overly pessimistic, with the body itself as a form of material culture a useful avenue to explore (Sofaer 2007), the shift of emphasis Warnier proposes from the body proper to bodily conducts and gestures does seem to be a more promising line of enquiry. As the term praxeology implies, practice is central. Of course, practice-based approaches are not entirely new: the 'habitus' of Bourdieu or the 'structuration' of Giddens are both cases in point, with the additional ambition of locating a level of analysis that can articulate between institutions on the one hand and individuals on the other. However, neither is particularly strong on material culture, nor is there a very ready integration with some of the perception/cognition approaches cited above. Warnier's praxeology, though, does have these advantages.

Warnier's approach to practice is predicated on the twin poles of movement and perception. The body orients itself in space through the perceptual integration of its seven senses (the five usual suspects, and proprioception and the vestibular sense of spatial orientation; Warnier 2006, 186), which are usually put into play as the body moves. While Warnier draws upon the work of Berthoz (1997) on sensorimotor perception, this perspective is actually held by a growing field in cognitive science and philosophy directed towards developing ideas of embodied, distributed, and situated cognition (e.g. Hutchins 1995; Clark 1997). A close marriage of perception and movement is also a core element within the ecological psychology of J. J. Gibson, though Gibson's somewhat extreme arguments for the *direct* perception of environmental properties has distracted attention away from the more far-reaching elements of his approach. This general outlook is also adopted by Ingold in anthropology (Ingold 2000; 2007a). Warnier, however, goes a step further, adding another component to the mix: following Damasio (2000), he asserts that sensorimotor conduct does not take place just for the sake of it, but that it is ultimately motivated and modulated by desires and emotions.[3] Thus Warnier speaks of the *sensori-affectivo-motor* conducts of the subject. But this is not all. In addition to these perceptual, physiological, and emotional dimensions, there is a fourth: material culture. Warnier's 'complete' picture thus consists of 'sensori-affectivo-motor conducts geared to material culture' (Warnier 2006, 187).

This is a significant step that Warnier takes because it implicates material culture as an integral component of the body. Warnier is, however, quick to emphasize that this is not an entirely new idea: it was already anticipated in the 1920s by Schilder, with his concept of the 'bodily schema' that did include objects (for example, a blind man's cane is essentially part of the body, perceptually speaking).[4] The implications for the study of material culture are considerable: rather than being seen as adjuncts to the body, various objects might instead be conceived as integral to bodily conducts and as part of the bodily schema (Warnier 2006, 187; see also Knappett 2006). Thus his praxeological approach incorporates material culture rather more explicitly than do some of the approaches in cognitive science, and indeed phenomenology.[5] Nonetheless, there is still scope for further nuance, as Warnier does not provide sufficient detail on the various kinds of interaction between the body and material culture. How does practice make some artefacts act as pivots or scaffolds, as in the scaffolding of information through the organization of kitchen space (Kirsh 1995)? How do artefacts 'work together' in assemblages (Gosden 2005; Knappett 2010)? How do artefacts become accumulated or enchained through practice (cf. Chapman 2000)? Some answers to these questions might be forthcoming through a more thoroughly interdisciplinary approach to the micro-physics of human practice and interaction, one that brings together the insights from cognitive science, psychology, and ethnography, for example. Indeed, I have already mentioned above the 'material engagement' approach in this regard, to which we might add exciting new perspectives from 'neuroarchaeology' (Malafouris 2008a; Knoblich and Sebanz 2006; Sebanz, Bekkering, and Knoblich 2006).

---

[3] For the connection with the senses, see also Howes 2006 on intersensoriality and material culture.

[4] Note also Heidegger's concepts of 'ready-to-hand', 'present-at-hand', and 'smooth coping', focused on the intimacy of connection between body and artefact in an activity setting, and the ease with which their interaction breaks down when activity stops (e.g. when a hammer breaks in mid-action). See Wheeler 2005 and Harman 2002.

[5] An example of a praxeological approach can be found in Knappett, Malafouris, and Tomkins (2010), in relation to the development of ceramic containers in the Neolithic and Bronze Age of the east Mediterranean.

SOCIAL CONTEXTS OF PRACTICE

Thus we can see how various strands may be brought together to create an approach to micro-scale practice that does justice to the role of the multiple senses, in tandem with action and movement, and bringing material culture within this envelope. However, with some important exceptions (e.g. Hutchins 1995; Goodwin 1994), many of these strands remain somewhat asocial. Gibson's understanding of affordances has long been criticized for this, and some moves have been made to 'socialize' the affordances concept (Reed 1988, 1991; Costall 1995). It can have problems capturing the conjoined nature of many human–environmental interactions, such that agents will experience environments together in groups. These limitations can arguably be overcome, while maintaining the key advantages of the affordances idea: it is relational and object-oriented. Warnier's praxeology too suffers from similar problems, tending to be individualizing.

An additional perspective on the interactions between body and environment, within a framework that is still broadly praxeological, can be found in the body of work loosely labelled 'cultural psychology' or 'activity theory' (Vygotsky 1978; Cole 1996; Wertsch 1988). Here we find a perspective that sees artefacts as pivots for micro-scale human action; and crucially, a pivot acts as a focus for shared gaze or joint attention (see Tomasello 1999), thereby bringing artefacts into the domain of *social* interactions. One might, for example, see a football, in the way it is used in conjunction with certain gestures of course, as a pivot for father–son relationships. For a more frivolous example, we can return to the case of the volleyball 'Wilson' in the film *Castaway*, mentioned in Chapter 1. Wilson becomes a kind of pivot for Hanks's reflections on his situation. This unique (and fictionalized) encounter does find more substantiated counterparts in ethnographic research, with Hoskins (1998) in particular (working in Indonesia) identifying some fascinating artefact biographies, with the artefacts operating as pivots for self-reflection as well as social interactions.

With the subject of pivots comes the theme of scaffolding, given their shared heritage of these concepts in the work of Vygotsky and others. That is to say, pivotal artefacts can have a role in scaffolded learning. A particularly good example for archaeologists is found in the work of Stout (2002) on adze-knappers in Indonesian Irian Jaya. Stout conducted ethnographic research among a community of knappers in order to formulate more effective archaeological models for understanding the acquisition of craft skills. He shows the ways in which apprentice knappers have their learning scaffolded by both social and material structures. That is to say, on the one hand the apprentice learns in a particular social environment that guides his behaviour.

And on the other, the material itself, and the way it is presented to him by skilled practitioners, also serves to guide and 'scaffold' learning behaviour. The approach elaborated by Stout builds on the ecological perspective outlined by Gibson (see above), what Stout also calls a 'perception-action' perspective (which has echoes of the enactive perception approach of Noë 2004, see above). This is particularly aimed at understanding skilled lithic production, with skill understood as an enacted phenomenon rather than a set of internalized mental templates. The acquisition of skill is thus not so much about internalizing formal sequences as learning how to adapt one's perception and action to particular circumstances. This process is facilitated by the deliberate manipulation of the social and physical circumstances themselves, which thereby provide 'scaffolding' for learning (Wood, Bruner, and Ross 1976; Stout 2002, 694). These scaffolds are locked to specific gestures and sequences of actions, and their spatial configuration is significant: hence Vygotsky's term the 'zone of proximal development' (Stout 2002, 694–5). This contextualization of skill serves to underline the difficulty of arriving at a proper understanding of skill other than in its physical and social action context.

To trace one more link in this complex set of connections, this idea of scaffolding has been related by Sinha (2005) to the concept of 'material anchors', as developed in cognitive anthropology by Hutchins (2005).[6] Hutchins explains that in many real-world instances we use material structures for grounding concepts. An example he uses is that of the queue: the concept is that of a series of individuals accessing a resource or service in the order of their arrival, the material structure that of people being able to line up. The material sequence can thus anchor effectively the conceptual sequence, obviating the need for the tricky cognitive task of each individual trying to remember the order in which different individuals appeared. What Sinha is seeking here is a combination of the focus on social interaction found in developmental psychology with the stress on individual cognitive capacity emphasized by Hutchins (Sinha 2005, 1553). On the one hand the cognitive load of each individual is lightened in queuing, while on the other, particular forms of social interaction are required to make this work (and we might all think of scenarios where queuing breaks down, benefiting a few individuals). The fact that Sinha is able to make a convincing link demonstrates the potential for interaction among these various approaches in related disciplines.

---

[6] We will revisit this in Chapter 7.

SUMMARY: A SOCIO-MATERIAL
NETWORK APPROACH

The above discussion shows that there are many useful connections that can be made between cognitive science, philosophy, psychology, and anthropology to develop a fuller and more detailed praxeology, using Warnier's work as the foundation. Nevertheless, there is still scope for further elaboration. First, a more fully *socialized* approach is needed, drawing on some of the above-mentioned concepts from cultural psychology and activity theory. Secondly, greater clarity is required on the specific processes by which objects/things might be implicated or included in bodily gestures. I have mentioned in passing ideas of pivots, scaffolds, assemblages, and so on, but these ideas demand more systematic elaboration. A third and related point is that the perspectives offered above tend to focus on individual artefacts; yet archaeologists frequently work with the idea of artefact *assemblages*, groups of artefacts that can in some senses work in concert to provide contexts for action and perception. This is a key point that will receive further attention in this chapter and subsequent ones. A fourth important point is that the above approaches invariably focus on artefacts that are *proximate* (Gamble 2007; Knappett 2010), within the immediate sphere of the senses and of bodily gestures. Yet human interaction with artefacts occurs across a range of scales, from the micro- through to the macro-level (see following chapters). This range of scales, and the complexities of their articulation, demands an approach that is capable of moving beyond the proximate (as discussed in relation to the work of Chapman, Gamble, Ferme, and Empson, for example, in Chapter 2). Thus, in moving forward we need to reconcile two aspects of micro-scale interactions: the face-to-face social interactions in which objects seem to be in the background; and the individual–object interactions in which sociality seems to fall into the background. At present these two dimensions are tackled rather differently, with relatively little overlap (though with exceptions, see above).

While not wishing to suggest that archaeology has a monopoly on material culture, which anthropologists have patently shown to be very far from the truth (Henare, Holbraad, and Wastell 2007; Miller 2005; Ingold 2007*a*), there is nonetheless an archaeological sensibility towards artefacts which has been seriously under-exploited. Archaeology may not be very strong on the social component of proximate interactions, but it does have some sensitivity for proximate material distributions; likewise, the socio-anthropological skill for identifying social interactions at the micro-scale sometimes brings with it an insufficient focus on artefacts. These two strengths need to be combined and harnessed. Admittedly, there are exceptions in socio-anthropology (and cognitive science, and so on) to this simplistic characterization, as shown above, and many are not only very much consistent with the approach developed here, but have also directly inspired it. But each is missing something: for example, there is a tendency to deal with individual artefacts and not with groups of things. What I will attempt here, nonetheless, is a combination of these different strands.

If we are to develop a scalable approach to the everyday, micro-scale, and proximate, then we need to conceive of the human and non-human actants as nodes and their interconnections as links. This network approach risks breaking up the continuous 'meshworks' of action at the micro-scale of the everyday (Ingold 2007*b*, 80–2), but in this process we can nonetheless reveal something of micro-scale practice. This is a deliberate methodological strategy, described in the previous two chapters; we have no other methodology that can capture the 'baroque' and chaotic interconnecting lines of everyday life. It may transpire that network thinking only really comes into play at broader scales; a possibility I shall explore through the course of this chapter and successive ones. But we must attempt to approach the micro-scale from a network perspective too, for the sake of comparability across scales.

MICRO-SCALE ARCHAEOLOGY

Archaeology suffers from a peculiar paradox. Because so much of the earliest archaeological interest lay in pyramids and palaces, there has been an enduring focus on institutions. Furthermore, the evolutionary and neo-evolutionary agendas, with their focus on bands, tribes, chiefdoms, and states, also drew attention to phenomena such as hierarchy and specialization. And yet the primary source of evidence in most archaeological excavation is the detritus of small-scale, everyday activities. When it comes to the study of the Palaeolithic, for example, this mismatch has been particularly damaging, with micro-scale activities denied their sociality (Gamble 1998, 427).

In other areas of archaeology an attempt to do justice to the micro-scale has been a defining feature of post-processual archaeologies, with phenomenology in particular evoked as a means of understanding individual human experience and agency (Brück 2005). This work has certainly played an important role in the discipline in challenging overly systemic approaches, and establishing more individualizing, intimate, and micro-scale perspectives. However, agency in archaeology has not been especially successful in creating methods for traversing and articulating scales, notwithstanding the frequent citation of ideas such as structuration and habitus from Giddens and Bourdieu respectively, each concerned with bridging the gap between agency and structure. Furthermore, agency has invariably been conceived anthropocentrically, ironic perhaps given the central role of artefacts in the archaeological process, though this is now subject to an interdisciplinary critique (Knappett and Malafouris 2008).

Artefact distributions at the micro-scale may be a familiar feature of archaeology, yet they need to be vivified by praxeological thinking, or a modified and 'socialized' version as outlined above. That is to say, artefacts ought to be considered wherever possible in the context of bodily conducts and gestures, and these within the setting of face-to-face social interactions. Given the leading role of Gamble in challenging some of our archaeological preconceptions in this domain, let us begin first with a consideration of this conundrum in relation to the Palaeolithic.

FACE-TO-FACE IN THE PALAEOLITHIC

A scatter of lithic débitage (waste material from the production of chipped stone tools) is one of the most basic, and indeed emblematic, micro-scale archaeological patterns. From the earlier periods of prehistory this is a key archaeological signature of human activity. A stone scatter can represent a moment in time in a particular space, occupied fleetingly by an individual or small group, the scene of some actions, before moving on (on mobility and practice, see Conneller 2007). Considerable work has gone into reconstructing the gestures and spatial interactions from such stone scatters, sometimes with results that can be surprisingly illuminating. The work of Pigeot (1990) at the Upper Palaeolithic site of Etiolles in northern France (see also Pincevent, Verberie), is a good example, able to show the spatial arrangement of skilled and apprentice knappers in socio-spatial relation to one another. The important ethnographic work of people like Dietrich Stout (2002) and Valentine Roux (Roux, Bril, and Dietrich 1995; Roux and Bril 2005; Roux 2007) on knapping apprenticeships helps to fill out the picture, showing the relationships between perception and action, and the scaffolding of tasks. The performativity of certain gestures of craft production has also been illuminated with regard to the creation of impressive obsidian blades, in much later contexts, such as the Bronze Age Aegean (Carter 2004; 2007).

The reconstruction of the lithic *chaîne opératoire* can be seen as a kind of network of connections analytically, even if not by the practitioner. Such a network would be rather cold, a sequence of steps pieced together. But what we are after is a network approach that shows the relations between human, gesture, and material at the micro-scale in rather more dynamic fashion. We need to consider the directionality of the links, their frequency, fidelity, and distance. Some of these parameters will not seem that relevant at this scale of analysis, but they will come into their own at the meso- and macro-scales.

So, how can we understand the frequency, fidelity, directionality, and distance of the connections in relatively simple situations such as those outlined above? We need also to consider these micro-networks as bipartite, composed of humans and non-humans as two modes. And if we depict connections graphically, we might also expect nodes to vary in their structural characteristics within the network. Let us try to work this through with a hypothetical example.

A mobile group of hunter-gatherers, perhaps Mesolithic or Magdalenian, stops briefly to set up camp. Various tasks need to be performed, but most members of the group have done them many times before. Some start to make the stone tools that will be needed in some of these tasks. The process of manufacture unfolds over time in a particular sequence. For those who are skilled, one step leads on to the next almost imperceptibly. For those less practised, however, the different stages do not flow together quite so effortlessly, with a lot more stop and start. They look over the shoulders of the skilled knappers and try to take on board their gestures.

Let us put together a hypothetical diagram for how the stone-tool manufacturing sequence might look (Figure 4.1). For the sake of simplicity, we might envisage four variables: selection of appropriate material, core preparation, blade length, and degree of retouch. Equally simply, let us also imagine that there is only a choice between two options in each of these stages, labelling them A or B for material, C or D for core, E or F for blade, and G or H for retouch. The pale-grey circle is the skilled knapper, the dark-grey circle is the apprentice. The circles with letters represent particular tools manufactured in a certain way, which is given by the code 'ACEG', for example, which means that those four choices were made in the sequence. Thus the skilled knapper only ever performs this sequence, at least as represented by these two tools. The apprentice, however, makes an ACEG, but also an ACE and an ACEH. An added dimension is included in the diagram which we also need to consider— there is a temporal evolution from left to right, and the encapsulating rectangle represents the snapshot of what was happening on that particular occasion at the camp site. On that occasion the skilled knapper made an ACEG tool, and the apprentice an ACE tool, not yet able to complete the last stage (with either

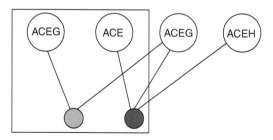

Figure 4.1. A simple affiliation network

G or H). However, on a future occasion both knappers make an ACEG; and further into the future still, the one-time apprentice has shifted to ACEH, perhaps as an improvement, or in the absence of the continung influence of the teacher.

This graph or 'network' is rudimentary, though as a bipartite affiliation network composed of two kinds of nodes—knappers and tools—it is already a lot more explicit about the nature of connections than are many one-mode networks. It has the added complication of depicting artefacts as multidimensional, and it includes a temporal component. There is no sense of Euclidean distance incorporated, though if there were, it would probably show that the elements are all closely spaced and proximate, as one might imagine them in Figure 4.2. Although very simple, there is already quite a lot to explain.

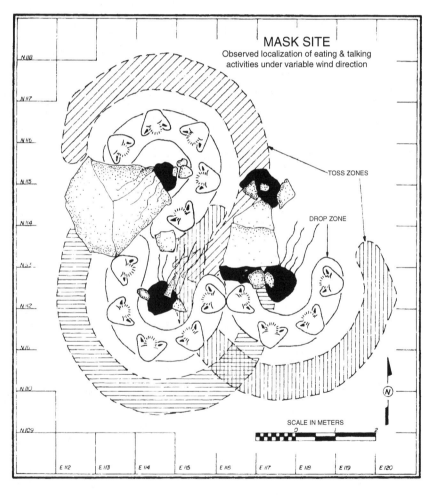

Figure 4.2. Proximate socio-material interactions

We may question how far this process of making affiliation networks gets us at the micro-scale. In the plan above we perhaps understand just as much about the socio-material processes. Those who do such micro-scale analyses of communication and gesture, such as Goodwin, do not tend to use networks to depict the scene or its interactions. Neither do those who use networks, such as in social network analysis, ever seem to occupy themselves with this 'micro-' scale of analysis. Unsurprisingly, these micro-situations are considered to be about 'agency', whereas networks are seen as a tool of structural analysis (Emirbayer and Goodwin 1994). But this is precisely why we have to try network ideas out at the micro-scale: to avoid this division such that some methodologies are reserved for certain scales of analysis. We must see how network thinking runs at the micro-scale, assess what the pros and cons are. It is essential in bridging the gaps between scales. It gives us some methodological purchase on the socio-materiality of the everyday. It is, essentially, a means of investigating more systematically the following kind of scenario imagined by Gamble:

> The limestone cliffs at Les Eyzies in the Dordogne is such a place for social occasions. Under their overhangs hunters moved throughout the Palaeolithic. While waiting for game to cross at the fords along the Vézère they made stone tools and later engraved antler, bone and the rocks themselves. These were places with associations based upon rhythms of encounters, seasons, hunting, growing-up, sleeping and eating around hearths and under rock abris. (1998, 439)

This concern with reconstructing something of everyday existence in the past is not confined to the study of the Palaeolithic, nor is it the sole preserve of phenomenological or agency approaches. We are faced with similar issues in accessing the micro-scale in all periods and places.

FACE-TO-FACE IN THE BRONZE AGE

The above excursion into the Palaeolithic has taken me beyond my specialization in later prehistory.[7] Perhaps in a future work it may be possible to compare and contrast the proximate or 'face-to-face' across diverse contexts in this fashion. Here, though, I return to more familiar terrain, introducing the first section of what will become, in this and following chapters, an extended discussion of one particular setting: the Bronze Age of Crete. It is somewhat arbitrary whether the focus falls on the Palaeolithic or later prehistory; and in many 'theoretical' works in archaeology the choices made are based on the

---

[7] I might equally have ventured into the early Neolithic, or to the New World, or into historical archaeology, all equally distant from my own primary area of study.

primary research area of the writer rather than a selection of an 'ideal' case study from across space and time. This work is no different, and I believe that if I am able at all to marry convincingly the theoretical angles proposed here with actual examples, it will be through the material that I know best. That said, and in defence of the seemingly arbitrary nature of the choice of subject matter, the Bronze Age of the Aegean, and Crete in particular, offers, in a 'protohistoric' context, an abundant and varied material culture from many different settlements and through a series of phases. Moreover, the material covers some striking socio-political changes, with the emergence of 'palatial' society at the turn of the second millennium BC. This transition sees some critical organizational transformations at the meso- and macro-scales, as we shall explore in subsequent chapters. But here the more immediate question is this: what, if anything, changes at the level of micro-scale practice with the shift from 'Prepalatial' to palatial society? I will now look at different kinds of practice in turn—divided up as production, distribution, and consumption—starting with production.

PALATIAL PRODUCTION?

Rather than try to cover all forms of 'production', that might include agricultural practices for example, here the focus falls on *craft* production. There are all kinds of craft production with interesting suites of micro-gestures, more or less observable archaeologically. In contemporary settings we can observe the gestures and the communicative utterances accompanying crafting actions (see Goodwin 1994; Stout 2002; Roux, Bril, and Dietrich 1995); but archaeologically we have to work from material traces to practices. Sometimes these traces may be 'on the ground' in the form of workshop installations. For palatial Crete, however, there is relatively little such evidence for actual workshops or other crafting locations (with the striking exception of Quartier Mu Malia, see below). Given the proliferation of sophisticated crafting activities, this absence is quite striking and suggests that craftspeople were working outside settlements, or perhaps on those margins of settlements that have barely been excavated. This then pushes us to look at other kinds of traces, those that we see in and on the finished products.

By adopting a *chaîne opératoire* approach we can seek to reconstruct the sequence of production steps involved in the manufacture of an object, and hopefully in the process identify some of the gestures and choices involved (Sillar and Tite 2000; Bar-Yosef and van Peer 2009). This approach is an important tool for forcing us to look at the dynamic processes underlying what can often seem dry and static artefacts; and for this reason alone it should be far more widely employed than is currently the case. It is not without its inevitable drawbacks, such as the assumption that craftspeople in the past had an operational sequence in mind first, which they then operationalized in practice. This may be the case for formalized modern technologies, but many ancient and traditional technologies may be rather more ad hoc. Furthermore, we are faced also with the obvious problem that reconstructing a full operational sequence may not be possible for additive technologies in the same way as for reductive technologies; we should not forget that the method was adapted primarily for reductive lithic sequences. For pottery, it may often be impossible to say much from the finished product about the gestures of clay selection and paste preparation, drying, and firing.

Admittedly, there are severe limits to our understanding of the details of craft gestures and activities in the Cretan Bronze Age. Nonetheless, we can see from the abundant finished products, especially the pottery, that there is quite some continuity in craft gestures from the Prepalatial to the Palatial period. In the Mesara region of south Crete, in the area around Phaistos (see map, Figure 4.3), clay paste preparation seems to change very little over a thousand years or so, from the mid-third to mid-second millennium BC (Day, Relaki, and Faber 2006). The same fine clays are processed and combined with river sand with remarkable consistency in grain size and clay–sand ratios. The coil-building of pots also seems very resilient, until, that is, a rather dramatic change comes with the introduction of the potter's wheel *c.*1900 BC (Knappett 1999*a*). Initially used only for small vessels, over the next 400 years the technique is extended to the full range of pottery produced across the island. Some wheel-heads have been discovered too, but the precise set-up is unknown. Nonetheless, the wheel technique, however set up, demanded new gestures, probably with knock-on effects for the spatial organization of workshops.

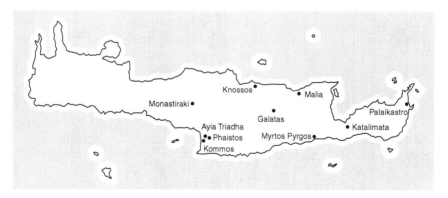

Figure 4.3. Map of Crete with some of the key Bronze Age sites

The decoration of pottery also changes quite markedly at the beginning of the Palatial period, with increasingly intricate and unique designs, embodied in the so-called 'Kamares ware' (Walberg 1976). The application of both white and red paint over a lustrous black slip would also have been considerably more time-consuming than most decorative techniques used previously.[8] This implies a slower rhythm to crafting practices, though the innovation of the conical cup, mass-produced with very little effort devoted to surface treatment, would seem to imply the opposite. We see the use of the very same clay pastes and forming techniques for both elaborate and simple forms, so presumably any given workshop would have had to adapt to both of these rather different rhythms.

If we attempt a network diagram of these continuities and changes, it helps to illustrate the character of the different kinds of nodes and links (see Figure 4.4). We can use the same method as that applied to the lithics above. Each artefact is assigned a simplified combination of letters representing its production sequence, covering fabric, forming technique, and surface treatment. We also imagine a simple range of shapes: cup, jug, jar, and cooking-pot, which we depict with a circle, square, hexagon, and rounded square respectively.

Fabric	A	Fine buff
Fabric	B	Coarse buff
Fabric	C	Coarse red-brown
Forming	D	Handmade
Forming	E	Wheelmade
Surface	F	Plain
Surface	G	Slipped
Surface	H	Dark-on-light
Surface	I	White-on-dark

Thus any of the four kinds of vessel we depict will have three letters, one each from fabric, forming, and surface treatment. In Figure 4.4 we see a cup that is in fine buff, handmade, and slipped; a jug that is fine buff, handmade, and dark-on-light; a jar that is coarse buff, handmade, and plain; and a cooking-pot that is coarse red-brown, handmade, and plain. The numbers 1, 2, and 3 are hypothetical pottery workshops.

What we can see is that one workshop makes cups, two workshops make jugs, one workshop makes jars, and one makes cooking-pots. One of the workshops makes both jugs and jars, which might be important in understanding the sharing of technical features and change over time. Indeed, the network as it currently stands is a snapshot and does not incorporate any

---

[8] This technique would have also needed a considerable mastery over firing techniques, and hence new gestures and practices in this domain too. See Faber, Kilikoglou, and Day 2002.

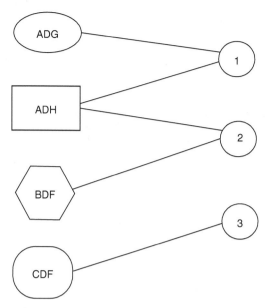

Figure 4.4. Imagined affiliation network for pottery production

temporal evolution, unlike our lithics network above. How might it look if we were to add this dimension (Figure 4.5)? Over time these general shapes continue from the Prepalatial to the Palatial period (though it is a lot more complicated than shown here), though there are changes in forming technique and surface treatment.

Although hopelessly incomplete, we can at least see how over time workshop 1 changes the decoration of cups to white-on-dark, but stops making jugs. Now jugs are only made by workshop 2, which in doing so changes the fabric to coarse, perhaps in line with its manufacture of jars. It also alters the surface treatment for both, now making jugs in white-on-dark and jars with a slip. Cooking-pots just carry on being made in the same way. These traditions are then taken up by the next generation of potters who, if one were to trace this on another step, may carry on in precisely the same vein. And in the next generation, it is then that a switch is made for the fine cups from handmade to wheelmade.

What this allows us to do in an extremely rudimentary way is envisage how the network or 'inter-artefactual domain' unfolds over time. It is in its current state little more than an exercise to show the kinds of complexities that emerge and how much we need to think explicitly about node qualities and connections. Although the above case is more hypothetical than factual, if we were to look closely at the evidence for pottery production from the Prepalatial to the Palatial, what we would see would be only very gradual, incremental changes

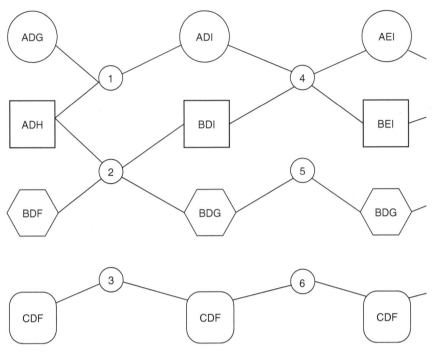

Figure 4.5. Imagined affiliation network for pottery production, with time evolution

from one generation to the next. Each change that is witnessed, whether it be the wheel or polychrome decoration, is well embedded in the network. To explore the nature of the micro-networks in a little more detail, however, we need to take into account a few more factors.

In many instances pottery shapes and decorative motifs seem to ape other media, such as stone, textile, or metal. This phenomenon, known as 'skeuomorphism', is certainly present in the Prepalatial period (see Nakou 2007), but seems to increase markedly in the Palatial era. We can tell from the various finished craft products that different materials were used in mimicking particular forms. So we can see obvious metallicizing features made in clay, stone vessels displaying metal features, clay vessels combining stone and metal mimicry in form and surface treatment, and so on. But we have very little evidence 'on the ground' for how these crafts were organized: did individual artisans turn their hands to many different crafts and materials (see Platon 1993), or were there a range of different material specialists working in close proximity, perhaps under palatial patronage in some instances? The building complex of Quartier Mu provides us with an important exception to this general picture, as here we do find a series of well-preserved workshop buildings all in use at the same time, in the eighteenth century BC (Poursat 1996; Poursat and Knappett 2005). There is evidence for pottery production, metallurgy, textiles, bone-working, sealstone-working, and so on, providing us with the opportunity to think about craft interactivity from the point of view of gestures and micro-scale spatial interaction. But even though we have high-resolution data from the Quartier Mu workshops, we do encounter some problems: the buildings in question are actually described by the excavator as 'maisons-ateliers': they are not only workshops but also living-quarters. The potter's workshop, for example, does have among its finds a potter's wheel and some small ceramic moulds, but it also contains many domestic finds; in fact, it is not clear that any potting went on in the building at all, as the wheel is not *in situ* and there is nothing else to tie pottery-production activities to this particular locale. A potter and his family may simply have lived here, stored some equipment, and worked elsewhere (in all probability, close by). The same goes for the 'atelier de fondeur', although it is anticipated that metallurgical production took place nearby, in a courtyard space to the west (see plan, Figure 4.6).

Figure 4.6. The Quartier Mu complex at Malia

Whether this was a performative process or not is difficult to say, though arguments of this kind have been made for Early Bronze Age Aegean metallurgy (Doonan, Day, and Dimopoulou-Rethemiotaki 2007). The 'atelier de sceaux', however, has lithic débitage on the floors and so probably was the scene of craft production. The probable grouping together of craft activities in and around these workshops, themselves closely connected to the main 'elite' buildings A and B, has a number of implications. It suggests that their residents may have had more than a passing familiarity with the craft gestures of these resident artisans. Furthermore, it indicates that artisans working with certain materials were probably very familiar with the gestures and practices of their neighbours: they could probably not only see them at work, but also hear and smell them (given the smoke and fumes produced by smelting or firing). Thus, their familiarity may have been sufficiently deep to allow for the sharing of craft skills, and certainly some scholars have argued that Minoan artisans worked in many crafts rather than specializing in just one (Platon 1993), though it is hard to say much about the interchangeability of gestures.

We can begin to approach this by considering possible overlaps, such as in the use of moulds. The two-piece moulds found in the metallurgy workshop tell us that moulding was a technique used in this craft, and we might suppose some broad gestural connection with the moulds found in the potter's workshop. However, these pottery moulds are rather specialized, used only for small appliqués on vessels, which are not very common in the ceramic repertoire of the site.[9] The techniques in use for the production of most ceramic forms were coil-building and wheel-fashioning, with moulding barely used at all. A rare exception is the use of two-piece vertical moulds for making basket skeuomorphs (Knappett 2002; see Figure 4.7).

Whether or not Minoan artisans turned their hand to many different crafts, there is clearly considerable cross-fertilization between crafts. And in the case of Quartier Mu at least, the different artisans must have had more than a passing knowledge of each other's gestures and skills. In comparison to the Prepalatial period, the gestures of production are surely different, given the increased range in the materials being handled by craftspeople generally, and the proclivity for drawing iconic connections between these materials.

If we now seek to depict these interconnections in *network* form, what can we learn? There is certainly a degree of directionality in the links, with some materials much more commonly mimicked then others: there is little chance of metal imitating ceramic, for example. There is also the question of the frequency of links, with ceramics aping metal vessels much more frequently than baskets. The fidelity of the connection is also of interest: some ceramics copy metal prototypes very precisely, while in other cases we see just an

---

[9] Though there is an interesting one-off find of a potter's wheel with multiple impressions made by a cockleshell, found at Skhinias, some 20 km east of Malia—see Eliopoulos 2000.

Figure 4.7. Ceramic basket skeuomorphs

individual feature, such as a ridged collar or a handle rivet. If we adapt the previously illustrated network by adding in a certain horizon the nodes of 'metal', 'stone', and 'basketry' (represented in Figure 4.8 by M, B, and S), further hypothesizing that these crafts were connected to only the workshop producing the fine wares (here represented by 4), then we can see that, even in this very codified form, the network of connections immediately becomes quite a bit more complicated.

And though we do not show either the directionality or the frequency of the interactions, these too would add further depth to the picture. A network is of necessity usually a reductive technique, a means of simplifying the picture to tease out some fundamental patterns. In the most basic terms, what we can see is that in the Palatial period these networks become more elaborate, with more connections and more kinds of connection. The 'agent–artefact space' of production expands, it would seem, with an increasing range of artefacts and specialists. Although in our affiliation networks we do depict both arte-facts and specialists (that is, workshops), we can project this two-mode network to one-mode, which is the kind of network to which we are generally more accustomed. This would appear as shown in Figure 4.9.

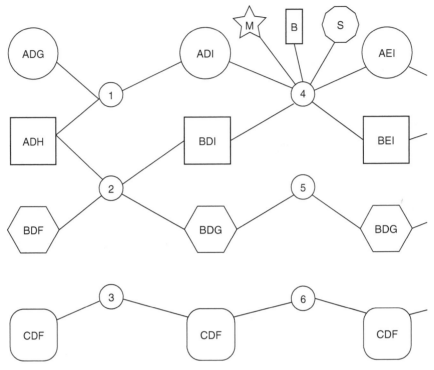

Figure 4.8. Skeuomorph network

As we can see, it does not take much to generate a denser knot in one part of the network. Here we posit, following the evidence from Quartier Mu, that this topological density is actually a spatial density too: proximate interactions at the micro-scale could have generated these connections. More connections do not, though, necessarily create greater assemblage stability; on the contrary, if compound blends are involved, more connections might actually engender instability. This we will return to in Chapter 7.

DISTRIBUTION

While in the previous section the focus fell on craft rather than other production forms, here we can nonetheless touch obliquely upon agricultural production in discussing storage practices. Such practices are here grouped under the heading 'distribution', as they intervene between production and consumption, even if not exchange or trade practices as such (which is what one might expect of the term). In contrast to production, there are rather more

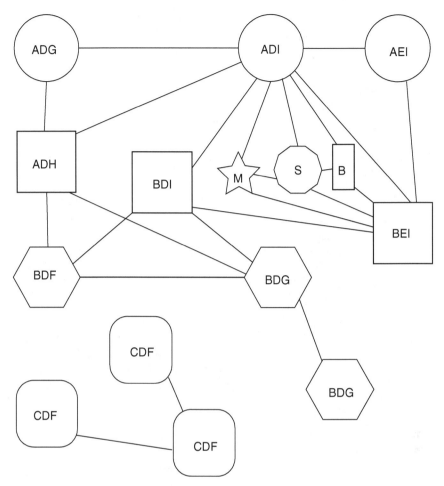

Figure 4.9. A one-mode projection of Figure 4.8

'on-the-ground' installations known to us that can be associated with the storage of agricultural commodities. Rooms devoted to storage called 'magazines' are variably connected to or closed off from other rooms (and here we may use ideas from space syntax or proxemics too—see Letesson 2007). These rooms afford certain kinds of bodily gestures, as do the storage vessels in them. Some can be tipped, some cannot; some can be manoeuvred using ropes and handles. Some are placed on run-off channels. There are particular arrangements that support the movement of greater or lesser amounts of different kinds of commodities. Among these commodities we can probably count olive oil, grain, wine, and pulses, though Cretan Bronze Age assemblages have seen relatively little archaeobotanical work and limited residue analysis (Martlew, Tzedakis, and Jones 2008; Koh 2008). While there are questions concerning when the olive and the vine were domesticated (Hamilakis 1996), it is probable that a similar range of products were stored in both Prepalatial and Palatial periods. Furthermore, one of the key storage containers, the pithos, is certainly already present from the beginning of the Early Bronze Age, and is very well represented in the Early Minoan IIB assemblages from the site of Fournou Korifi (Warren 1972).

Despite this apparent continuity from the Prepalatial to Palatial period, we do see some significant changes. One is in the actual morphology of the pithos. The Palatial period does see larger pithoi, capable of storing more produce, but also more difficult to manipulate without a team of people on hand. The arrangement of the handles also changes: Prepalatial pithoi have offset handles. That is to say, the top row of three to four handles is not arranged directly above the lower row. In the Palatial period the handle arrangement changes so the two rows are aligned, as seen in Figure 4.10.

Although no experiments have been conducted to assess how this changes the manoeuvrability of the pithos, it must surely have had some effect. A further change is not so much in the pithos itself but in the rooms in which they are used. For the Prepalatial period there is as yet little to no evidence for specific installations or rooms (magazines) devoted to storage. Yet one of the defining features of the first palaces is the storage magazine, often arranged in rows and with considerable projected storage capacity. The early magazines in the palace at Malia (see Figure 4.11) have purpose-built channels leading down to a ceramic basin sunk into the floor for catching run-off (presumably of olive oil).

This palatial arrangement of storage magazines is also seen outside the palaces, for example in the Quartier Mu complex at Malia (Figure 4.12), where Building A has a series of four small magazines opening off a 'ceremonial' room; and in the Crypte Hypostyle, where five large magazines are linked by a small staircase of four steps to a ceremonial benched room (Poursat 1992, 51).

These magazines have low plaster platforms, including run-off channels, but are not full of large pithoi as one might expect. One of the rooms—magazine I 7 in Figure 4.6—has a series of medium-sized jars, with a total capacity of c.250 litres (Poursat and Knappett 2005, 159), while another is entirely empty of storage vessels but has only a pile of about thirty loom-weights. These are not the only storage rooms in Quartier Mu—there are also some magazines of a rather different, oblong shape in the SW of the complex (rooms III 8–9 and 16–17—see Figure 4.6). These had magazines above them on the upper storey, which evidently had a number of pithoi which collapsed into the lower floor when the building was destroyed; the upper storey of room III 8, for example, had eleven pithoi, four jars, and five amphoras in total at the time of the destruction (Poursat and Knappett 2005, 162–3). The larger oblong rooms with pithoi were probably more difficult to move around in, but were perhaps accessed less frequently; the small square magazines had smaller

Figure 4.10. Pithos from (Proto)palatial period, with handles aligned

vessels, and were as a result easier to move around in, and were perhaps accessed more often, and in a different way, for providing smaller quantities for consumption in the adjoining ceremonial rooms. A final point on the storage practices in Quartier Mu concerns the small 'house-workshop' buildings that are set up on the periphery of the complex. Some of these, such as the potter's workshop (Atelier de Potier), are used for storage, and calculations

Figure 4.11. Early magazines in the palace at Malia

Figure 4.12. Magazine in Quartier Mu with low plaster platforms and vases *in situ*

suggest that this building alone had pottery storage vessels—both pithoi and amphorae—with a capacity of *c*.1,000 litres (ibid., plate 72).

With the advent of the Palatial period on Crete, therefore, we do observe some changes in the micro-scale of storage practices. Rooms designed for and dedicated to storage are seen, often, but not only, in palatial settings. The pithoi used in storage increase in size, and have new design features in the arrangement of the handles, presumably to increase manoeuvrability (or for a new system involving ropes?). Storage rooms, if the Quartier Mu evidence is not just a one-off, seem to be shaped with capacity of storage and frequency of use in mind. All of this indicates a fuller control over commodities in this phase between production and consumption. Further evidence for the micro-scale, gestural control over commodities is seen in the practice of 'direct object sealing' that comes in during the First Palace period, seen at Malia but also especially at the palace of Phaistos (Schoep 1999*a*; Weingarten 1986, 1990). Doors to storage rooms and storage chests are secured with clay and then 'sealed' with sealstones bearing particular symbols or designs, presumably associated with powerful individuals. Sealing practices do continue into the Second Palace period, but appear to be less concerned with the direct physical control of the everyday practice of storage. Evidently there is a dimension to palatial storage that concerns redistribution of commodities between different communities. This takes us away from the domain of the micro-scale to that of the meso-scale, so we will revisit some of these issues, and particularly the role of bureaucratic practices therein, in the following chapter.

Just as we used simple networks to codify some of these micro-scale patterns in production, so we might attempt the same for distribution practices. First, we would need to create a table enumerating the different features of storage, which might include the following features:

Pithos	A	Small, 1 row of handles
Pithos	B	Medium, 1 row of handles
Pithos	C	Large, 2 rows of handles
Room	D	Simple
Room	E	Magazine
Room	F	Magazine + features
Sealings	G	Pithos or room
Script	H	Inscribed pithos

'Magazine with features' describes a magazine with dedicated installations such as platforms and run-off channels. For 'sealings', some pithoi, or the rooms they are stored in, see evidence for sealing practices, as described above. And some pithoi are inscribed in the Linear A script as part of the administrative process in the Palatial period. The next stage is to postulate three different kinds of stored product: for example, olive oil, wine, and barley. These are represented in the network (Figure 4.13) by nodes of different

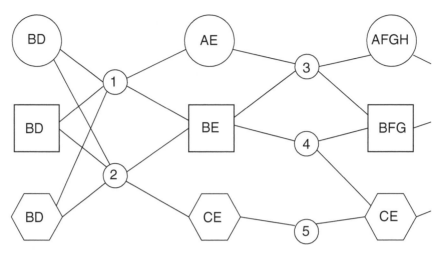

Figure 4.13. Imagined network for storage practices

shapes: circle, square, and hexagon respectively. The different combinations of choices are denoted by the letters in each shape—and these are very much hypothetical, for want of evidence. To make an affiliation network we need actors, even more hypothetical. Here we use numbered nodes to represent different actors involved in storage: let us imagine they are units roughly equivalent to households. Finally, the network mimics a very coarse time evolution, from left to right.

The column on the left shows the three different staples all stored in the same way (medium pithoi, plain rooms), and with each staple stored by both households 1 and 2. This is what one might very crudely imagine for the Prepalatial period. Then in the middle column the situation changes, with household 1 deciding over time to only store olive oil and wine, and household 2 wine and barley. Moreover, they do so now in dedicated magazines, and with pithoi tailor-made for each job. These practices are picked up by the next generation, of households 3, 4, and 5, although now 5 specializes in barley and 4 in wine, while 3 covers both wine and oil. Over time they in turn adapt their practices, with 3 developing even more specialized facilities, such as run-off channels, and using sealings for the administration of both wine and oil, with the added use of inscriptions only for the control of oil. Meanwhile household 5 carries on as before, dealing only in barley, and 4 branches out so as to no longer specialize only in wine by storing barley too. These final changes are of the kind one sees in the Palatial period, and one might consider 5 to be a 'normal' household while 3 has evolved into a villa, only below the palaces in the political hierarchy.

It cannot be stressed enough that this is a hypothetical reconstruction resembling the data only in the very broadest of brushstrokes. Yet, through this exercise we can see more connections between certain actors and artefacts, as well as particular patterns of directionality. The lines of lived experience—in this case the manoeuvring of large storage vessels in small rooms—do not necessarily lend themselves to division into nodes and links; and yet even a very codified network diagram can help throw up new patterns and facilitate interpretation. Though I will not pursue this further here in relation to distribution, I will now try to stretch this network idea further in relation to changing patterns of consumption between the Prepalatial and Palatial periods.

CONSUMPTION

The poor preservation of organic remains places limitations on how much we can say about consumption practices. We have little information on the foodstuffs that would have been consumed in Bronze Age Crete, and how they would have been prepared and served.[10] Moreover, we also know little about wooden and other organic artefacts that might have been used in the preparation and presentation of food and drink. So our discussion takes as its starting-point the inorganic craft products, and particularly the pottery, used in consumption. Note, however, that these caveats have not stymied discussion of consumption, with a flurry of recent studies in the Aegean Bronze Age on one particular practice—feasting—much discussed as an important socio-political act (e.g. Halstead and Barrett 2005; Wright 2004; Hitchcock, Laffineur, and Crowley 2008). Yet feasting has not been much considered from a praxeological perspective, one that focuses specifically on the gestural micro-scale and the active role of objects.[11] We can examine a number of strands of evidence. Certain kinds of vessels are habitually used, it seems, in feasting, principally cups and goblets of various kinds, and jugs, notably of beaked and bridge-spouted types. We can examine the affordances offered by these different types: their capacities, their graspability, the visibility of their decoration. We can look at the functional sets that group some of these pots together, and indeed the spatial arrangements of the rooms in which they are commonly found. We can consider the ways in which the Central or West Courts of palaces are thought to offer venues for feasting, and we might consider the 'Early Magazine A' evidence in this context (Macdonald and Knappett 2007). But these are very different spaces, evidently, with different gestural possibilities, to those presented in other settings, such as private or semi-private houses. What should we expect praxeologically when we find

---

[10] Though see Martlew, Tzedakis, and Jones 2008; Isaakidou 2007.
[11] The work of Hamilakis is an exception, however. See Hamilakis 1996; 1999; 2008. See also Simandaraki 2008.

conical cups in houses such as those at Palaikastro? Or the stacks of cups in Quartier Mu Malia, close to the lustral basin?

For the Prepalatial period there are indications of the use of large quantities of drinking- and pouring-vessels in feasting ceremonies of some kind; however, even at a site like Knossos it is incredibly difficult linking these assemblages to any kind of activity area (Day and Wilson 2002, 148–52). Many of the deposits are in secondary contexts, dumped in wells or the like, though we do see Vasiliki drinking-wares in small foundation deposits, as at Malia (Driessen 2007). We do not even know if there was a precursor to a central court in the Early Bronze Age at Knossos, though recent work suggests there may have been (Tomkins 2012; also at Phaistos, see Todaro 2012). Nonetheless, some differences in the ceramic drinking-vessels can be seen compared to those of the Palatial period. There are not the obvious vessel hierarchies that we observe even from the very beginning of the Palatial period (e.g. Macdonald and Knappett 2007, 161–5). Also later in the Palatial period there is the phenomenon of the conical cup, mass-produced and ubiquitous; there is simply no kind of equivalent to this in the Prepalatial period. As Day

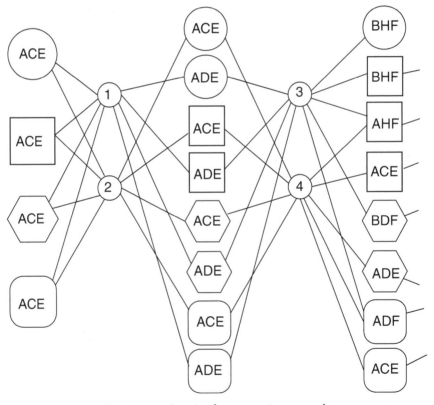

Figure 4.14. Imagined consumption network

and Wilson (2002) concede, the scale of feasting in the Palatial period proba- bly did increase considerably. All in all, the 'praxeology' of feasting probably did undergo significant transformations, involving new spaces and larger numbers of people; but some of the gestures of pouring and drinking may have remained relatively constant, at least judging by the continuities in vessels such as the goblet and the beaked jug.

As we have done for production and distribution, we can represent some of these consumption patterns in network form (Figure 4.14). Let us again simplify matters as much as possible, by choosing four kinds of vessel used for drinking and pouring liquids: goblet, cup, beaked jug, and bridge-spouted jar, represented by four different shapes (square, circle, hexagon, and rounded square). Then we need to codify different patterns associated with these shapes, as in the following table:

Material	A	Clay
Material	B	Metal
Quality	C	Low
Quality	D	High
Locale	E	Household
Locale	F	Palace

The numbered nodes in the affiliation network represent actors. There is a simple time evolution in the network from left to right. We also suppose a proliferation of artefact types over time.

The left-hand column displays the four basic vessel types, each of which is made of clay, of low quality and consumed in household settings by both actors. From this rather 'egalitarian' scenario there is an evolution to the middle column, which sees the two actors differentiate themselves through an increase in agent–artefact space. There are now two kinds of each vessel, high- and low-quality, with actor 1 consuming high-quality vessels and actor 2 low-quality. Into the next generation, represented by actors 3 and 4, this differentiation is passed on and developed still further, as we see in the third artefact column. Now there is only one kind of goblet, and it is a high-quality metal vessel consumed only by actor 3, and now in public, palatial settings rather than private household ones. In general, actor 3 now consumes pre- dominantly high-quality metal vessels in feasting while actor 4 uses clay; but in some instances there is overlap, when actor 3 also uses some high-quality pottery of the same kind as actor 4. However, actor 4 never uses metal vessels. Again, as with the previous networks, this time evolution simulates in a very rudimentary way some of the possible changes from the Prepalatial to the palatial period.

Of course, we can make this kind of network far more complicated, in various ways: by adding multiple actors, or by showing the much fuller range of vessels that would actually have been in use. For example, the manipulation of liquids is not something confined solely to feasting. We can see a preoccupation with liquids in other rituals, such as those involving rhyta. The rhyton is a seemingly peculiar kind of vessel in that it has two openings: one primary opening into which liquid is poured, and a secondary opening (always *c.*0.5 cm wide) from which the liquid flows (Koehl 2006). While in many of the various kinds of rhyton that exist the secondary hole is commonly in the base, in figural rhyta the hole may be in the muzzle of the animal (see Figure 4.15).

(a)

Figure 4.15. Bull's-head, globular, and conical rhyta

(b)

Figure 4.15. Continued

(c)

Figure 4.15. Continued

Rhyta are a long-lived phenomenon in the Aegean Bronze Age, present in both Prepalatial and Palatial periods. One interesting contrast between the two periods is that Prepalatial rhyta are almost exclusively figural, often taking the form of bulls and sometimes women, and are most commonly found in tombs (Koehl 2006, 280). The relatively small size of these rhyta, and the arrangement of the handle in relation to the two openings, would have necessitated a particular set of gestures. The gestures associated with palatial rhyta must have been different, meaning that the praxeologies of rhyton manipulation changed. The ovoid rhyton with a handle like the one shown in the centre in Figure 4.15 could have been used to siphon liquid from one container to another, with the thumb clasped over the primary opening used to create a vacuum. The conical rhyton, another common palatial type, could have been used as a kind of strainer for filtering liquids, perhaps wine (Koehl 2006). Such rhyta are often found in small clusters within palatial and other settlements, as is the case at Gournia for example, and at Palaikastro in Block Delta Room 18. Koehl has argued that they were stored in cult repositories and brought out for particular processions leading to public courts; an example of a fresco depicting a rhyton seemingly included in such a procession comes from Knossos (ibid., plate 60). The micro-scale gestures needed for effective rhyton use can in some sense be construed from the very particular design features of the vessels themselves, supplemented by experimental work into their affordances (ibid. 259–76). Certainly the rather different shapes and affordances of the Palatial period rhyta point to a new set of gestures in contrast to those of the Prepalatial period. Moreover, the contexts of use do seem to have changed too, from consumption primarily in tombs to a much wider use of rhyta in settlements. Rhyta may not have seen an everyday use, but perhaps more intermittently in specific cult practices; nonetheless, it seems likely that such practices were performed seamlessly within the daily fabric and rhythms of palatial and urban life.

MICRO-NETWORKS?

As people in the past went about their daily lives, producing, distributing, and consuming things, much of their experience would have felt continuous, embedded, and unthinkingly 'everyday'. Perhaps an intermittent 'event'—let us say a cult procession in which rhyta featured in some way, or maybe a burial rite—served to break up the everyday routines. This micro-scale of the everyday, a world of face-to-face interactions, of repeated movements in certain spaces in the company of familiar sets of objects, can be incredibly enduring, not just from one day to another but over the long term. If we look at the material culture through many centuries of the Greek Neolithic there are relatively minor changes. Yet we *do* see changes in the micro-scale between the Prepalatial and Palatial periods discussed above. We might not be able to tell in these prehistoric contexts how the form or content of conversational communication changed, or what altered in the way people related to one another. But we can see that new artefacts and new spaces are introduced, and these imply also new gestures and practices. It is with the beginning of the Palatial period that new methods of craft production appear on the scene, with the potter's wheel having some serious ramifications in terms of acquiring new gestural skills, division of labour, and temporal rhythms of working. More-over, the more thoroughgoing connections among different crafts either meant that some craftspeople were turning their hand to a variety of materials, or that specialists were exposed to one another's actions more directly with cross-fertilization among media encouraged. In distribution, and specifically the management of agricultural commodities, the micro-scale storage prac-tices change in the Palatial period, with new, larger storage vessels and more specialized storage spaces. As for consumption, there is some continuity in the gestures of feasting, though the nature and scale of the social gatherings in which they were embedded may well have changed. There are many other dimensions to consumption, but the only other area touched on above, that of the consumption patterns associated with rhyta, also saw some obvious gestural changes from the Prepalatial to Palatial periods.

And what of the networks we have used as tools for analysing materiality as the sets of interactions and affiliations between actors and artefacts? Though very rudimentary in the form taken here, they do have a role to play in helping us conceptualize interactions, even if only heuristically. They allow us to afford some attention to the *frequency* of the interactions between a producer and his or her materials, and the degree to which that relationship is of high *fidelity*, that is to say richly textured and consistent. Other variables we have consid-ered in passing are the *directionality* and *distance* of the connections. But what we see by thinking in network terms is how unlike a network the micro-scale of continuous lived experience may often be. It is only by stepping out to another scale that we begin to discover the network qualities of these very same artefacts and connections. And in terms of making sure we articulate these different scales, the same kinds of network thinking should be carried forward to the meso- and macro-scales.

SUMMARY

This chapter has provided a perspective on the micro-scale of individual lives that is very different from the 'agency' perspectives often used to access the micro-scale of the everyday. But how is it different? First, it includes artefacts as part of a social praxeology, and is non-anthropocentric in a way that marks it out from most 'agency' approaches. The perspective is really 'enactive' (see Law and Mol 2008), in that the actors and artefacts come together in affiliation networks and bring one another into being. Secondly, ideas of structuration and habitus may seek to articulate the micro-level of agency and the macro-level of structure, but they do not possess the kind of explicit methodology like that of the network for traversing scales. And thirdly, this approach can cope with both absolute physical space (geometry) and socially constructed, relative space (topology), in ways that are not anticipated in agency, habitus, or structuration approaches. We will see the importance of combining physical and social space as our scale of analysis expands in the two chapters that follow.

5

Meso-networks: Communities of Practice

WHAT IS THE MESO-SCALE?

The previous chapter was about proximate interactions, at what we called the micro-scale. This involved, for example, interactions among people and objects within a household. Now in this chapter we 'scale up', shifting to what we term here the meso-scale. What does this encompass? It means examining interactions between households in a single community, and between communities within a region. Evidently there is nothing hard and fast about how we define these scales from one context to another, and to some degree they emerge through empirical analysis. The same is true for the macro-scale, to which we turn in the following chapter, in order to describe the interactions between regions. This definition of three scales of analysis is not without its problems. One could very well argue that there are multiple scales: why not five, or even ten? Another approach entirely would be to say that we should not predetermine any scales whatsoever. While both of these perspectives have their merits, I have chosen to select these three scales as a rough guideline, providing some order to the exploration of scale.

Interactions at any scale involve human movement. If the micro-scale is defined as the 'proximate', that is, that which is within immediate reach of most of the senses within a single moment, then the meso-scale stretches beyond this. But how far? It is through moving that humans perceive and act; and humans have a range of movement in given time-frames and within technological constraints. On foot, a human could not possibly cover a modern city in a single day, but this might be more feasible by car, for example. As for prehistoric scenarios, let us continue where we left off in Chapter 4, by taking examples from the Aegean Bronze Age. Current estimates for even the largest Cretan Bronze Age town, Knossos, suggest a population of 12,000–18,000 (Whitelaw 2004). We can imagine that an individual would be able to 'take in' (on foot, let's say) most of a town of such a size in the space of a day or two. But this assumes the possibilities for human mobility without considering what the motivations for mobility might be. For the contemporary urban 'flâneur', there need not be any motivation. For a Mesolithic hunter-gatherer, the reasons for mobility would be quite different.

Although the dynamics of human mobility do necessarily underwrite our thinking about the micro-scale, they are not our primary concern. What we are after here are the dynamics of *cultural* mobility. That is to say, how do cultural practices in one household space come to be repeated in other households in a community, and from one community to another? A particular way of coil-building a pot, or using a pithos for storage, may be performed in one household. The practitioners are probably indirectly aware of other individuals engaged in the same practices not too far away; and similarly, they might be aware that others do similar kinds of things but with different gestures, or different objects. So a micro-practice, with its particular gestures, forms part of a meso-scale picture too. But how is this known and experienced? Why do some cultural practices seem to cluster in space, while others leapfrog space, finding discontinuous distributions, confounding the 'nearness effect' (Hägerstrand 1967)? Spatial proximity is not always a good indicator of social proximity: houses on opposite sides of a town may be much 'closer' in their practices than immediate neighbours. Thus, at the meso-scale we need to be mindful that the spatial and the social need not overlap neatly.

These are some of the problems we face in understanding cultural dynamics at the meso-scale. How *do* practices come to be distributed across space and time, beyond the proximate? In an individual's bodily gestures fashioning a pot on a wheel, manoeuvring a pithos in a room, or holding a cup to the lips to drink, the knowledge of how to act is embodied in a set of motor skills particular to that individual. Nonetheless, those motor skills, that 'savoir-faire', are most probably shared among a number of actors, who may not be physically proximate, and who may indeed have never even met that particular individual. How do such particular gestures come to be 'common' knowledge in a given group? Or to put it another way, through what forms of interaction are they communicated (Finnegan 2002)? Such questions are of course not trivial: they go to the heart of an enduring conundrum in sociocultural studies, concerning the nature of cultural traditions and how they are spread and sustained over space and time. Although phrased rather differently, in terms of presence and absence, or proximity and distance, some scholars in sociology and geography have recently gone as far as saying that social science generally has focused much more on the proximate than on the distant (Urry 2004, 27: 'the social sciences have developed weak analyses of the more distant yet intermittent connections that hold social life together'; Callon and Law 2004, 7). Given the scope of the problem implied by such comments, it is naturally not a question of solving this conundrum in a few easy steps; my aim here is to establish some parameters that might help us approach some of the key features, and to do so in a way that explicitly recognizes the need to articulate micro-, meso-, and macro-scales in the process.

The most important general idea to keep in mind concerning the meso-scale is that it requires a shift away from proximate interactions. It implies, in other words, a 'release from proximity' (Gamble 1998, 431; 2007, 211; citing Quiatt and Reynolds 1993, 141). Gamble underlines the significance of arte-factual resources in this process, in their ability to anchor ideas across space and time, and also discusses the variable uses of such resources across different kinds of networks. Here network ideas are also employed but drawing on a wider range of network concepts as outlined in Chapter 3. When we used such concepts in Chapter 4, it emerged that the 'meshworks' of lived experience did not tally particularly closely with a networked division of links and nodes; nonetheless, it was a network analysis that threw this pattern into sharp relief. In this chapter, however, I explore the possibility that it is at broader scales, beyond face-to-face experience, that network thinking comes into its own, both experientially and analytically. This will be still further accentuated in the next chapter on macro-scale interaction.

SITUATED SEMIOTICS

But networks alone are not enough to understand the ways in which artefacts can span experiential scales. We learnt in the previous chapter how artefacts operate as pivots or scaffolds for face-to-face social interactions. But how do they anchor interactions across broader scales? If an artefact can in practice invoke a person, gesture, or feeling that is not immediately proximate, then it is acting as a sign at some level. And entering into the domain of signs means engaging with semiotics. The semiotic perspective proposed here is situated and pragmatic, specifically drawing upon the semeiotic of C. S. Peirce. The particular suitability of Peircean semeiotic for gauging the meaningfulness of artefacts and materiality has been argued recently in both archaeological and ethnographic contexts (e.g. Keane 1997, 2003; Knappett 2005; Preucel 2006).

These and a host of other works explore Peirce's triadic sign system of icon, index, and symbol. Without rehearsing the arguments anew, we can briefly summarize these different forms of sign relation in terms of how they make absence present. Indexes make absence present through a direct connection of some kind, often causal in nature. So a footprint is an index of a foot and thus a person, due to a prior causal, contiguous relationship. There was inevitable proximity at some point between sign and referent. While a footprint may have been left by a foot many hours or even days earlier, other indexes have a closer temporal connection between sign and referent: smoke and fire, a cry of pain, or a weathervane. An icon, however, involves a sign–referent relation of physical similarity. This does not require the same kind of proximity or causality. A referent may be viewed from afar and then a sign created. The individual leaving the footprint may be viewed, and then drawn or painted. This may even occur some days or weeks later. Icons can transcend the proximate much more readily than can indexes. And when we consider symbols, these can be even further removed. A symbol is a sign relating to its referent via a system, a set of conventions; there may be very little direct connection between sign and referent. Symbols have limitless potential to range across time and space.

In much semiotic analysis, particularly Saussurean, it is very easy to get carried off into the representational world of symbols and lose sight of the pragmatic. And vice versa, in engaging with the pragmatic one can lose touch with the representational. Warnier in his praxeology is keen to avoid this very problem. In art history it sometimes arises in the guise of presentation versus representation. One way to try to ensure they are not polarized is to always situate these semiotic processes in the context of human practices (that is, praxeology). One example that I always find useful comes from the work of Rowlands (1993) on the role of monuments and rites in remembering. Following Connerton (1989), Rowlands differentiates between 'inscribing' and 'incorporating' practices; the former rely on the inscription of meaning in a monument to sustain memory and 'transmit' culture, while the latter leave no visible trace, memory instead being incorporated and internalized by the participants through the ritual practice in question. Rowlands uses examples from the British Bronze Age, with Stonehenge and other monuments in the landscape being associated with inscribing practices, while the practice of discarding bronze weapons in the Thames being an example of an incorporating practice: presumably a deeply meaningful ritual act to the assembled actors, but leaving no material trace and only transmissible subsequently through oral narrative, if at all (see also Bradley 1990).

While it might seem with the above example that the inscribing practice is more likely to lead to a more enduring 'memory' of the event than would an incorporating practice, things are not as they first appear. The monument associated with the ritual event may endure, but once the event has passed, and the actors have dispersed, the monument then takes on a life of its own. It may endure and signal to those not present at the event that something occurred there; but the knowledge of what actually happened may be rather imperfect for those not present. The monument gives more of an opportunity than might otherwise have existed for reinterpretation. Perhaps counter-intuitively, artefacts can be less fixed than ideas. One need only look at contemporary conceptions of monuments such as Stonehenge and Avebury.

I think it is useful to recast the above distinction between inscribing and incorporating practices in semiotic terms, specifically using Peirce's triad of icon, index, and symbol. Let us very loosely imagine the artefacts associated with the ritual events in both cases, at a monument like Stonehenge and at the edge of the Thames as a valuable bronze weapon is about to be tossed into the river, never to be seen again. In both cases the material culture is an integral part of the act; the stone circle and the bronze sword are indexes of the practices in which they are bound up. However, what the participants in the Thames sword act do by tossing the sword into the Thames is to 'freeze' the semiotic status of that artefact. The stone circle, however, becomes not only an index but also an icon. It is conspicuous, there to be seen, imitated, assimilated as an image. It can be transmitted culturally far more rapidly than the incorporating practice, albeit with far less texture and fidelity.

The point I wish to make is that different kinds of practices occupy space and time quite variably, and this must have something to do with their transmission dynamics (Knappett 2010). This in turn relates to the iconic, indexical, and symbolic status of these practices, because as signs these have different potentials for transcending space and time. Thinking along such semiotic lines provides a way forward for tackling the articulations between different scales, which we have a taste of with the inscribing/incorporating distinction made above. Some authors, particularly in Actor-Network Theory, have seen the need for some kind of semiotic perspective to achieve a multi-scalar perspective, without actually going much further than this, and certainly without using Peirce (e.g. Callon and Law 2004, 7). Indeed, one of the only authors to make progress in this direction is Webb Keane (1997; 2003), who explicitly uses Peircean semiotics in his ethnographies. Yet though the situated semiotics that Peirce's system allows is incredibly potent for understanding transmission, it does need to be socially embedded, which I do here by harnessing it to the idea of 'communities of practice'.

COMMUNITIES OF PRACTICE

The semiotic perspective shows us the material links that might have certain effects on human interactions across different scales. But we also need to give some more thought to the ways in which these socio-material interactions create and are created by 'communities of practice' (Lave and Wenger 1991; Wenger 1998; see also Lave's 1977 work on tailors in West Africa). This is a relational rather than a strictly spatial approach to the definition of a community, in that a community is defined by the relations between members, which are in turn established not by norms but by day-to-day practices. This practice-based approach, though based on ethnographic method, spans different disciplines, with impact upon educational theory and psychology, as well as in what one might label design and human–computer interaction (HCI): consider the work of Sellen and Harper (2002) on the ways in which various office-based communities of practice utilize the affordances of paper in such a way that computers seem destined *not* to create paperless offices.

These and other examples underline how practice-based communities are first and foremost 'relational'; these communities, as Amin and Cohendet (2004) show with the example of Silicon Valley and the influence therein on Taiwanese CEOs, can transcend physical space even at the global level. However, the physical spatial component cannot be forgotten in the equation; spatial clustering *is* also important in the dynamics of innovation in Silicon Valley, as it is in other industrial districts.

The 'communities of practice' idea has also been utilized in ethnoarchaeological studies, with a stronger emphasis on spatial distribution. The exemplary work of Gosselain (2000) in West Africa (see also Gelbert 2003; Gallay 2007) has examined the spatial distributions of different aspects of pottery-crafting techniques and the extent to which they tally with linguistic or ethnic identity over broad swathes of West Africa. Gosselain emphasizes the impact of the learning processes associated with different practices on their spatial transmission, with some practices requiring more in-depth learning than others likely to be transmitted vertically rather than horizontally. In some instances the 'savoir faire' is not that difficult to acquire; there is information available that could allow for certain steps to be taken and new practices adopted. However, that information needs to be validated, and only acquires this quality if it flows along trusted channels; information has to be trusted for practices to be copied.[1] Gosselain's analysis might be more at the level of the macro- than the meso-scale, but this slippage just goes to show the relative character of different scales and the easy interplay we should allow between them. It is not always a question of the need for embodied, motor skills, however.

Gosselain's work provides an empirical basis for the theoretical distinction between horizontal and vertical transmission, used in neo-Darwinian approaches to cultural transmission (Shennan 2002, 50). Horizontal transmission occurs from peer to peer in social groups, and generally involves practices that are both conspicuous and readily imitated. This could be easily copied forms of pottery decoration, for example. Vertical transmission is generally from parent to child, or at least between related family members of different generations. This kind of transmission tends to be more sustained, more face-to-face, and can carry more complex and difficult-to-learn information. Returning again to pottery, a good example here would be forming technique, given the long apprenticeship needed to learn the wheel, for example (Roux and Corbetta 1990). The two forms of cultural transmission imply different kinds of interaction, rates of change, and patterns of distribution of particular gestures and their associated material culture.

---

[1] This comes out very clearly in the work by Layton on innovation among French farmers in the 1950s (Layton 1989).

There is an important point to make here concerning the actual role of the artefacts themselves in these processes of learning and transmission. In the idea of 'communities of practice' as devised by Lave and Wenger, there does seem to be ample consideration of the active role of materials; after all, communities are defined by both 'participation' and 'reification'. Yet these two processes are implicitly hierarchical: humans come first and participate in practices, and in the course of so doing they create artefacts, thereby reifying practices in material form. Reification comes across, therefore, as a secondary process. I would like to place humans and non-humans on a more even footing, in line with the arguments of ANT and symmetrical anthropology. The artefacts themselves are not merely secondary results of processes of transmission, but can actively structure or 'scaffold' the learning process (Stout 2002). So perhaps our 'communities of practice' need to be conceived of as both human and non-human. This requires us to think seriously about collectives of artefacts, that is to say, assemblages. Archaeology should be one of the better-placed disciplines for providing insights on the nature of assemblages: as well as all the descriptive work in archaeology on assemblages, more thematic treatments of late include those of Chapman (2000), Knappett (2006), Gamble (2007), and Gosden (2005). Further treatment of the idea of assemblages as groups of artefacts that serve to span space and time will be worked through in Chapter 6 as well.

So, the interactions producing cultural transmission should be considered more thoroughly as human and non-human. Furthermore, in so doing they might usefully be depicted in network form, with attention to directionality, frequency, fidelity, and distance. This is precisely what is done in social network analysis, in the domain of sociology rather than anthropology (on the whole, though White and Johansen 2005 is an exception). By looking briefly at this sociological literature, we should be able to see useful links between the 'communities of practice' perspective and ideas of 'affiliation networks' (e.g. Wasserman and Faust 1994). It is also in sociology that we see work on diffusion through social networks, of relevance here to our concern with how practices are transmitted over space and time at the meso-scale.

AFFILIATION NETWORKS

It is interesting that the ethnoarchaeological and ethnographic work described above does tend to give some thought to the spatial dimension of social connectivity and knowledge-sharing. In social network analysis, on the other hand, the emphasis seems to fall very largely on relationships in a topological sense, as shown, for example, in the typical graphs of friendship networks in schools, or of research collaborations (e.g. Jackson 2008, 6–8). The networks depicted in such work are often at the meso- or macro-scale, but very rarely at the micro-scale (see previous chapter). When aimed at the macro-scale, they are frequently directed towards the discovery of communities within the greater whole, or what are sometimes described as 'blocks' (see Chapter 3). In some cases, joint participation in specific social occasions, such as fans attending a football match or activists taking part in a demonstration, is used to identify the community or block (Faust 1997; 2005). Here the connections are not shown directly between actors, but indirectly via participation in overlapping situations: each situation is represented by a node, as is each actor. Links are only drawn between different kinds of node in what is called a 'two-mode' or 'bipartite' network. This process of drawing up 'affiliation networks' is compatible with the 'communities of practice' perspective because of its focus on social situations involving specific 'practices'. Communities are defined on the basis of joint participation in daily practices.

Yet social network analysis is sometimes criticized for falling short in only *describing* such networks and not *explaining* their form and functionality (Newman, Barabási, and Watts 2006). These same authors stress the importance of, for example, understanding the processes whereby diseases (or, for that matter, computer 'viruses') spread through networks, or how fads and fashions spread through populations (see Watts 2002; Bettencourt 2002; Bettencourt *et al.* 2006). This focus on what are essentially diffusion models is not exactly unknown in social network analysis, however, where it has devoted particular attention to the spread of innovation (e.g. Rogers 2003; Valente 2005).[2] This work has served to underline the importance of different kinds of actors in the dynamics of innovation diffusion, in distinguishing, for example, between early and late adopters.

These approaches, however useful, do have some limitations as far as our current perspective is concerned. First, the sociological approaches mentioned here are focused on particular forms of interaction, such as the diffusion of innovation, whereas our interest in cultural knowledge and practice is more general. For example, many of the cases used in this literature concern information that can be picked up and spread relatively easily; there is not much explicit acknowledgement of the differences between horizontal and vertical transmission, nor of the differences between easily acquired and transmitted information and those 'savoir-faires' that are much more difficult to acquire (see Gosselain 2000). Secondly, in what is at root an *archaeological* approach, I am keen here to recognize the significant role played by artefacts and assemblages in the sharing and transmission of cultural knowledge over space and time. Artefacts do not feature much in these sociological accounts.

---

[2] See Collar 2007 for a recent example using network ideas to understand the diffusion of religious ideas in the ancient Near East.

COMMUNITIES OF PRACTICE IN PREHISTORY

Identifying communities of practice in archaeological settings has its own challenges. But if we are able to identify distributions of spaces, features, and artefacts across and between settlements, then we have a chance. If we are defining communities by sets of practices (or praxeologies), then by tracing the spatial recurrence of practices (or not) and their material scaffolds, we may be able to trace different kinds of communities and hence understand something of the character and pattern of interaction at the meso-scale.

The way I shall proceed follows the scheme outlined in Chapter 4: I shall try to demarcate practices of production, distribution, and consumption, and trace them using network thinking to show in simple fashion the parameters of frequency, fidelity, directionality, and distance of links.

PRODUCTION

Let us imagine a large Cretan Bronze Age town: we might return to Malia, for example, discussed in the previous chapter. Pottery seems to be one of the most abundant kinds of artefacts in this and other similar towns, such as Knossos or Phaistos. Some vessels are certainly imported from other sites, situated far and wide, even off-island. But let us assume that the majority are locally made, within the town. Is there any reason why all the potters in a town should make what consumers want by using identical techniques? Should a jug or a pithos always be exactly the same? Certainly, consumers may have specific expectations. And indeed, at many Cretan Bronze Age sites the techniques used are very similar within that site. Forming technologies are quite standardized. They do, understandably, change through time, but at any given moment all potters seem to be doing pretty much the same thing.

There is one interesting exception to this in the Palatial period on Crete. At Knossos, the largest town, there is more variability. In the Middle Minoan IIA phase, for example, *c*.1850 BC, some potters are making jugs using the wheel technique, a recent innovation, while others continue coil-building. This, if we follow Gosselain's earlier comments, is quite some difference. It is this kind of difference that could suggest quite separate communities of practice at Knossos, as far as pottery production is concerned. Pottery-forming is the kind of practice that is learnt in-depth and inter-generationally: through vertical transmission, that is. We can see patterns of this kind in relation to wheel techniques in other settings too, such as on the Greek mainland in the Middle Helladic period, where only some potters are using the wheel in certain communities (see Spencer 2006); or on Cyprus, where such technologies are also unevenly distributed within individual settlements during the earlier part of the Late Bronze Age (Crewe 2007*a*, *b*).

The case of Knossos aside, there is on Crete a remarkable homogeneity in technical choices for pottery production, both within settlements and indeed between settlements. Many sites within a broader region will tend to follow the same practices. And it is not just the choice of forming technique, but also the methods of paste preparation and firing that would appear to be resilient and consistent. Interestingly, this pattern, very broadly speaking holds true across the Prepalatial–Palatial transition; which could have some significant implications for our understanding of the effects of palatial political growth on production communities. This is not to say, however, that all the pottery produced from one workshop to another, or from one settlement to another, is the same. These deep-rooted practices that are presumably learnt through vertical transmission tend not to show up very conspicuously in the finished product. Aspects that are more easily imitated and transmitted horizontally, peer to peer—such as shape or decorative motif (see Gosselain 2000), are in many instances extremely variable from one unit to another. These are 'stylistic' dimensions that are more prone to deliberate 'tweaking' by the producer, and have an entirely different dynamic. One brief example: at Malia in the First Palace period local potters make beaked jugs in two different fabrics, red and buff (Figure 5.1). The red fabric jugs are either plain or decorated with white-painted motifs such as horizontal bands and a frieze of spirals at the shoulder; while the buff jugs are burnished or more often decorated with dark paint that sweeps up vertically from the base to the shoulder (Poursat and Knappett 2005, plate 18–20). This probably represents choices being made by at least two different workshops to create beaked jugs with different styles; nonetheless, they employ the same forming techniques, and the pottery appears to be fired with the same skill and control, suggesting that they are nonetheless part of the same community of practice.

Although perhaps stretching the extent of the 'meso-scale', which is in any case not an absolute measure, we might compare this pattern with the production of beaked jugs at the same time at the site of Myrtos Pyrgos, on the south coast of the island. Here too beaked jugs are made in a buff fabric, with very similar techniques and identical shape and dark-on-light designs (Cadogan 1978; Knappett 1999*b*; Cadogan and Knappett in prep). There are no red clays locally so red fabric jugs are not represented, though there are jugs in a buff clay with a dark slip and white-on-dark decoration (Cadogan and Knappett in prep). It is not only the dark-on-light buff fabric jugs that are so similar at the two sites: a whole range of other table wares, such as straight-sided, carinated, and hemispherical cups, and bridge-spouted jugs, are also highly similar in both technology and style (Cadogan 1978; Poursat 1988; Knappett 1999*b*). This points not only to the participation of potters at both sites within the same community of craft practice, but also to a deliberate

(a)

Figure 5.1. Beaked jugs from Malia

(b)

Figure 5.1. Continued

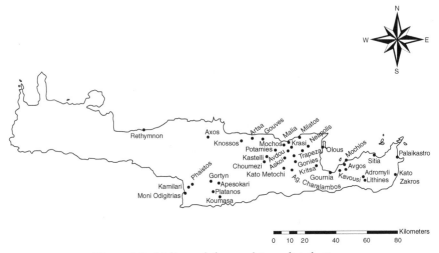

Figure 5.2. Malia workshop sealstone distribution

signalling of cultural and perhaps ideological or political links between them and no doubt the consumers of the pottery too. There is a definite directionality and considerable fidelity in the iconic connections seen here, with Myrtos Pyrgos potters imitating Maliote products.

We ought to be able to take this example of Malia and Myrtos Pyrgos further, beyond the pottery alone. There are indications that the metallurgy practices are similar too (Cadogan 1990). The stone vases, however, indicate a 'highly conservative, local repertoire', with only a limited number of imports and explicit connections with Malia (Bevan 2007, 119). This observation ought to act as a warning against the tendency to try to fit all patterns of material culture variation into a single unit, in this case the purported state territory of Malia. With the idea of communities of practice, however, there may be multiple, overlapping communities according to the practices in question. If we consider another form of evidence, the *c*.500 sealstones attributed to the Malia workshop, many are from Malia itself and its immediate environs, though a handful are also found in the centre and the east of the island, as we can see in Figure 5.2 (Driessen and Frankel 2012; Poursat and Papatsarouha 2000). These same authors also note the apparent similarities in the distribution of these sealstones with that of the Cretan Hieroglyphic script, suggesting a connected administrative community of practice.

Other 'communities' may be traced regionally in the Protopalatial period. Both Malia and Myrtos Pyrgos import oval-mouthed amphorae from the Mirabello and Mesara regions (Poursat and Knappett 2006), with the former arguably in a Malia 'state' but the latter certainly not. Moreover, Mirabello amphorae also find their way to Palaikastro in this period, well beyond the limits of what one might imagine to have been Maliote political control (Knappett and Cunningham 2012). Knossian amphorae do not turn up at any of these sites, and seem to belong to a different 'community' altogether. Yet, there is some movement of Kamares ware from the Mesara to Knossos; although in nothing like the quantities suggested (Day and Wilson 1998), there is nonetheless a connection here that points to a distinct community of practice.

As mentioned earlier in relation to Knossian workshops and the use of the wheel, spatial proximity is not a secure means of predicting a community of practice. The connections I mapped out in network form in Chapter 4 were purely relational and non-geometric in nature, though I did suggest that proximity did in fact play a role, as in Quartier Mu. Those same networks could be drawn here in this chapter, even though their distribution reaches beyond the proximate, and spans regions. One way in which we can emphasize this spatial flexibility is to compare the Protopalatial patterns described above with those in the following Neopalatial period, when the regional extent of communities of practice changes markedly. On the one hand, the community of craft practice in terms of shaping techniques continues to be island-wide, with no discernible regional differences in the application of the wheel to larger and larger vessels. However, it is in this period that the sharing of ceramic styles is much wider, with the emergence of 'tortoiseshell ripple' for example (Evans 1921, 592–3), a distinctive dark-on-light decoration perhaps imitating wood graining, produced by potters in very similar fashion at sites all over the island. Of course, we can also consider similarities in its consumption, which we come to below. Other dark-on-light motifs, such as spirals, become prominent, and are produced with a glossy finish that again points to the sharing of surface treatments and firing regimes among distant potters. While some of the motifs might themselves be readily imitated, the overall effect owes a lot to difficult technological practices, the sharing of which probably indicates a community of practice.

Other forms of production also see more widespread sharing at the 'meso' level in the Neopalatial period, such as for stone vases (Bevan 2007), and in architecture. There is good evidence from the Neopalatial period at Myrtos Pyrgos that construction techniques, such as extensive use of gypsum and ashlar, showed strong connections with Knossos (Driessen 1989/90; Driessen and Frankel 2012). We shall revisit some of these themes in the section to follow on meso-scale consumption patterns.

Of course, these island-wide patterns that we begin to see in communities of craft practice take us to another scale, the macro-scale. This is something of an arbitrary distinction between the meso- and macro-scale, evidently; but we can carry these points forward into the next chapter, when we go off-island and consider the spread of communities of craft practice at this broader scale, with reference to Akrotiri on Thera in particular.

DISTRIBUTION

Here I will use the example of the storage of agricultural goods, midway in their biography between being produced and consumed, and thus in some way in the process of being distributed even while being 'stored'. In Chapter 4 I cited some of the examples of storage practices, such as at Malia, in an effort to define individual cases of storage and the gestures, practices, and materials involved. One might equally well imagine other domestic practices with particular gestures, such as cooking, grinding, weaving, carrying, and so on. But how do such gestures come to be shared in different house(hold)s, if at all? Some of these practices might involve embodied gestures learnt over time, the kinds of gestures that are transferred from one generation to another (vertical transmission). Thus similarities between houses might point to family ties. Other practices might be much more easily imitated, and they may be observed and known about; if the information is trusted, then this might lead to imitation and transference. If the information is not trusted, however, then neighbouring houses might easily perform quite different domestic practices.

Let us then pick up the thread where we left off in Chapter 4. There I argued that there were significant changes in the micro-scale of storage between the Prepalatial and Palatial periods, particularly with more structured storage spaces and presumably more structure in the accompanying practices too. But how similar are storage practices across and between settlements in these different periods? Is it possible to identify any intra- or inter-site variation in the distribution of commodities? This is difficult to establish as fully as we might wish, given that storage installations have not really been found in sufficient numbers or with adequate preservation at many sites. This is especially true of the Prepalatial period: for many sites we can estimate the size of the settlement but we do not have high-resolution data from different sectors of the settlement indicating functional specialization or the like. As for comparisons between sites, our best bet is to look at regional variations in storage ware typologies, such as pithoi.

The study by Christakis of Cretan Bronze Age pithoi (2005) finds that the evidence from the Prepalatial period is patchy. Nonetheless, he comes to the conclusion that there are broadly similar patterns across the centre and the east of the island; this despite the observation that at Myrtos Fournou Korifi two distinct pithos traditions are identified, one Mirabello and the other South Coast (Christakis 2005, 78; Whitelaw *et al.* 1997). It may be that with more evidence from north-central and south-central Crete, and any evidence at all from east Crete, that further regionalism might be identified in Prepalatial pithos types. This holds some importance because Christakis contrasts this Prepalatial pattern with what he sees as the beginnings of regionalism in the

First Palace period. Indeed, the Mesara does now produce pithoi with painted motifs, a practice barely seen anywhere else on the island; moreover, the pithoi here tend to be more ovoid and with multiple handles (Christakis 2005, 73). In the area of Malia and east-central Crete pithoi are more ovoid-conical and often have trickle decoration and raised ridges (Poursat and Knappett 2005). Further east we are still somewhat in the dark on pithos types, at least until the Second Palace period.

So if we are to take the pithos as a material type serving to anchor certain sets of storage practices across space and time, what can we then say about changes in these practices between the Prepalatial and Palatial periods? Is it at all possible to identify a change in the scale or nature of communities of practices at the meso-scale? The evidence is imperfect, but does allow a different reading to that offered by Christakis. We cannot rule out the possibility that regional variation was just as pronounced in the Prepalatial as it was in the First Palace period. It seems that in both periods there is an overarching island-wide community of practice such that pithoi are used for the storage of commodities; and these vessels have approximately the same capacities and material properties of manoeuvrability and graspability. Yet within this broad picture there are micro-traditions regionally which suggest smaller communities of practice within the overarching one. These micro-traditions are perhaps in part sustained not only by frequent communication among users, but also by the movement of the pottery itself; imported pithoi are found at Fournou Korifi in the Prepalatial period, for example (Whitelaw *et al.* 1997), and at Malia in the First Palace period, in quite some numbers (Poursat and Knappett 2005). Arguably this picture does not change much from Prepalatial to Palatial periods, though it seems probable that these regional communities of practice become more politicized, sustained by different kinds of motivations. Come the beginning of the Second Palace period this politicization of regional communities of practice comes to the fore, with the strong influence of north-central practices of pithos production and use on communities in the Mesara (Christakis 2005, 76). This affects not only pithos types, but a much wider sphere of action, including other pottery categories, architecture, and wall paintings.

The use not only of pithoi but also of amphorae and jars for storage and distribution does seem to show some continuity from the Prepalatial to Palatial periods, and from one part of the island to another. But are all of these types equally used in different kinds of settlement, and in different parts of an individual settlement? There appears to be a general pattern whereby finely crafted pithoi are found in palaces and elite mansions, whereas more simply manufactured examples crop up in ordinary households (Christakis 2005, 80). Moreover, at palatial sites there do seem to be higher concentrations of large pithoi in the central parts of the settlement than in the outlying areas; at Knossos, for example, the Giant Pithoi from the heart of the MM III palace are a case in point (Evans 1921, 232–3), as storage vessels of these dimensions are certainly not found anywhere non-palatial. For some sites, such as Palaikastro for example, we hardly find any pithoi in the settlement, certainly so for Block M during the First and Second Palace periods (Knappett and Cunningham 2012). This relative absence of pithoi begs the question of whether this scale of storage was going on elsewhere in the settlement, perhaps in the putative palace (see Boyd, Whitbread, and MacGillivray 2006). Certainly nearby sites such as Petras and Zakros have found extensive palatial storage facilities with large pithoi dating to the Second Palace period (Christakis 2008). Palaikastro probably used similar techniques and storage wares at both of these sites, given they are all in the same region. Though these patterns do indicate some important differences in the scale of storage in palatial versus non-palatial contexts, and a greater prevalence of more finely made specimens in the palaces, there is sufficient continuity between the extremes to say this does not amount to separate communities of practice. One need only look at the very striking continuity of storage practices between the main buildings and the workshops of Quartier Mu Malia to realize this (Poursat and Knappett 2005).

If we can, then, argue for an extensive community of practice (with some sub-communities) across and between settlements as far as storage is concerned, what might help explain such a pattern at this meso-scale? On the one hand we should consider the actual movement of storage wares across the landscape, a pattern for which there is certainly evidence in both Prepalatial and Palatial periods. On the other hand, there is also the role of standardized vessel types in anchoring shared practices. Despite the regional and temporal variations in typology and decoration that do exist, there is nonetheless a remarkable resilience of the basic type across many centuries. Even though as many as 122 distinct 'forms' have been identified (Christakis 2005), the underlying morphology is incredibly repetitive (ibid., figs. 1–26). There is a kind of iconic continuum which serves to hold the notion of bulk storage in place. That said, the size of the pithos can vary considerably within this standardized form, with capacity ranging across two orders of magnitude, from 30 to 3,000 litres (ibid., table 1). This is an extraordinary range, and does not even include the miniature pithoi which are iconically identical to the larger forms but which would barely contain even half-a-litre (Knappett 2012). By including the miniatures, we increase the range across three orders of magnitude. This simply does not happen for any other ceramic type. That the type can maintain its coherence across such a scalar range is indicative of the strong anchoring role the pithos plays as an 'icon' of storage. One would nevertheless imagine that small and large pithoi offer quite different affordances in terms of manoeuvrability and actual patterns of use; yet pithoi do seem to be used in much the same way irrespective of size.

However important the pithos as an icon of storage practice, we need to broaden our discussion and go beyond ceramic types. We have indicated some differences between palaces, mansions, and ordinary households in the capacity and crafting of pithoi; another difference is that storage practices in palaces and mansions tend also to be the subject of some bureaucratic control. Various administrative practices employing scripts and seals are used to achieve this control. Although there is some discussion of the possible early occurrence of such practices in the Prepalatial period (Weingarten 1990), it is really in the Palatial periods that these kinds of practices come into their own. At first, in the First Palace period, two scripts are used in administration, Linear A and Cretan Hieroglyphic, in different parts of the island; but eventually, in the Second Palace period, Linear A becomes the sole script used all over the island. In parallel with this is an extension of administration beyond palatial sites to include smaller, secondary centres.

When considering communities of practice in seal- and script-use, we are immediately concerning ourselves with a relatively small segment of the population. These are not everyday household practices, generally being confined to 'elite' contexts and with the assumption of a very limited literacy and script-use being in the hands of a select few. Nonetheless we can certainly identify distinct communities of practice in the First and Second Palace periods. We see the same pattern as we see in many other areas of Cretan Bronze Age material culture: an overarching island-wide pattern within which are found distinct regional sub-communities. For example, in the First Palace period there is an unmistakable regionalism, with Linear A in use in south-central Crete and a completely different script, Cretan Hieroglyphic in use in the east-central and eastern parts of the island; at Knossos we seem to see an overlap with both scripts occurring (Schoep 1999*a*; Knappett and Schoep 2000). These scripts are also tied up with rather distinct bureaucratic practices, with four-sided bars used for Cretan Hieroglyphic in contrast to the page-shaped tablets for Linear A (Olivier and Godart 1996; Godart and Olivier 1976–85). And yet in both areas there is a pattern of staying rather close to the commodities that are being processed, with the use of 'direct object sealings', medallions, hanging nodules, and the like (Hallager 1996). We can see the sharing of such practices from one site to another; for example, the practice of direct object sealing at Monastiraki, in the Amari valley, parallels the administrative processes at Phaistos very strongly (Weingarten 1986). Likewise, the administrative techniques found at Petras duplicate those from Quartier Mu Malia (Tsipopoulou and Hallager 2007). Subsequently there is a very strong trend towards an island-wide community of practice with the establishment of Linear A as the single script, albeit with regional variations in actual sealing practices and so on still very much apparent (Schoep 1999*b*). This is another example, as with the pithoi, of the spreading influence of Knossian communities of practice in the Second Palace period, despite the irony that Linear A is seemingly an innovation from the Mesara.

For the pithoi, I discussed the role of iconicity in anchoring communities of storage practice at the meso-scale, particularly between sites (and indeed the role of miniatures in accentuating the iconic status of this type). What, though, are the effects of bureaucratic practices using scripts and seals on the meso-scale sharing of practices? These technologies too constitute a form of 'object-ification', of galvanizing what might previously have been more fluid patterns of resource exploitation. The flows of commodities through the landscape are stopped and given a more explicit value at a particular time and place. The technologies employed are systematic rather than purely experiential (rather like a kinship system—see Read 2010), and hence readily transferable from one place to another. We can see this happening in practice within regions in the First Palace period, and then across the whole island in the Second Palace period. While the practice is at first both iconic and indexical, with an establishment of contiguity between sign and object necessary in direct object sealing, this indexical component is surrendered in the Second Palace period for a more iconic, and indeed distant, relationship; and this distancing is, paradoxically, capable of providing more effective control. It is perhaps this shift that facilitates the spread of the system off-island, but we will return to this in the following chapter on the macro-scale. This broader scale will also allow us to bring in questions of networks more effectively: the semiotic processes that are part and parcel of the connections maintaining communities can also be understood as part of a move away from meshworks towards network thinking. The establishment of the pithos as icon and of script and sealing practices can be thought of as objectifying, node-creating, network-building practices.[3]

CONSUMPTION

Picking up from the previous chapter, where we found that there are considerable changes in the micro-scale of consumption (e.g. in feasting, use of rhyta) from Prepalatial to Palatial, now we can ask how these practices look at the meso-scale, in terms of their distribution across and between settlements. How are these practices shared and transmitted across communities of practice at the meso-level? Are they, perhaps, more amenable to horizontal transmission than some other practices? What role do the artefacts themselves

---

[3] Note that some pithoi are themselves inscribed in Linear A, with examples at Petras, Palaikastro, etc.

play in anchoring practices at this scale? Is anchoring more important in horizontal than vertical transmission?

The broad pattern of similarity across Crete in consumption practices mirrors that already identified for production and distribution too. There is a remarkable homogeneity which holds true for the Prepalatial and Palatial periods; this is something that Minoan scholars easily take for granted, but all it takes is a glance across to the mainland, the Cyclades, or coastal Anatolia to see how very different consumption patterns can be (principally concerning pottery) in neighbouring areas. The unity of Crete at this level is very striking, and underlies the general sense of a unified Cretan Bronze Age culture (though this changes in the Final and Postpalatial periods). Nevertheless, there are of course strong regional patterns within this overarching homogeneity, and it remains a challenge to understand the dynamics of this relationship between different scales. We also have to ask ourselves how varied consumption practices may be *within* any given settlement.

Let us begin at the site level. How varied are consumption practices, as far as the evidence allows us to say, within a site, from one household or building to another? If we begin with the Prepalatial, we are, as is often the case, hamstrung by the gaps in the settlement evidence. It is really only the site of Myrtos Fournou Korifi that offers some insights, thanks to the careful excavation of Peter Warren (Warren 1972), and subsequent detailed analysis by Todd Whitelaw (Whitelaw 1983; Whitelaw *et al.* 1997; Whitelaw 2007). Here it is possible to interpret patterns in ceramic distribution in terms of differential household choices. For example, dark-slipped vessels with white painted chevrons are only found in one household in the community. Furthermore, 'households in the north and east of the community prefer the locally produced piriform jars, while those in the south prefer vessels imported from the Gulf of Mirabello area' (Whitelaw 2007, 73). Other such inter-household patterns are surprisingly difficult to find for the Prepalatial period, as we have very few well-excavated destruction horizons.

We do have more evidence for the Palatial periods, as one might expect. And one might also expect to find pronounced differences in consumption patterns at palatial sites between the palace, the elite urban centre, and the urban periphery. However, though there are differences, they are not nearly as pronounced as one might have suspected. Certainly, there does seem to be something of a concentration of the finest palatial ware—eggshell Kamares ware—within the palaces (for example, Knossos Royal Pottery Stores), but is by no means absent outside the palaces themselves (Walberg 1976; Macdonald and Knappett 2007). At Knossos there is even a rather counter-intuitive pattern observed in the Second Palace period such that the palace seems to have *less* fine pottery than does the surrounding town (Evans 1921, 552–3; Hood 1996). However, this is often explained in terms of missing metal vessels: it is these far more valuable objects that would have been used only in the palace for elite consumption, and yet such vessels are rarely encountered in the archaeological record because of their high value and capacity for recycling.

Variable consumption between town and palace has also been the subject of a recent study at Phaistos (Militello 2012). Another site where a number of town buildings have been excavated, but not a palace, is Palaikastro. Here recent excavations allow for comparisons from one building to another, with the end of the Second Palace period (LM IB) being the best-represented in terms of destruction deposits and material-culture assemblages. The material from the buildings in question—Buildings 4 and 5—is not yet published, except in preliminary reports (e.g. MacGillivray *et al.* 1989; 1991), though that from House N is (Sackett and Popham 1965). Though a detailed study to compare these buildings is certainly required, something that will be made possible once full publication has been completed, indications are that there are no significant differences from one building to another in consumption practices. What is very striking, however, is that in this very period a previously flourishing set of town buildings, in the area dubbed Block M, has gone completely out of use (MacGillivray, Sackett, and Driessen 2007; Knappett and Cunningham 2012). This seems in some way connected with strategies pursued by the residents of this block earlier in the Second Palace period; the construction of a Minoan Hall in this block, an architectural form of central Cretan type, and the only one of its kind yet found in Palaikastro (Driessen 1999), indicates a strategic alignment with elites in the centre of the island (that is, Knossos). This so far seems to be a decision made only by the residents of this particular block, which may indicate a different community of practice within this large town site.

That said, other aspects of consumption within Block M seem largely in line with what is observed in other parts of the town at this time (MM III and LM IA), with local ledge-rim bowls and conical cups very much to the fore as the principal pottery vessels (Knappett and Cunningham 2012). One might also mention the work currently being done for Malia using geographic information science (GISc) to analyse distribution patterns of artefacts across a site (Hacigüzeller, n.d.).

If we now consider a different scale of variation, shifting from intra-site to inter-site patterns, an obvious case study presents itself for the First Palace period: the so-called Malia-Lasithi state. This polity is hypothesized principally on the basis of very similar pottery types at a range of sites in east-central and east Crete, but primarily Malia on the north coast and Myrtos Pyrgos on the south coast (Poursat 1988; Cadogan 1990; Knappett 1999b). The former is a large palatial site, presumably at the centre of a political territory; while the latter, it is suggested, fell within Malia's territory. The strongest similarities in the pottery are in the fine wares—mostly finely crafted, elaborately decorated drinking- and pouring-vessels—that would surely have been used in elite

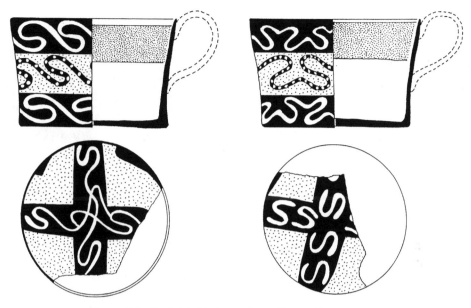

Figure 5.3. Straight-sided cups from Myrtos Pyrgos

conspicuous consumption. Not only are there many cup and jug shapes that are identical at the two sites, but there are also very specific decorative features that are incredibly close. The straight-sided cups illustrated in Figure 5.3, in a trichrome ware with running meanders, are found in identical form at both sites, though locally made in each case.

This does have implications for the organization of production and communities of production practice, of course; but here we are focused on consumption. What this surely indicates is the alignment of the elites at Myrtos Pyrgos, a relatively small site, with those of Malia. They must have shared very similar consumption practices, though this does seem to have been a relatively short-lived, strategic arrangement, perhaps lasting no longer than a generation. The fact that these consumption practices, whatever their precise form may have been, were anchored in very specific and elaborate items of material culture is suggestive; perhaps it points to a very dynamic, shifting scenario, with competition from all sides, meaning that the practice needed to be highly specified by the material culture involved. These vessels do fit into a wider Cretan practice of 'feasting' in the First Palace period, with the same cup types—hemispherical, straight-sided, and carinated cups especially—repeated also at palatial sites such as Phaistos and Knossos (see Levi and Carinci 1988; MacGillivray 1998; Macdonald and Knappett 2007). Yet the specifics of the decoration mark these Malia and Myrtos Pyrgos

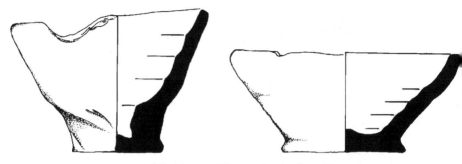

Figure 5.4. Middle Minoan III conical cups from Knossos

examples out; such trichrome styles as those illustrated above never occur at Phaistos or Knossos.

In the Second Palace period, however, this kind of practice seems to change. The pronounced regionalism is eroded by a strong cultural influence from Knossos as its power expands through the Middle Minoan III period and into Late Minoan IA. A totally new form of table ware appears from the very beginning of Middle Minoan III, at sites all across the island—the 'conical cup'. This takes a wide variety of shapes, not always conical, but the basic idea is always the same: a small handleless cup that is made rapidly and sometimes carelessly on the wheel, and which is always plain and undecorated (Figure 5.4).

During MM III there is some degree of regional variation in these types, but by LM IA a rather standardized form is in use (van de Moortel 2002). It has been convincingly argued that these vessels are used in acts of 'token hospitality' (Rupp and Tsipopoulou 1999), with some small quantity of food or drink being offered to guests, in settings ranging from private to public, before the vessel is then discarded, perhaps after only one use. Arguably the standardized form of the conical cup served to anchor this widespread practice and allow the growth of a community of practice in 'feasting' that spread across the island (and indeed off-island) as never before. Could it be that the very simplicity of the form, and the practice it served to anchor, is what enabled the maintenance of this community at such a scale? It is in marked contrast to the elaborated, precisely designed forms and decorations of the drinking-vessels of the First Palace period, which may also, as a corollary, have been accompanied by more diverse forms of feasting across the island.

We should not consider either conical cups or their predecessors in isolation; these vessels were used within wider assemblages, and indeed within particular spaces. The degree to which these assemblages and spaces also become more standardized and thus more capable of securely anchoring consumption practices also merits detailed attention. In just touching upon these issues here, however, we might draw attention to the rhyton as a particular kind of vessel presumably used in at least some consumption practices alongside conical cups; while also mentioning some of the possible architectural spaces in which conical cups and rhyta were employed—courts and halls.

Rhyta do seem to increase considerably in number in the Second Palace period (Koehl 2006); indeed, they are a little thin on the ground during the First Palace period, less so even than the Prepalatial period. Their affordances and probable associated gestures were discussed in the context of the micro-scale in Chapter 4. What we now need to assess briefly is the extent to which the rhyton occurs in predictable types in the Second Palace period, to the extent that it could be said to iconically and indexically anchor and announce its associated practices (across time and space). The rhyton evidently embodies great specificity in its design, almost at the other end of the spectrum from the 'design-devoid' conical cup. The Type II Handleless Piriform rhyton, first appearing in MM IIIA, is widely distributed across Crete by LM IA, becoming 'one of the most popular rhyta in Aegean culture' (ibid. 24–5). Another rhyton type first appearing at the beginning of the Second Palace period and going on to become a widespread type is the Type III Conical (ibid. 45–7). While both these types of rhyton appear in a range of materials and decorative styles, their forms are really quite consistent across regions and periods. They are perhaps a kind of iconic standard that helps to scaffold their associated gestures and use contexts. The iconicity of some rhyta is still further accentuated by their 'pictorial' zoomorphic form, such as the Type II Head-shaped rhyton taking the form of a bull's head (ibid. 32–6).

These various kinds of rhyta occur in a range of find contexts, but in the Second Palace period can be associated in particular with 'cult repositories', such as that in House Cm Room 58 at Gournia (Koehl 2006, 288–9). The idea is that these rhyta, in this case fourteen in number, were stored for use in a cult procession of some kind leading to a hall or court.[4] In the LM IA period there is a growth in the number of Minoan Halls across the island (Driessen 1982), suggesting that this relatively standardized architectural unit may too have played a part in scaffolding a particular set of practices (the same may be said of central courts too). Not only do rhyta find a connection with such spaces, but also conical cups: the Minoan Hall of Block M at Palaikastro, for example, has a cupboard or small storeroom of conical cups and bowls close to its entrance (Knappett and Cunningham 2003). It is as if a series of connections are needed between different materialities to guide and structure practices across and between communities; and that these are established iconically through the repetition of recognizable forms. This process becomes quite

---

[4] Striking plaster reliefs of bulls, griffins, and human figures are found in connection with the East Hall of the Palace of Knossos, and may also have lined corridors and staircases leading up to the central court. See Evans 1930, Hägg 1995, Blakolmer 2006.

pronounced in the Second Palace period, seemingly as part of a process of 'political culture' under the guidance, explicit or otherwise, of Knossos (see also Chapter 7).

DISCUSSION

In the above discussion of patterns of production, distribution, and consumption at the meso-scale, a taxing problem bubbles under the surface throughout. The problem is that in social science we have not proved particularly adept at understanding how humans operate beyond the scale of face-to-face interaction. How *do* humans manage to interact with one another across space and time, when they are not co-present? How are cultural practices and social ideas shared across communities of practice that extend beyond the proximate? Part of the reason why such questions seem so baffling to us is that the role of artefacts in such processes has been under-theorized. Certainly, scholars have recognized that artefacts have the capacity to communicate (Finnegan 2002, 137–75); but this has not been sufficiently thought through in conjunction with a 'scalar' approach. At the micro-scale, for example, artefacts frequently act as pivots in structuring interactions (Goodwin 1994). But there are all kinds of processes at work in the ways that artefacts stabilize the world of phenomena (things) in the world of ideas (objects) (van der Leeuw 2008). Making images of things can situate them as objects, and this can occur through depicting the thing in a wall painting, displaying the thing (Gosden 2004*a*), or making a miniature version of the thing (Knappett 2012). Naming things can also stabilize them conceptually, in the process denying some of their thingly qualities (Schwenger 2006), as can fragmentation (Chapman 2000). What these and many other processes do is to create a virtual community of objects that can transcend time and space, and which can be drawn upon across communities. Not all objects and technologies are the same, of course, with some more or less prone to different modes of transmission, and variably caught up in physical and topological relationships. But what we can see, I would argue, in the case studies used above is an increase over time in the degree of political investment in strategies of objectification. Over time, practices from one community to another are brought into line through the structuring effects of iconic objects. What this in effect achieves is a network of objects and not just a meshwork of things (see Ingold 2007*a*, *b*, on meshworks). Networks of iconic artefacts seem to sustain communities, holding them together across space and time, thanks to both their persistence and their capacity for acting as material anchors (for conceptual blends).

Networks emerge not just as an analytical tool for us, but as a way of congealing technologically the complex continuous meshworks of lived experience, of creating artefactual nodes as fixed points of a kind around which action can be scaffolded. The lived lines of experience can be grasped at the micro-scale, as they inhabit space and time at the scale of the body. But sensing beyond the moving body, expanding the scale, we lose control, lose comprehension; in this expanded agent–artefact space network understanding is a means of finding some order. The network is in a sense a tactic; indeed, one might even understand it as interfering with other spaces (see Moreira 2004 on interferences among topologies he dubs 'region, network, fluid and fire'). But while there may be many ideas emergent recently on topologies, there is still very little to help us connect action at different scales. When relationships among socio-technical entities are understood as semiotic connections, however, in the sense of being iconic, indexical, and/or symbolic, then we are provided with a means of bridging the local and the global, the present and the absent, means which are not often recognized in the social sciences (e.g. Callon and Law 2004; though Keane 1997 is a notable exception).

In the chapter that follows I extend the scale of analysis to what I call the 'macro-scale', dealing principally with interregional interactions and the role of artefact networks in sustaining such far-reaching human communities.

6

Macro-networks: Regional Interactions

INTRODUCTION: LONG-DISTANCE LINKS

In the two previous chapters, on the micro- and meso-scales respectively, I used case studies from Bronze Age Crete focusing on production, distribution, and consumption in the Prepalatial and Palatial periods. These case studies allowed for the evaluation of network thinking at the micro- and meso-scales. It is at the macro-scale, however, that network thinking comes into its own. Socio-material networks grounded in iconic 'objects' facilitate macro-scale interaction, allowing for the transcendence of spatio-temporal distance. Indeed, such objects may play a role in the subset of regional interaction that involves actual cultural transmission, alternatively depicted as 'colonialism' (Gosden 2004*b*).

It is thus probably no coincidence that it is at this scale that we encounter the most explicit use of network models in archaeology (see Chapter 3; Rihll and Wilson 1991; Broodbank 2000; Mackie 2001; Graham 2006; Sindbaek 2006; Terrell 2010). These network approaches stay close to the geometric properties of the networks under study, rooted in actual physical space; it is perhaps for this reason that network models take shape at this scale, as the idea of interaction as taking place in a physical container is still largely current (*à la* New Archaeology). Nonetheless, even when rooted in physical space they do have relational properties: the networks of the Cycladic Early Bronze Age (EBA) archipelago, for example, are based on an understanding of a social technology—paddling or rowing—and the distances that would be feasible to travel with such a technology and with limited populations (Broodbank 2000). Similarly, if we look at early commercial aircraft networks, Dakar in Senegal and Natal in Brazil were crucial nodes in linking the continents of Africa and South America, representing the shortest route between the two (1,890 miles). This was only relevant with the limited range of propeller technology, however, and with commercial jets the significance of these physical locales is dramatically reduced (Munson 1972). The seemingly absolute physical network takes shape according to available technologies, which are socially shaped and mediated. These and numerous other possible examples should alert us to the point that the physicality of such macro-scale networks is not to be discounted or overlooked; but that it is in some sense relational. The topology of the network changes fundamentally with new aeronautical technology, or with the invention of the sail.

These two dimensions of many human networks—the absolute (physical) and the relational (social)—are difficult to reconcile. In many network studies the approach follows either one route or the other (see Chapter 3). This relates to a much wider issue concerning conceptions of space in archaeology and the social sciences, with a marked polarity between these two dimensions. We need to find a middle path between physical and social determinism: physical space does not determine social action any more than social practices entirely create the spaces in which we live. Finding means to articulate the two is, though, a challenge. A large part of the problem lies in the habitual separation of the social from the physical or material, with insufficient attention paid to the constitutive role of particular materialities and their spatial configurations in mediating and guiding human practices. The social is ineluctably material and spatial. What is required, though, beyond this basic recognition, is an exploration of the potential of different kinds of technologies for working with or transcending the impositions of physical distance in the creation and sustenance of 'virtual' communities.

Technologies that have such capacity do not come free. Network connections across space and time bear some cost, whether that be in terms of capital, labour, or time investment. Think of the investment needed—sheer physical energy in paddling or rowing—to sustain the EBA networks in the Cycladic archipelago. This changed with the introduction of sail technology; though the investments were less physically strenuous for individual sailors, there was much more capital investment required, as well as the learning of specialist boat-building skills. Given the existence of costs, and the general tendency to offset cost with some benefit (assuming some minimum optimization in human actions), what benefits do we imagine might accrue from contacts that span physical distance? Broodbank provides a clear social context for this in the EBA Cycladic archipelago, with the need, on the one hand, for exogamy to keep small island communities viable, and on the other hand the prestige and power gained from knowledge of the distant and exotic (Broodbank 2000, 81–96). But macro-scale interaction is not necessarily in and of itself beneficial at the individual level, even though we tend to simply assume it happens without asking why.

WEAK TIES AND SMALL WORLDS

There are two issues here: *how* macro-scale interaction emerges in relation to the micro-scale, and *why*. Let us first tackle how. Oddly perhaps, given the boom in network analysis, relatively few studies explicitly tackle the relationship between different network scales. This is a blind-spot with some history, though: sociology's apparent inability to 'relate micro-level interactions to macro-level patterns in any convincing way' was lamented thirty-five years ago by Mark Granovetter in his groundbreaking 1973 paper 'The Strength of Weak Ties' (Granovetter 1973, 1360). While many studies had, he argued, focused on the cohesive nature of small networks bound together by strong ties, few had gone beyond these micro-scale studies to explore how different clusters were then interconnected into larger entities (moving towards the macro-scale). His response was to focus attention on those elements in interpersonal networks that he saw as the bridges between the micro- and macro-scales: he characterized these bridging connections as 'weak ties', in contradistinction to the 'strong ties' that held the cliques together as clusters within social networks. The counter-intuitive assertion that followed was that the weakness of these bridging ties was actually a strength. That is to say, in terms of access to information, concerning available jobs for example, the member with some strong ties within groups but also weak ties across groups may be better placed than a member with only strong ties. In other words, one might say that to keep these cross-cluster ties weak, ties that are inevitably also longer-distance ones than the intra-group ties, is advantageous and contributory in some sense to the resilience of that member's position within the network.

While Granovetter followed up on this seminal article in a 1983 paper, many network studies continued to focus on specific social clusters at a given scale; this remains a valid and ongoing enterprise (e.g. Christakis and Fowler 2007, on obesity networks; or Broodbank 2000, on Cycladic networks). However, Granovetter's distinctive trans-scale approach received renewed impetus with the paradigmatic work of Watts and Strogatz (1998) on 'small-world networks', though in this paper they refer to the 1960s work of Milgram rather than citing Granovetter. While it had long been acknowledged that social networks were neither regular nor random, Watts and Strogatz provided the first mathematical model able to show how regular and random components might be combined; in particular, they showed how to achieve the uncanny combination of clustering (i.e. cliques) and short path lengths characteristic of so many social networks, through a minimal random rewiring of a regular lattice. This effectively showed how social networks can exhibit both local clustering and global connectivity, thereby articulating micro- and macro-scale dynamics.

Watts and Strogatz's elegant model does have its limitations. It creates networks with small-world properties through 'rewiring' of fixed lattice substrates, adding what they see as long-range, random short-cuts. It is these that allow for global connectivity with short path lengths, the so-called six degrees of separation. In a subsequent paper, Watts does make explicit comparison between this work and that of Granovetter,[1] likening these random short-cuts to Granovetter's weak ties:

> Granovetter (1973), following Rapoport, had introduced the distinction between 'strong' and 'weak' ties, where the former could be construed as arising from local ordering principles like homophily (Lazarsfeld and Merton 1954) and triadic closure (Rapoport 1953a), and the latter from occasional random contacts, which Granovetter called local bridges, but which are clearly analogous to Watts & Strogatz's shortcuts. (Watts 2004, 246)

However, while the analogy does have some validity at a general level, there is nothing to suggest that Granovetter's weak ties are in any way random, merely because they are long-distance and infrequently maintained. The process of random wiring may create the same *effects*, but it is hardly a realistic social process. Another key component of real social networks is their searchability: it is not just that a member may be connected to any other member on the network via a few links, but that the member is capable of executing that search with local knowledge alone. Kleinberg (2000) offers an adaptation to the model that does take searchability into account; it turns out only some small-world structures offer 'efficient navigability'. This is freely acknowledged by Watts (2004, 247), who goes on to add that a further limitation of both the Watts–Strogatz model and the Kleinberg variant is that they 'rely on the presence of some underlying lattice substrate' (ibid. 248), which is unrealistic for social networks.

STRUCTURE AND FUNCTION, CAUSE AND EFFECT

This question of a network *structure* lending itself to searchability raises a difficult point concerning the *function* of networks. Searchability may be an effect of network structure, a function that the structure affords. Yet this need not mean that the function causes the structure. In Granovetter's study, for example, structure and function do find some connection, in the sense that structural properties were seen to afford functional advantages, although these functions were not necessarily deemed to be causal of the structural properties. For Watts and Strogatz, the small-world network structure arises from random rewiring, and so there is little sense of any kind of functionality driving

---

[1] Social network analysis returns again and again to Granovetter's paper; it is indeed one of the most heavily cited papers (15,293 citations recorded on www.googlescholar.com, 22 Feb. 2011).

the structure. Other, more recent studies exploring small-world properties also seem uncertain on the nature of the relationship between structure and function. One example is the work of Onnela *et al.* (2007) on mobile-communication networks, in which they identify a particular topology of weak and strong ties in a large dataset of mobile phone-call records. However, this overall network structure, of strong local clusters bridged by weak ties, remarkably reminiscent of what Granovetter describes, is generated by local concerns: as the authors clearly state, 'the purpose of the mobile phone is information transfer between two individuals' (ibid. 7334). The overall connectivity in the network, with its strong and weak ties, is an unforeseen effect of local patterns, it would seem, rather than a property that individual users are seeking to exploit or direct. Network searchability or diffusion is then an effect rather than a cause of network structure; users are not employing the network, on the whole, with searchability in mind. In Onnela *et al.*(2007), although they are able to map communication networks in a unique way, a clear account of the processes driving the observed structures is missing.

One problem, potentially, is the lack of any sense of cost. There is no mention of the cost of phone-calls, and the sense that there are limited resources: links are not cost-free. Users presumably have to choose how to spread their resources, and are likely to 'optimize' in some way, investing most in their closer ties, while not completely ignoring the more socially (and perhaps geographically, given cost structures) distant ones. This criticism is also one that has been levelled at the Watts–Strogatz model, in which there is no sense in which the rewiring that creates short path lengths is in any way modified or limited (Urry 2004). By thinking in terms of the optimized use of resources, we provide a way in which we might begin to *explain* some of the properties of small-world networks in more socially realistic ways. As will be shown below, optimization is a fundamental feature of the model developed in this book. This begins to address the question of not only *how* the micro- and macro-levels interact, but also *why* there should be any utility for small groups in engaging in large networks at all. There must be some function driving structure.

GEOMETRY AND TOPOLOGY

The work of Watts and colleagues has been absolutely fundamental in opening up the study of social networks to a much wider disciplinary field; so any extended critique reflects the influence of their work. Here we need to touch upon the question concerning the relationship between physical and social connections in networks. I mentioned at the beginning of this chapter the general tendency in social sciences, and very marked in archaeology, to treat

networks as either geometric, physical phenomena or relational, social formations. This is part of a much wider issue of the way in which space is treated in
different academic discourses. The way in which Watts reacts to the limitations he sees in the Watts–Strogatz model, with its use of fixed physical
substrates, is entirely predictable given these deep-seated disciplinary divi-
sions. He essentially jettisons the physical substrate in favour of bimodal
affiliation networks, in which the network connections are relational rather
than physical. These networks are much more realistic socially, but the shift
that Watts undertakes involves the removal of the physical spatial component
altogether. In this he has solved the problem of fixed physical substrates by
dodging the physical issue entirely. Perhaps recognizing this, he does then
create the option of qualifying the distances between groups according to
social dimensions, examples of which he gives as geography or occupation. It
seems odd to reinvent geography here as a social dimension, but one sees how
it has to be brought back into the equation at this late stage, having been
jettisoned at the outset.

In recognizing that the Watts–Strogatz lattice substrates are socially unrealistic, Watts seems to surmise that the problem must lie with physical
substrates, period. Indeed, physical substrates are problematic if they are
seen as determining social action. However, it is probably more straightforward to integrate the physical substrate in the early stages of a model, rather
than introducing it subsequently through the back door. A geographical
substrate of nodes in a network (whether sites, or individuals) can be created,
with the potential for the actual relationships between those nodes, and indeed
the character/size of the nodes themselves, to be generated subsequently
through the dynamics of the model. In this way the social and the geographical
can be co-created in what is actually a more realistic network: many social
networks do, after all, have a non-trivial existence in geographical space.
Rather than pulling a rabbit out of the hat, in the manner of Watts's sudden
production of affiliation networks as the solution to his small-worlds problem,
a model can be created that has many of the same advantages (nodes and links
of varying identities; non-reliance on deterministic lattice substrate) without
throwing out the baby of physical networks with the rest of the small-worlds
bathwater.

MODELLING MACRO–MICRO INTERACTION

There are ways of tackling macro-level interactions that do consider the
articulation of both absolute and relational space (geometry and topology),
and which also incorporate a sense of balancing cost–benefit (optimization)
and some notion of causality. The modelling work I present here owes much

to an in-depth and ongoing collaboration with physicists Tim Evans and Ray Rivers (e.g. Knappett, Evans, and Rivers 2008; Evans, Knappett, and Rivers 2009). Our approach uses insights from statistical physics to generate dynamic networks that utilize an underlying substrate but which can reshape this substrate in wedding it to social affiliations. We thus avoid the polarization of the social and the physical inadvertently introduced by Watts. Added to this, our form of model-making can offer the further advantage of optimization, as mentioned earlier; we incorporate a measure of cost for the growth of sites and the addition of network links through an optimization function. Our optimization model produces quantitative outputs that are controlled (though not straightforwardly determined) by a series of input variables. This dynamic approach thus provides us with a much more powerful means of analysing the processes of various network topologies, among them small worlds; we can explore the relationships between these different forms, and the input conditions under which small worlds might emerge. Our focus is on the *dynamics* producing both clusters (cliques) and links between clusters, and as such is directly aimed at the inter-scale articulation so often bypassed in analyses that tend to be either macro or micro in focus. Moreover, our framework provides the means of explaining what may be driving the formation of small-world networks, as opposed to any other kind of network structure, rather than merely describing the structure and then analysing its subsequent functionality as a separate process.[2]

Our model tackles the Aegean Bronze Age. But before addressing questions of production, distribution, and consumption along the lines of the previous chapters, we need to first focus on the outlines of the model and the kinds of pattern it produces. We begin with a series of sites that are placed geographically where sites are known to occur in the latter part of the Middle Bronze Age (Figure 6.1). These are certainly not all the sites in the southern Aegean, but many of the main ones known to us.

The aim is to have sites represented in the main clusters of activity: Crete, the Cyclades, the mainland, and the Dodecanese/coastal Asia Minor. The level of knowledge for these different areas is quite uneven; archaeologically, we know a lot now about sites on Crete, but relatively little about the Dodecanese and coastal Asia Minor. Nonetheless, the distribution of these sites is sufficiently realistic. What happens at the end of the Middle Bronze Age is that the different clusters, which have long been interacting among themselves, and which fall into quite separate 'cultures', start to interact much more fully than before. What might explain this? Why should there be long-distance interactions between these clusters all of a sudden? Furthermore, these

---

[2] We are partly enabled in this by our use of a gravity model that allows us to make some block renormalizations and hence overlook some of the problems of the micro- to meso-scale interactions (we generalize about this scale in order to focus on another).

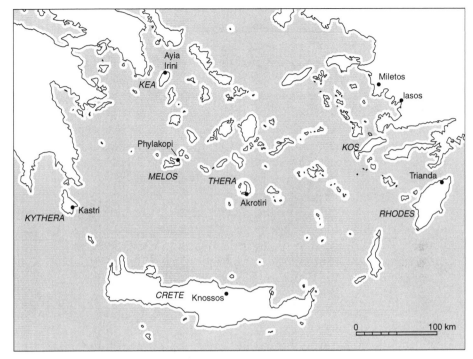

Figure 6.1. Some of the main sites in the Aegean during the Palatial period

interactions now involve not only exchange of materials, but some level of acculturation, such that Cretan cultural practices exert influence over these other areas, in a process dubbed 'Minoanization' (Broodbank 2004). The beginning of this process appears to coincide with the growth on Crete of Knossos as the dominant centre; but is this mere coincidence, or is this centralization in some way responsible for new cultural dynamics at the macro-scale? Or vice versa, is the centrality of Knossos to be explained by its position in expanding interaction networks?

Armed with these kinds of question we set about examining the kinds of interactions that might be favoured on a network connecting up the thirty-four sites chosen for the study. They have a particular distribution in space, but we did not want to include any more information as 'input'. We sought to create a model that would not only permit a link between any two sites on the network, but that would also enable us to characterize the potential strength and directionality of that link. Furthermore, we wanted the potential for sites to have varying characteristics too, so sites can develop within the model to become large or small. Thus, according to the variables in the model that we establish as inputs, a very wide range of model outputs can be achieved.

Before describing the components of the model in more detail, let us first outline another kind of network analysis that has been performed in the Bronze Age Aegean. In his study of the Early Bronze Age of the Cyclades, Broodbank (2000) seeks to explain how and why a handful of relatively large sites emerge on certain islands in the course of the third millennium. His thesis is that these sites have some kind of centrality or nodal status in networks of interaction; but it is difficult 'eyeballing' such properties in this fractured archipelago. Thus Broodbank applies a simple, systematic method for teasing out possible patterns of connectivity. He uses proximal point analysis (PPA), which involves placing a certain number of nodes across the physical spaces of the islands (Broodbank uses estimates of population density in placing his hypothetical nodes), and connecting each node to only its three nearest neighbours. Some nodes on the edge of the island archipelago will only have outward connections to their three nearest neighbours. Some nodes that are more centrally placed, however, will not only have their three external links, but may also have incoming links from other islands. In Broodbank's analysis, a handful of nodes accrue five or six total connections, making them more 'central' in the network. Moreover, at a certain population density some of these nodes accurately predict the location of actual central sites as observed in the archaeological evidence.

So Broodbank's networks involve sites of equal size, each site connected to its three nearest neighbours. This is appropriate to the problems faced in the EBA Cyclades for which Broodbank was seeking answers. But we are faced in the 'Palatial' period with a rather different scenario at a totally different scale. PPA cannot give us the sophistication in terms of outputs that we need: that is to say, variable site size, variable strength and directionality in the links, and the potential for any given site to be connected to any other. The way we provide this sophistication is through a quantitative model that has been devised using an optimization function. This is programmed in Java and wedded to visualization techniques employing Pajek software (Knappett, Evans, and Rivers 2008; Evans, Knappett, and Rivers 2009). What we can do in the model is alter the weighting of the costs and benefits of investing in local resources as opposed to investing in external connections ('trade', loosely phrased). If we set up the inputs so that trade is, in entirely relative terms, associated with considerable costs, in conjunction with a particular cost–benefit function for local investment, then we are given an output that shows an entirely disconnected network (see Figure 6.2).

This output will not look the same if we rerun it multiple times: because it is stochastic rather than strictly deterministic, each output could and should be subtly different, though following the same general pattern. If a different set of inputs are entered, for example favouring investment both in trade and in local resources, then the output tends to be an entirely unrealistic scenario of

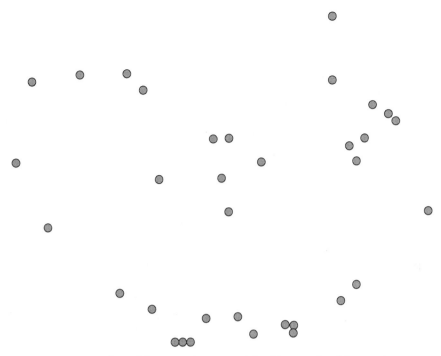

Figure 6.2. Network model output showing minimal interregional interaction

many huge overblown sites and multiple interactions criss-crossing the entire network (Figure 6.3).

It is only by entering inputs that balance these two extremes of under- and over-connectivity that we are able to generate outputs that are more 'realistic'; that is to say, with more connections within clusters than between clusters, and with some sites larger than others. Figure 6.4 is one such output.

What we are interested in with these networks are the conditions under which those that seem realistic to us are produced. Realistic in this case means mimicking the archaeological data for the period: which does indeed show strong connectivity within clusters (for example, within Crete), but more sporadic activity between clusters. In the Figure 6.4 network we do get some site variation too, but perhaps not enough; and the largest sites are in the Dodecanese/Asia Minor cluster, whereas we would expect the largest to be on Crete. We can alter the parameters so that the largest sites are on Crete, but in so doing we clearly need to pay attention to what goes into creating the different network topologies. This is the strength of our model: it allows us to see the kinds of processes underlying different network shapes. We also need to pay attention to the robustness of different network types. For example, is the above network resilient to minor changes in the model, or is it transitory and hard to reproduce? What kind of transition do we see

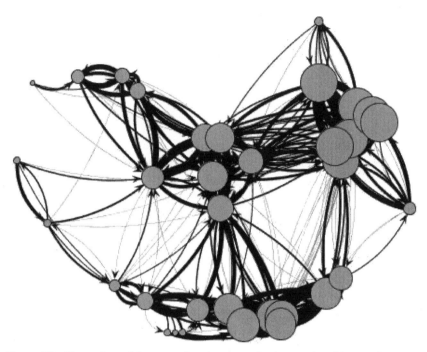

Figure 6.3. Network model output showing extensive interregional interaction

between scenarios like this and scenarios of total disconnectivity? Are they gradual, or rather sudden and like 'phase transitions' in physical systems?

What we can see is that if there *are* going to be links between clusters creating overall network connectivity, then this tends to be achieved through a kind of small-world structure, with a handful of weak ties between clusters. The way in which this differs from previous 'small-world' research is that it shows how such networks could actually be generated by particular cost–benefit regimes (contra Granovetter 1973; Watts and Strogatz 1998; Onnela *et al.* 2007). The particular distribution of weak and strong ties across the network that we observe is an output resulting from a series of inputs that offer benefits from trade balanced against costs. The network as a whole is an optimized solution to a given set of input constraints. Essentially, macro-scale interaction at this interregional level is neither the norm nor the exception; but it seems likely to occur in particular scenarios. What are the conditions we have created, though?

Let us look into this a little further. First, we have set up a particular distance scale in our model that makes 100 km of travel a kind of threshold; connections between sites below this limit are going to be favoured. The reasoning behind this comes from the limited information we have concerning transport

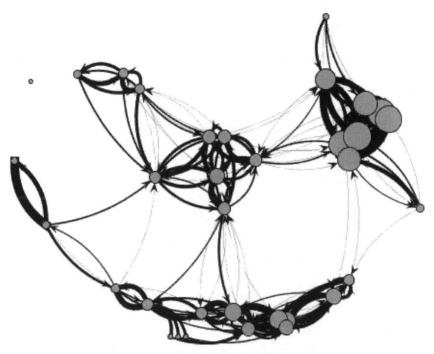

Figure 6.4. Network model output showing moderate 'small-world' interregional interaction

technology at the time; indications are that the sail was introduced in the Aegean at around the beginning of the second millennium BC, and so we imagine that by *c.*1700 BC (our period of study here) the sail was in use and allowed for long, uninterrupted journeys. Of course, if we imagined that the technology available only allowed journeys of 10 km at a time, this would fundamentally alter the topology of the network. Secondly, we talk in rather abstract terms about the benefits and costs of 'trade'. It is perhaps not difficult to imagine the costs of making lengthy and potentially dangerous sea trips across the Aegean; though these costs were, we might assume, much less onerous with sail-boats than they had been with paddling/rowing-boats. But what could the benefits have been? Here it is essential to remember that the Aegean is extremely patchy in terms of resources. This is true for various kinds of resources, with agricultural productivity on Crete, for example, holding much greater potential than on many of the small rocky Cycladic islands. It is also well known that obsidian—an excellent stone for blade production—occurs only on the islands of Melos and Yiali. But for this period in the Bronze Age it is the uneven distribution of metal resources that is perhaps the most fundamental. Silver and bronze, for example, were used in the Palatial period on Crete in prestige consumption; yet Crete itself does not have any silver, copper, or tin. These and other metals, such as gold and lead, are only found in very restricted areas, such as Lavrion in Attica, and in distant locations in Anatolia in the Near East. This would presumably then have been a major benefit to be had from investing in 'weak' ties in the broader network; weak ties may have been sufficient for gaining access to metal, or even just acquiring information on the whereabouts of traders with metal ingots.[3] So here we begin to see some of the socio-technical costs and benefits in the network—cost of sailing balanced against benefit of acquiring metal resources—that help to give our model some explanatory power. 'Optimization' in a model may be a crude measure, and may be anathema to those social scientists opposed to seeing humans as solely rational actors (though this is to misunderstand optimization); yet it does provide a framework for explaining 'small-world' networks that is missing in other approaches that only describe the pattern.

CULTURAL TRANSMISSION

And we can take our argument in a different direction. Previously I suggested that interaction is one thing and cultural transmission another.[4] The former can exist without the latter: in the Middle Bronze Age southern Aegean there is certainly interaction between regional clusters without any transmission as such. That is, until towards the end of the period, *c.*1700 BC, when interaction becomes something more. Rather than the different clusters only exchanging commodities, as seen in the movement of pottery (Knappett and Nikolako-poulou 2005), one cluster, Crete, starts to affect the others in new ways. That is to say, the local material culture at sites in the Cyclades and elsewhere takes on features more commonly associated with Crete. This process has been inter-preted in a variety of ways, ranging from colonization of these different locales by actual Cretans, to 'acculturation', whereby local communities choose to adopt certain Minoan practices and artefact styles (Branigan 1981; Hägg and Marinatos 1984; Wiener 1990; Broodbank 2004). This set of processes of 'Minoanization' continues until the collapse of the Minoan palatial system at the end of the Late Minoan I period, in the mid-second millennium BC. But

---

[3] Note that those nodes with the weak links to distant clusters seem to be equivalent to what have been termed 'gateway' sites in the archaeological literature (see Hirth 1978). Such gateways to the more tightly knitted clusters could easily have been the sole entry points for exotic resources such as metals.

[4] Note that 'cultural transmission' can also refer to the processes of inheritance through time that contribute to cultural lineages. Here I am more concerned with spatial, synchronic processes.

what new forces initiate and sustain this process, following at least two centuries of interaction without cultural transmission?

We might choose to address this question at the micro-scale, and say that individuals or groups in these various Aegean communities saw new motivations for affiliating themselves culturally with Crete at this time. Thus, perhaps they started adopting Cretan practices to align themselves with Cretan elites, in order to cement their position in burgeoning trade networks. So maybe the new pattern can be attributed to a series of micro-level initiatives, with the macro-level pattern generated from the bottom-up. However, we might also see Minoanization as a process with its own macro-scale dynamic, with changes in network connectivity allowing or encouraging affiliation in ways that were not previously possible. Did the 'small-world' networks that appear to form more prominently at this time play some sort of role in the new modes of cultural transmission? This we can also explore using modelling techniques. We can release random walkers onto our networks and observe the links and nodes that are most frequently traversed or visited. It is then possible to compare the patterns of 'transmission' on different kinds of networks; is it the case, for example, that networks with 'small-world' properties are able to transmit cultural traits more readily than more tightly clustered networks? What effect does the proportion of large, well-connected sites in a network, those that might act as hubs, have on the transmission of traits through the network as a whole? Though we are still examining these kinds of issues, it is an exciting step in exploring the possible influence of the macro-scale characteristics of regional networks on micro-scale transmission processes.

This is indeed a relationship that has recently been highlighted as in need of investigation, with Coward stating that 'we must learn to tack between the large scales of cultural transmission and the small scale of social relations to gain the best possible understanding of cultural transmission past and present' (Coward 2008, 1495). Those studies that have tackled the large scale of cultural transmission of late have tended to select traits that are readily transmissible and which only require the most basic of social relationships for transmission. This renders the link between the micro and the macro seemingly straightforward. Western fads and fashions seem to be a popular field in this regard, with studies of the spread of baby names, or the style of tennis fist pumps (Bentley, Hahn, and Shennan 2004; see also Bettencourt 2002). These cultural models have much in common, explicitly or not, with studies in epidemiological transmission, key in charting and understanding the spread of infections (Bettencourt *et al.* 2006). Epidemiological models rely on relatively simple characterizations of the virulence of the infection in question and the susceptibility of individuals in the population. The spread of a virus is similar to the spread of a cultural fad or fashion, in that they both rely on little more than contact and susceptibility (see so-called SIR models, in which a population is characterized in terms of susceptible, infected, and recovered individuals). The cultural models devised by Bentley and others, working very often on the basis of random copying, deal with cultural traits that are quite easily transmissible, requiring little learning (see also, in archaeological contexts, work on stylistic drift—Shennan and Wilkinson 2001; Eerkens and Lipo 2005).

Modelling cultural transmission in this way is very seductive, because one can readily see how random copying is a real form of cultural transmission in the case of fads and fashions. However, this is not the whole story when it comes to cultural traits. Many traits require extended learning, invariably 'embedded in networks of social relations between individuals' (Coward 2008, 1494). Thus fads and fashions may spread like wildfire, almost virally, but this does not account for anything like the full range of possible forms of cultural transmission. A fuller acknowledgement of the different rates of change and transmission of cultural traits is overdue; a recent example comes in a paper on evolution of canoe design, in which the positive and negative selection pressures on the transmission of different cultural traits is recognized (Rogers and Ehrlich 2008). The authors see the slower dynamic of change for canoe 'functional' traits as opposed to canoe 'stylistic' traits as a matter of environmental fit; natural selection for functional attributes creates conservatism, while stylistic attributes that do not affect survival or reproduction are not so constrained. However, following Coward's line of reasoning, there may be other processes at work here too—the learning processes for functional and stylistic traits may be rather different. It is conceivable, for example, that the former are subject to vertical transmission, from parent to child, broadly speaking, whereas the latter are more readily transmissible, and hence open to so-called 'horizontal transmission', from peer to peer (Shennan 2002). Ethnoarchaeological work on pottery production in West Africa has also shown how material culture features can be susceptible to different dynamics according to their practice and learning contexts (Gosselain 2000). Gosselain shows how pottery-shaping methods are much less prone to the rapid 'stylistic' change of decorative traits, in large part because they are performed within house compounds and are not at all conspicuous in the finished product. If the work of Rogers and Ehrlich on canoe design were considered in this light, with attention to the social context of learning for functional and stylistic features, then one might be able to assess whether the more significant functional features are more protected and subject to the greater control possible within vertical transmission.

CULTURAL TRANSMISSION:
MATERIAL SCAFFOLDING

However important the character of the connections between individuals is in these learning networks, it is all too easy to overlook the active participation of material culture therein (it is, for example, largely overlooked in Mesoudi, Whiten, and Laland 2006). This is a key point: cultural transmission does not just serve to propagate ways of doing and items of material culture; it is in itself structured and mediated by material culture. At the micro-scale, Stout (2002) has demonstrated this very effectively in relation to the acquisition of stone-knapping techniques, with the material themselves scaffolding the learning process. But materiality also plays similar roles at the macro-scale, and this has barely been considered in the consideration of macro-scale network dynamics. This is precisely where this chapter heads next, by looking at some of the patterns of production, distribution, and consumption in the Bronze Age Aegean, and how they are transmitted, learnt, or rejected from Prepalatial to Palatial periods. Previously our scope was the island of Crete, but now we move beyond Crete to tackle the wider scale of the southern Aegean, just as we did in the network modelling discussed above. But what I shall now do is examine the active role of material culture, and in particular iconic *objects within networks*, in the establishment of macro-scale interaction and transmission at the interregional level. It seems that in these 'colonial' encounters one cannot underestimate the power of colonializing artefacts in establishing and perpetuating these networks (Gosden 2004*b*).

PRODUCTION

It is interesting that while the wheel-fashioning technique for pottery was spreading rapidly across Crete, and developments in the technique through the course of the centuries that followed were identical from one site to another, off-island, in other cultural groups, a quite different pattern was unfolding. In the equivalent periods, *c.*1900–1700 BC, there was absolutely no use of the wheel technique in the Cycladic islands. A completely different channel of wheel innovation had opened up in mainland Greece at the end of the EBA, through contacts with Asia Minor in all likelihood, but this was only taken up in a very limited way and eventually petered out (Spencer 2006). This total lack of receptivity of Cycladic communities to the wheel innovation is not due to some lack of contact; there is evidently contact with Crete, for example, with ample imports testified in levels dating to this period at the site of Akrotiri on Thera, among other sites (Knappett and Nikolakopoulou 2005).

This contact alone, presumably intermittent in nature, was evidently insufficient in any case for the transmission of a practice like wheel-fashioning, so difficult to learn. That said, even more imitation-friendly traits, such as simple decorative motifs, are not transmitted either.

But all this changes at a certain moment, around 1700 BC (in MM IIIA). Those southern Aegean networks that had previously just been about the exchange of materials and products now become networks of affiliation too (Knappett and Nikolakopoulou 2005; 2008). It is in part a quantitative shift, with 10 per cent of ceramic assemblages on Thera now imports from Crete, whereas previously this had only been 1 per cent. But this alone cannot be driving the qualitative changes. We see imitation of certain pottery styles from Crete, most conspicuously tortoiseshell ripple (Figure 6.5), but also the use of white dots on a dark ground.

(a)

9 3 9 1

Figure 6.5. Imported and local tortoiseshell ripple, bridge-spouted jars

(b)

9424

Figure 6.5. Continued

New Cretan shapes appear as well, such as ledge-rim bowls and bridge-spouted jars. But perhaps most significantly of all, we also see the first use of the wheel technique, for the manufacture of a handful of Cretan shapes, principally plain straight-sided cups and plain ledge-rim bowls (see Figure 6.6).

This must have required some exposure of local artisans to Cretan potters, as this technique needs some investment and close guidance to be picked up; the kind of learning that is often from parent to child, or what is also called vertical transmission, inter-generationally (Shennan 2002). It is as if some potters on Thera are being educated into the Cretan community of practice. How and why was this happening at this time? We do not know the precise mechanisms, but we can speculate about the expanding influence of Knossos and the decisions being made in the Cyclades to align themselves in the right

10540

Figure 6.6. Locally produced plain ledge-rim bowl from Akrotiri Thera

networks. But we must remind ourselves that this is a very partial process of cultural learning: the vast majority of the locally produced pottery continues to be made by hand, even well into the LM IA period. This represents some kind of resistance, conscious or unconscious, to the Cretan technique, however 'superior'. We might compare this process with that seen at other sites in the southern Aegean, such as Kastri on Kythera, where Minoan-style pottery is made using Cretan wheel techniques throughout the First Palace period (Coldstream and Huxley 1972); at Miletus, where there is also some early use of the wheel, but possibly under Anatolian rather than Cretan influence (Raymond 2001); and also at Phylakopi on Melos, where it has been argued that the continued use of hand-building techniques was related to questions of local island identity (Berg 2007).[5]

DISTRIBUTION

As far as storage is concerned, there is clear evidence for the influence of Cretan practices beyond Crete, with the actual importation of numerous Cretan pithoi to Akrotiri (Nikolakopoulou 2002). Fragments of imported Cretan pithoi are also found at other sites, such as Miletus and Iasos. The indication that cultural transmission accompanies this is that these imports provoke local imitations too, at Akrotiri at least (Nikolakopoulou 2002). However, it seems that these vessels are incorporated within existing storage practices, as the spaces for storage in the settlement at Akrotiri do not appear to owe anything

---

[5] In other contexts—the early Middle Helladic of the Greek mainland, and the early Late Cypriot—recent work has also focused on the role of ceramic wheel technology in the elaboration of local identities: see Spencer 2006, Crewe 2007*a, b.*

specifically to Minoan Crete (Nikolakopoulou 2002; Palyvou 2005; Christakis 2008). That said, it is difficult establishing how much these LC I storage practices owe to Minoan Crete, given the limited evidence of this kind from earlier periods in the Cyclades. One might also consider the evidence for any corollary changes in agricultural and storage practices. Archaeobotanical work indicates that only the last stages of food production (e.g. flour) tend to be represented in the LC I settlement; this has been used to argue that the community was more of a consumer than a producer in LC I, in contrast to the scenario during the MC period (Sarpaki 1987; 1992; 2001). This may have been facilitated by a reorganization of the landscape and of agricultural production in LC I, possibly enabled by informational technologies such as bureaucracy, imported from Crete in the form of Linear A and sealing practices (Karnava and Nikolakopoulou 2005). This change could have occurred as a result of the community's participation in Cretan-driven trade networks, allowing Akrotiri to focus its attention on exchange. The site does display evidence for a wide range of regional contacts, with imports from Cycladic islands such as Naxos and Melos, the Dodecanese, the Greek mainland, and Asia Minor (Miletus).

CONSUMPTION

The processes of interregional interaction and acculturation in the Palatial period bring new forms of Cretan material culture and consumption practices to sites across the southern Aegean. The most obvious candidate is a new standardized and very simple form of handle-less drinking-vessel called the conical cup. This is invariably made locally rather than actually imported, and comes to be used at many sites in very large quantities (Wiener 1990; Bevan et al. 2002). Simple in form, rapidly produced, and remarkably standardised (Knappett 1999c; Berg 2004), the conical cup is a new kind of object. While during the First Palace period there were some simple forms, they were just one option among many; now in the Second Palace period the conical cup is dominant, easily the most common ceramic shape on almost any Minoan site. Its simplicity made it easy to replicate for producers, while for consumers it seems to have been easily assimilated, becoming iconic of the practices with which it was associated. In this regard the conical cup may have had the capacity to 'carry' Cretan consumption practices across time and space in ways that were previously not viable with the more diverse drinking-vessels of the First Palace period. It does not seem to be quite so closely linked to public spaces and halls in off-island contexts as is the case on Crete, but this is largely because such contexts are rather few and far between beyond Crete.

Nonetheless, conical cups do seem to be used in a similarly wide range of settings, for example at the site of Ayia Irini on Kea (Wiener 1990).

Another form of material culture used in distinctively Minoan consumption practices is the rhyton (see earlier chapters). At Akrotiri on Thera we see a range of rhyton types in use, some actually imported from Crete, while others are local products and imitations (Koehl 2006). As was mentioned for the use of the wheel, and the local imitations of pithoi and conical cups, this too signifies a considerable degree of cultural transmission from Crete to the Cyclades. Koehl suggests that rhyta were used on Thera much as on Crete, if not even more broadly, and that this indicates 'a profound influence' of Crete on Thera (ibid. 298).[6] Rhyta are found elsewhere in the southern Aegean too, such as Kastri on Kythera (Coldstream and Huxley 1972), Phylakopi on Melos (Renfrew 2007), and Ayia Irini on Kea, where the rhyta from House A during period VII (equivalent to LM IB on Crete) are from both Crete on the one hand and the Greek mainland on the other (Koehl 2006, 310–11). The different types of rhyton seem to act as effective scaffolds for Minoan consumption practices over space and time; though far more complex in shape than the conical cup, and thus less obviously iconic in some sense, their effectiveness may come from being tightly associated with very specific practices, as signalled by their particular affordances for containing and releasing.

DISCUSSION

If we look at changes over time in the Bronze Age Aegean, as we have done in previous chapters, we see that macro-scale interactions undergo a significant transformation; this occurs somewhat later than those at other scales, not so much at the transition from Prepalatial to Palatial, but at the transition from the First to Second Palatial period. The change is essentially one from exchange to affiliation (Knappett and Nikolakopoulou 2005): whereas previously interactions at this scale had involved the exchange of various kinds of product, they began to involve actual cultural transmission and the sharing of practices and material culture. This can be explained at a number of levels. It is probably driven partly by the needs of the Cretan elites, and partly by the desire of local communities across the southern Aegean to participate in exchange networks in a more intensified and competitive arena, one that necessitated some show of alignment or allegiance. This pitches explanation at the level of individual agents and communities. There may be another level of explanation too: that it was changes to network configurations at the meso-

---

[6] Note the distinctively local types at Akrotiri though, like the boar's-head rhyta.

and macro-scales that facilitated these new kinds of interaction that bred affiliation. The relationship between the macro- and the micro-levels in explanations of cultural transmission is in need of much fuller exploration, as has been pointed out above (see Coward 2008). But there is a third dimension to consider: how were these various agents and communities enabled to interact in these new ways, far transcending the normal constraints imposed by face-to-face interaction, and achieving what Gamble calls the 'release from proximity' in ways barely before seen (e.g. Gamble 1998)? Here I would argue that the role of artefacts—of networks of *objects*—in enabling these affiliation networks cannot be overestimated. The emergence of new modes of objectification—feasting using a set form, the conical cup; administration using one script (Linear A), and production using one method (the wheel)—opened up more distant areas, in what one might describe as a process of object-led colonialism (Gosden 2004*b*; Knappett and Nikolakopoulou 2008).

In these three chapters we have explored some aspects of the *how* of human interaction across different scales. In the next part of the book it is time to ask *why* humans interact through objects and things at these different levels.

Part III

Why Networks? Objects, Things, and Time

7

Networks of Objects

INTRODUCTION: WHY EXTEND?

The history of humanity has arguably been a process of extension: extending the spatio-temporal limits of interaction, so that humans have more and more means of connecting beyond the level of the face-to-face (Gamble 2007, 38). In the preceding chapters we have encountered some of the material methods humans use to promote and support social interaction. In this we have ranged across different scales of interaction. Beginning in Chapter 4 with the micro-scale, we considered how objects support proximate interactions, as in the case of the pithoi and other features for storage in Minoan Crete. Then in Chapter 5 we moved out to the meso-scale, to see how objects help hold together communities of practice. And in Chapter 6 we zoomed out one more level, to the macro-scale, with objects having far-flung effects (with one example being conical cups across the southern Aegean). Our concern in these chapters was to establish some of the means by which objects are bound up in social interactions across different scales. But we did not devote much attention to a more difficult question—that of why such interactions across scales should involve object networks at all. When posed as starkly as this the question seems impossible to answer. It really conflates two questions: why should humans wish to extend the spatio-temporal range of their action anyway, and why use objects to do so?

There are, no doubt, different ways of breaking these impenetrable questions apart. But the approach I would like to pursue here takes its direction from some of the network research mentioned in Chapter 6. The stochastic model developed for exploring site interactions in the Aegean has various pros and cons, but one very significant advantage is that it works with an optimization assumption (Knappett, Evans, and Rivers 2008; Evans, Knappett, and Rivers 2009). It is by casting individual links in terms of their costs and benefits to the network as a whole that the model becomes dynamic. Cost–benefit analysis and optimization are often perceived negatively in archaeological analysis because of their association with overly mechanistic approaches to human adaptation in the processual paradigm (Johnson 1977).

However, if handled with sufficient sensitivity and in a heuristic sense, a straightforward, qualitative thinking through of object interactions in terms of costs and benefits may gave us a way to begin broaching the questions of why people interact at increasing scales, and why through objects. Or put another way, what are the benefits of object networks?

In tackling these 'why' questions, we should probably begin with the micro-scale and the proximate. In Chapter 4 some of the 'hows' of micro-scale interaction were discussed, in terms of social interactionism, material inter-actionism, and praxeology. This did inevitably touch on some of the underlying cognitive mechanisms for socio-material interaction, such as scaffolding and conceptual blending. Here we will revisit some of this terrain, asking what benefits there are to interacting with and through objects at the micro-scale. Answers to such questions have been put forward in cognitive science, though not so much in archaeology. Then we will turn our attention to ever-increasing scales, asking what benefits (and indeed costs) attach to interactions through object networks at these levels. Our definition of 'benefit' will not be in narrow economic terms but is set very broadly, allowing us to imagine social, political, cognitive, and metaphysical benefits. We will not, as for example in cost–benefit analysis, be seeking to *quantify* the benefits of one set of interactions over another.

WHY OBJECTS?

Why use objects to think with? According to Clark, the human mind has evolved to its current efficient state by using the world as its own best model (Brooks 1991; Clark 1997). Structure in the world is engineered and manipulated in a process of cognitive 'offloading'. The more the brain can use 'off-line' resources, distributing mind processes in the world, the more it can do. The environment can in many ways be used 'as is', but of course humans have long been adapting their environments and transforming 'things' into 'objects' for the purposes of smoother cognitive operation. Clark has called this 'super-sizing the mind' (Clark 2008). While there are thorny philosophical issues involved, such as the 'parity principle' (Clark and Chalmers 1998), what we are particularly concerned with here is the degree to which objects produce cognitive benefits.

Clark refers particularly to the work of Kirsh in exploring the cognitive benefits to be had from using material objects in specific tasks (Clark 2008, 214). For example, Kirsh's study with Maglio on the steps involved in playing the computer game Tetris revealed that expert players chose to manipulate the zoids in order to ascertain their shape, even though this may entail more moves: what seemed costly in a pragmatic sense can actually be beneficial in epistemic terms, contributing to success in the game (Kirsh and Maglio 1995). Kirsh (2009), in a recent overview, underlines how, in a range of situations, actors employ the resources available to solve the problems before them. One example he uses come from the work of Carraher, Carraher, and Schliemann (1985) on the numerical abilities of Brazilian street-market children. To calculate the price of ten coconuts, each costing 35 cruzeiros, a girl did not add a 0 to the 35, but instead thought in terms of a common batch of three coconuts costing 105 cruzeiros, did this three times, then added one. Using the add-0 technique in the classroom these same children fared less well: what might, from one perspective, appear to be the same mental task actually emerges as two quite different tasks in these two situations. The market situation provided scaffolds that the children could exploit in achieving their tasks, scaffolds that were not present in the classroom. Clark (2008, 118–20) does, however, counterbalance this by referring to a study by Gray and Fu (2004), in which it emerged that actors seek the most cost-effective route in a task (in terms of time), whether that involves on-line or off-line resources. Off-line elements are not more efficient in every case.

CONCEPTUAL BLENDS

Often cited together with Clark is the work of Ed Hutchins (e.g. Hutchins 1995; 2005). Hutchins conducted ethnographic work on the cognitive tasks involved in navy-ship navigation (Hutchins 1995). He showed that instead of navigation being a mental set of operations performed with the assistance of equipment such as charts and rulers, it could be argued to exist as an integrated distributed system within which the 'external' props were as fundamental as any 'internal' mental architecture. From this we can progress to the idea presented in his 2005 paper, 'material anchors for conceptual blends'. Conceptual blending, as the name suggests, describes the process whereby elements of two conceptual spaces are projected into a third space; the new concept that arises from this projection is a 'blend' of the two input concepts (Hutchins 2005, 1556). Most work in conceptual blending theory (also 'conceptual integration') is focused on the blending of concepts in language. However, the theory does not specify that the blend has to operate between two conceptual structures—it also allows for blending between a conceptual structure and a material structure. In this there are similarities to the study of metaphor: here too the emphasis has generally fallen on language, yet metaphor can work on a much broader basis that includes the human body and material culture (Lakoff and Johnson 1980; Tilley 1999; Gamble 2007). Conceptual blending theory and metaphor (or 'conceptual metaphor theory', Grady, Oakley, and Coulson 1999) are related, although the former has greater flexibility and scope in not being limited to a simple mapping between target and source domains (Fauconnier and Turner 2008).

Conceptual blends using material culture are useful because the material structure can provide stability (essential particularly during complex mental manipulations) that is not always easily achievable with purely conceptual models. Hutchins provides an example: a line of people queuing for theatre tickets (2005, 1559). The conceptual structure is that people can acquire tickets in the order that they arrive. The material structure is a line of people—bodies located in space in a material, grounded way. It is the blending of the physical line with the conceptual sequence that creates the conceptual blend of a 'queue'. Hutchins maintains that this process of blending does not occur solely in mental space, with the *idea* of a sequence blended with the *idea* of a line: 'the process include[s] perceptual processes and therefore include[s] the bodily interaction with the physical world' (ibid. 1560). Hence the real world is part of the blend, and serves as a 'material anchor' for the conceptual blend. Hutchins goes on to produce many other examples of material anchors for conceptual blends, such as fictive motion ('the fence runs all the way down to the river'), method of loci (using a sequence of landmarks to map a sequence of ideas), the intelligent use of workspace, the Japanese hand calendar, and navigation in Micronesia.

SCAFFOLDING AND STIGMERGY

Sinha (2005) draws connections between this concept of material anchors and that of scaffolding, as used in the Vygotskian tradition of activity theory, and in cultural and developmental psychology more broadly (e.g. Vygotsky 1978; Wood, Bruner, and Ross 1976; Cole 1996; Wertsch 1998). In this framework too artefacts are seen to be key to human activity, mediating human interactions by acting as pivots. Artefacts are seen as particularly crucial in processes of learning and apprenticeship, such as when adults use cognitive and material 'scaffolds' to facilitate the building up of knowledge. Sinha argues that this kind of thinking in developmental psychology can be useful to conceptual blending theory, as indeed can blending thinking to developmental approaches (2005, 1540). He considers that the social interactive focus of developmental psychology can help situate the individual cognitive capacity for blending (ibid. 1553).[1] Hutchins too seeks to understand the broader setting of

---

[1] A similar criticism—that conceptual metaphor theory and conceptual blending theory are insufficiently social in their outlook—is also levelled by Brandt and Brandt (2005). They advocate a cognitive-semiotic approach as a means of contextualizing metaphor more satisfactorily within social situations in which actors are communicating.

individual conceptual blends, commenting that each individual model is part of an 'ecology of conceptual blends that have accumulated and been layered, one over the other, to produce complex emergent properties' (Hutchins 2005, 1576).

Susi and Ziemke (2001) also see links between different domains of cognitive science and philosophy in the ways in which artefacts are seen to play a role in cultural dynamics. Although they trace Vygotsky's influence in 'activity theory' rather than developmental psychology, they nonetheless see both this and distributed cognition (Hutchins 1995; but note that their paper is earlier than the emergence of ideas on conceptual blending, e.g. Hutchins 2005) as theoretical frameworks for exploring interactive cognition. To these they add a third, that of 'situated action', represented by the work of Suchman (2006) and Lave (1988). They identify some differences between these three approaches, principally in their scales of analysis, which range from the 'activity' in activity theory, to the 'setting' in situated action, to the 'distributed, socio-technical system' in distributed cognition. Nonetheless, Susi and Ziemke argue that insofar as all three emphasize the importance of the environment, they are compatible with their own idea of 'stigmergy'. This describes the coordination of activities among agents achieved indirectly via the environment. This is not a new idea per se, in that it was developed nearly fifty years ago to understand the coordinated behaviour of social insects such as ants and termites (Grassé 1959). These insects do not communicate directly, but indirectly through pheromone trails they leave behind as they engage in particular activities. So, when foraging the ant leaves a particular pheromone trail that other ants will then encounter as they move around their environment. If an ant comes across enough pheromones (beyond a particular threshold) indicating 'foraging', then that ant will alter its behaviour accordingly, perhaps also switching tasks to engage in foraging. The idea in comparing humans with ants is that we too may be considered to 'record' activities in the environment, in the form of material culture, also as a means of coordinating collective behaviour. Susi and Ziemke's idea of applying stigmergy to human–environment interactions is innovative, and they suggest that it could provide a useful link between the various approaches in cognitive science outlined above. Although not making explicit use of the stigmergy idea, related approaches can be found in the domain of human–computer interaction (HCI) research in computer science.[2]

---

[2] Rambusch, Susi, and Ziemke 2004; Susi 2005; Susi and Ziemke 2005; Hirose 2002; Taylor *et al.* 2006; Harper, Taylor, and Molloy 2008.

NICHE CONSTRUCTION AND
EPISTEMIC ENGINEERING

Distributed cognition, activity theory, situated action, and stigmergy all emphasize the contribution of the environment to the cognitive processes tied up in learning, perception, and action. Each of these strands of thought has its own trajectory and its own pros and cons, more on which below. And at the risk of creating further confusion through yet another link, one could suggest that these strands all have some possible connection with a powerful idea recently put forward in biology, that of 'niche construction' (Odling-Smee, Laland, and Feldman 2003). Various species adapt their own environments in ways that have knock-on effects, preferably beneficial, for future generations: rabbits make warrens, beavers construct dams, and termites make nests. These kinds of physical and social modifications of the environment create 'downstream' effects for future generations, but in most species there is little evidence of any kind of cycle of discovery and improvement (Sterelny 2003, 150). Humans, however, do engage in such 'cumulative' innovation, which can create a 'ratchet' effect, as named by Tomasello: one innovation can become the basis for yet further innovations (ibid. 150–1). Yet these innovations need not be solely physical and pragmatic (for example, making a larger, heavier axe) but can also be informational or 'epistemic' (ibid. 154–5). Humans might create new labels for things that might fundamentally change how they are understood. Or they might rearrange their workspace, and Kirsh has shown how effective this can be, not pragmatically as such, but epistemically (Kirsh 1995). This point is also made in connection with the playing of the computer-game Tetris, as mentioned above—how a seemingly unpragmatic action may have significant benefit because of its epistemic value (Kirsh and Maglio 1995). Because humans face particular 'cognitive resource bottlenecks' (Sterelny 2003, 155), such as limited working memory (see also Read and van der Leeuw 2008), it makes sense to use the structure that is in the environment to free up on-line resources. By drawing together the work in cognitive science by Kirsh (and Tomasello, for that matter), with that in evolutionary biology by Odling-Smee, Laland, and Feldman on niche construction, Sterelny creates a rich set of connections concerning the epistemic consequences of tool use and stigmergy.

SO WHY OBJECTS AFTER ALL?

At the risk of wedding theories with hidden incompatibilities, it looks like we can gain from combining elements from cognitive science, cultural psychology, and evolutionary biology. Each of these approaches has their respective strengths that go some way toward explaining human interactivity with environments and artefacts:

1. *Material anchors for conceptual blends*—this perspective, developed by Hutchins, opens up conceptual blending theory so that it can include material as well as conceptual structures. Its focus is, however, on the *individual* cognitive role of material structures, with less explicit attention devoted to social relationships or temporal change.

2. *Scaffolding*—Sinha recognizes that this perspective is not as strong as conceptual blending theory as far as individual processes are concerned, but it does offer a stronger perspective on the *social* interactive role of material structures.

3. *Stigmergy*—this approach brings with it a strong focus on the use of the *environment* in coordinating collective behaviour.

4. *Epistemic engineering and ratcheting*—these concepts incorporate a strong developmental, or *temporal* focus.

Though these strands of thought have emerged from different, though overlapping, disciplinary backgrounds, they do all share some common ground. In each case it is apparent that the human interaction with artefacts brings benefits, whether that be in terms of individual cognitive processing, social relationships, environmental adaptation, or learning and transmission (over time). As argued earlier, simple optimization principles can provide the dynamics for explaining why cultural interactions take certain forms rather than others. What we should next consider is whether the focus in such work on micro-scale, proximate interactions can be extended to cover multiple-scale interactions that reach beyond the proximate. Can we interrogate object *networks* in the same manner, in terms of the benefits they offer human interaction?

AGENT–ARTEFACT SPACE

The answer to the above question would seem to be yes, if we take on board some exciting new work emerging from interdisciplinary approaches in economics. In the context of seeking more convincing accounts of innovation processes in industrial settings, and particularly the phenomenon of innovation cascades, Lane proposes that one key mechanism for innovation is exaptation rather than adaptation (Lane, Pumain, and van der Leeuw 2009): that is, innovation occurs through new attributions of functionality, such that existing products or relations between products are exapted and attributed with new meanings.[3] An example of exaptation is the CD, or compact disc: initially developed for improving sound quality, it was exapted and used for storing computer data (Villani *et al.* 2009, 415). Once new patterns of activity congeal around these new products, then fresh opportunities present themselves for exaptation, thereby creating a cumulative process described as 'bootstrapping' (Lane, Pumain, and van der Leeuw 2009), that is, the system 'hauls itself up' by its own bootstraps, without external help. This notion of bootstrapping is akin to the 'ratchet effect', whereby human cultural developments build cumulatively, a feature not observed in other animals (Tomasello 1999). The ratchet effect in turn informs the idea of *cumulative downstream epistemic engineering* elaborated by Sterelny (2003). There are some important differences though, that we should highlight. First, Lane's approach to innovation is conceived as a response to those who argue (as do many in the niche-construction literature) that biological models are advanced enough to explain processes of cultural change and innovation (Mesoudi, Whiten, and Laland 2006). Thus, possible links to ideas from biology such as niche construction and stigmergy have not been much explored. Secondly, the approach is explicitly grounded in the field of non-linear complexity science, and thus network models used in understanding complex adaptive systems have been instrumental in the growth of this novel approach to innovation (Lane, Pumain, and van der Leeuw 2009; see also Bettencourt *et al.* 2006).

Hence, with these network ideas the relational and spatial features of exaptation are much more fully explored than in much of the literature mentioned above. Integral to this is Lane's concept of 'agent–artefact space', which conveys the sense in which a given technology, whether it be stone-tool technology or a Silicon Valley technology, consists of sets of knowledge distributed across various entities—be they agents or artefacts—with various kinds of interconnections. For an innovation to take hold—that is, for an isolated invention to spread across the network space—there has to be some kind of alteration of that space, which may be physical or conceptual. The space is dynamic because not only can its structural properties be the very source of invention and creativity, but its structures are also subsequently altered by such change. As more artefact types are created, so are new kinds of agents; and these in turn may create new interconnections that in turn spawn yet further problems requiring solutions. As the agent–artefact space changes and grows, more kinds of attributions and exaptations are enabled, leading to more innovation. Hence *benefits* accrue. The extent of overlap between these ideas (Lane, Pumain, and van der Leeuw 2009) and those from biology such as niche construction require further detailed exploration, it would seem. That aside, however, the Lane approach is powerful because it provides the network

---

[3] Consider parallels between exaptation and conceptual blending (Fauconnier and Turner 2008; Hutchins 1995).

and non-linear methodologies for charting the dynamic processes in agent–artefact space across multiple scales.[4]

ARCHAEOLOGY AND MATERIAL ENGAGEMENT

What impact, if any, has this kind of work had on archaeology? Ideas of embodied, extended, and situated cognition have certainly been filtering into the branch of the discipline known as cognitive archaeology. This is particularly so in connection with Palaeolithic archaeology (e.g. Stout 2002), but also in broader terms. Renfrew (2004) and Malafouris (2004; 2008*a*, *b*) have been developing the notion of 'material engagement' to try to capture the sense of symmetry and mutual enaction of the mental and the material.[5] In addition to individual publications, these two scholars have been developing interdisciplinary connections with different domains of cognitive science through a series of colloquia and associated publications, such as *The Cognitive Life of Things* (Malafouris and Renfrew, 2010), and *The Sapient Mind: Archaeology Meets Neuroscience* (Renfrew, Frith, and Malafouris 2009).[6] The former put cognitive-science researchers such as Don Norman, Andy Clark, Ed Hutchins, David Kirsh, Chuck Goodwin, Tom Ziemke, and Mike Wheeler side by side with archaeologists interested in cognitive issues; and the latter involved Chris Frith, a leading neuroscientist, as a co-editor, and included papers from scholars across the fields of archaeology, psychology, and neuroscience.

Though this is undoubtedly an exciting and potentially extremely fruitful development, the emphasis seems to be on the *how* of material engagement rather than the *why*. A dynamic framework, such as might be provided by a cost–benefit function, is missing, or at best implicit. There is a further limitation, in what is admittedly an early stage of the development of material engagement as a concept: the scale of analysis is confined to the proximate, which is indeed also a characteristic of much of the cognitive science cited above. However, there are solutions to these problems. One is provided from the 'exaptive bootstrapping' ideas described above. Though these ideas have been principally developed with modern economics in mind, they developed in the context of an EU project (ISCOM) co-directed by an archaeologist,

---

[4] The approach of Arthur (2009) would appear to be consistent with that developed by Lane, Pumain, and van der Leeuw, particularly in its turning away from biological models for cultural change.

[5] The recent focus on 'materiality' in archaeology and anthropology is another domain in which the active role of objects in human social interactions is acknowledged and explored. See e.g. Miller 2005, Meskell 2005.

[6] See also Knappett and Malafouris 2008, an edited volume including chapters from Clark and Sutton, philosophers in extended/situated cognition.

Sander van der Leeuw.[7] Thus, such ideas (and see Arthur 2009 too, also broadly applicable) have grown with input from archaeology, and are amenable to application to a range of situations beyond those of modern economics alone. The interdisciplinary possibilities of the ideas from this project becomes further apparent when one considers the considerable involvement of most key project members in the Santa Fe Institute (one of the ISCOM co-directors, Geoff West, is a former president of SFI). SFI has a strong tradition of the participation of archaeologists in research on complex systems (e.g. Kohler and Gumerman 2000).

A second solution comes not from theory but from the empirical basis making up much of archaeology: typologies. The discipline is practically founded on typologies, reaching back to the pioneering work of Scandinavian archaeologists such as Thomsen and Montelius (Trigger 1989). We are going to use this to our advantage. Much of the typological work in archaeology has been descriptive rather than explanatory: we do not have very good models for explaining *why* human groups create ever-increasing artefactual categories. However, when reframed in the context of the above concepts from cognitive science such as scaffolding and conceptual blends, and when activated through cost–benefit functions, we can put the incredible wealth of typological data that is out there to good use. We can begin to use archaeological data in new ways—to ask what are the benefits of object networks to human interaction.

ASSEMBLAGES AND OBJECT NETWORKS

The above-mentioned approaches—such as niche construction and supersizing—are certainly powerful means for explaining why there is distributed thinking through material culture. It brings cognitive *benefits*. But it does not really have much to do with objects in *networks*. It mostly concerns individual artefacts in proximity, at the micro-scale. We need to ask *why* distribute such objects and images across broader scales, using network thinking. What does this achieve that makes humans need or want to do this? What does multi-scale, materiality-based interaction afford human individuals or groups? If we want to consider the benefits of assemblages, then we need to combine some of the concepts discussed above with some archaeological examples.

How can we use Aegean case studies to throw light on the *benefits* of assemblages? (NB Clark does raise the issue of how difficult it is to *measure* benefit). It might be better to begin with an easier question that involves trying

---

[7] Note also the strong involvement of cultural anthropologists in the program and its publication (Dwight Read, Doug White), and of another archaeologist (the author; see Evans, Knappett, and Rivers 2009).

to understand the relative costs–benefits of individual types in assemblages (as in our stochastic model, we might try to see how the overall shape of the typological network emerges from the relative costs–benefits of different types). We could try to discover why some types persist once they are introduced, while others are more vulnerable and become obsolescent in the space of a few generations.

CONTAINER METAPHORS IN THE AEGEAN

One good place to start is with the very first appearance of ceramic vessels at the transition between the Mesolithic and Neolithic in Greece. This is frequently understood in terms of a 'Neolithic revolution', with ceramic containers being one of the key components in a bundle of innovations that permitted settled village life. The archaeological proclivity for seeking out origins and revolutions has recently been critiqued by Gamble (2007), and it is one reason behind the often stark separation between periods, such as Mesolithic and Neolithic, or indeed Bronze Age and Iron Age. Thinking in terms of revolutions also makes it hard to fathom where the ceramic-container innovation could have come from and why. Tomkins makes the important point that the earliest Greek Neolithic pottery, particularly at Knossos, seems to feed off existing container categories, most probably in wood and other organic materials such as basketry (Tomkins 2007; Knappett, Malafouris, and Tomkins, 2010). This argument is based on features in the earliest ceramics that appear to be skeuomorphic, such as polishing techniques mimicking wood-grain, and corded decoration techniques seemingly aping basketry.[8] Thus the innovation of the ceramic container can be seen as a process of exaptation, taking an existing idea of 'containment' and combining it with another idea, the modelling and firing of clay, already in use for making solid forms as figurines 30,000 years ago (Gamble 2007, 194). This can be seen in terms of conceptual blending too (see Hutchins 2005), and indeed metaphor. Whether we use exaptation or conceptual blending as our model, we can argue that the innovation of the ceramic container is in some sense 'efficient' (in terms of cost–benefit) because it exploits existing cognitive resources. We could eventually make the same arguments for other seemingly 'revolutionary' inventions, such as the emergence of metal containers, or indeed stone vessels (Bevan 2007, 62–99), each of which 'piggyback' on existing categories.

---

[8] For connections between pottery and basketry in a different context, the American Southwest, see Ortman 2000.

SHAPE AND DECORATION

The above case of 'containers' concerns broad categories and technologies. We might also examine the dynamics of types within ceramics, for instance; we can look at the relative 'fortunes' of cooking-pots, storage wares, and fine tablewares in terms of their respective costs–benefits and hence longevity. It is something of a rule that table wares change more rapidly over time than do the others, in part because they break more often, and also because they are used often in conspicuous consumption (and thus answer to different social practices than the other two broad categories). To set the ball rolling, we might simply state that another reason for this is that the cost–benefit ratio of a particular cooking-pot or storage type is very stable over time, whereas for table wares they are evidently much more variable. That said, not all table wares are equally persistent. Some survive and adapt for many generations; others do not. Here we could contrast the Minoan hemispherical cup with the carinated cup: the former endures for as much as a millennium, while the carinated cup comes and goes within 200 years. The carinated cup apparently differs from the hemispherical cup in very little (such as size, capacity) other than being more explicitly linked to metal. It mimics metal forms, and thus is tied up in wider, or just other, dynamics from the hemispherical cup. It is, following Hutchins (see above), something we could label a 'compound blend'. Insofar as it 'piggybacks' on *more* existing cognitive categories, it could be considered efficient at some level; however, it is linking up to categories that may have been unstable, and thus prone to obsolescence. As benefits faded, the cost–benefit ration became unfavourable and it fell out of favour. One could say much the same of 'eggshell ware': a high-cost, intricate form of pottery that first sees the light of day in MM IB and barely lasts into MM IIB. Its high skill-demands and cost made it a marginal product even at its peak, but again its strong basis in mimicking of metalwork meant it was treading a risky path in terms of benefits, which presumably shifted, leading to its demise (at around the same time as the carinated cup, perhaps not coincidentally). This is not to say, however, that intricate forms are necessarily doomed to short lives. The rhyton is an intricate form that manages to survive for quite some time— presumably its cognitive and social benefits kept on outweighing its costs.

Also note decorative styles have their logics of change too—some seem much more stable, such as trickle decoration on storage wares. This combination occurs over and over again from the Early Bronze Age (e.g. Fournou Korifi, south Crete) through to the Late Bronze Age, a period spanning nigh on 2,000 years. The cost–benefit balance in this association must have been incredibly stable; it is a simple technique that mimics the trickling of oil or some other liquid for which such containers must often have been destined, and so signals directly the likely contents of the vessel—potentially of value in a range of situations, from exchange and transport to everyday use. Another kind of decoration—white dots on a dark ground—might seem almost as straightforward, but it comes and goes, lasting only a century or so at the end of the Middle Bronze Age. It was not employed on pithoi, but predominantly on table wares such as straight-sided cups and bridge-spouted jars. In our simple formulation this means the cost–benefit balance must have been much more unstable, a feature we may understand as soon as we recognize that those white dots were probably aping particular effects on certain stone vases. But how is this so different to the mimicry of the liquid trickles on storage jars? Perhaps not all that different, except that the stone being imitated was rare and non-local, in all likelihood obsidian from Yiali. When we look at the chalice found at Zakros (albeit in a later period than most white-dotted ware) we can perhaps understand. This decorative technique would surely have been particularly dependent upon the prevalence of and taste for such stone vases, and thus more vulnerable as wider networks of circulation inevitably shifted over time. The oil trickle is inherently local and embedded in everyday agricultural practices, whereas the white dots turn out to be quite exotic in their derivation. Moreover, the white dots on ceramic table wares are a form of compound conceptual blend. We can look at further examples of how such blends may be more costly than others in terms of cognitive investment, or at least how the pay-off between cost and benefit is differently weighted, or more likely to fluctuate.

ASSEMBLAGE DYNAMICS: AEGEAN EXAMPLES

While we can focus on individual shapes or decoration and how they come and go, we do need to remember that it is the network/assemblage properties that are key in the fate of any individual case. It is fascinating how so much work has been done on typologies, but how little we understand of their dynamics—it is a question hanging in the air since Montelius and others in archaeology, Warburg, Focillon and Kubler in art history (see Olivier 2008; Kubler 1962), and now in economics and complexity science resurrected in a new guise (Arthur 2009; Lane, Pumain, and van der Leeuw 2009). We have seen in Chapter 6 how some scholars have tried to fill this gap—the failure to explain typologies and artefactual assemblages—by proposing biological models for cultural change, often variants on Darwinian thinking (e.g. Mesoudi, Whiten, and Laland 2006). However, biological models can only capture some of the sense of cultural dynamics, and leave a lot unexplained.

In Chapter 7 we looked at the interregional transmission of particular consumption practices from Crete across the southern Aegean, focused specifically around the conical cup and the rhyton. It was also noted that these

types spread across the southern Aegean at the same time as a number of other
cultural features in the domains of architecture, administration, and art. What
we did not consider, however, was the extent to which these different forms of
material culture might have acted together as *object networks*, thereby producing stronger interactive possibilities than could have been achieved with
only one or two of these forms and practices. There are benefits in such cross-
cutting patterns, where the whole exceeds the sum of the parts. In each of the
above-mentioned domains we encounter 'iconic' artefacts that objectify Cretan interests in 'efficient' manner. In the words of Gosden on colonialism, it is
the objects that do the work, with the capacity to get a hold of people, working
on minds and bodies (Gosden 2004*b*).

It is surely no accident that the conical cup is also the first 'colonial' cup.
That is to say, it is the first kind of drinking-cup that effectively 'colonializes'
diverse spaces in the Palatial periods, rapidly transmitted across Crete and far
beyond. This at the very time that Knossos seems to gain the upper hand in the
power-struggle between the Cretan palaces, with Phaistos and Malia much less
prominent from *c.*1700 BC onwards, while Knossos goes from strength to
strength. The colonial conical cup would on the face of it seem to be the
least likely candidate for such a transformation—after all, is not Cretan pottery
distinguished by its elaborate decoration and exquisite craftsmanship? It is
precisely such forms—those of Kamares ware—that find themselves
distributed across the Aegean and the Near East, prior to the conical cup,
albeit in small quantities. No, the plainness and extreme simplicity of the
conical cup seem to be its great advantage rather than its weakness. These
provide it with distinctive iconic qualities, insofar as it is very readily recognizable. While its categorical status is significant, because it is this quality that
makes it easily objectifiable in network form, we must not forget that it also
had specific affordances in use. Though employed in a wide range of contexts,
and thereby defying easy functional categorization, the best explanation so far
proposed is that it functioned in 'token hospitality', used once for a ritual act of
consumption before being discarded (Rupp and Tsipopoulou 1999). This too
fits with the purpose of an iconic object—conical cups would rarely acquire
biographies that could serve to rework and compromise the simple networked
role for which it was designed.

The presumed functional association of conical cups with liquid consumption might also have seen them used in concert with rhyta on many occasions.
These too are found in a range of contexts, from the domestic to the cultic,
from palaces to sanctuaries and burials. Unlike conical cups, though, rhyta are
very rarely plain; they are highly elaborate in form, decorated in a range of
motifs, some of which are evidently skeuomorphic. And unlike conical cups,
which do not tend to see production in stone or metal, rhyta are manufactured
in both of these materials, including some of the most stunning vessels known
from the entire Aegean Bronze Age. In a very different way to conical cups,

therefore, rhyta have their own iconic network properties, serving to connect up particular practices of consumption with exquisite imported materials such as rock crystal, gold, and silver.

The connections go further. It is not only that rhyta are associated with liquid consumption—evidence suggests they were used in consumption practices that incorporated ceremonial processions. Koehl (2006) underlines how particular assemblages of rhyta, such as that from Gournia, are deposited in contexts close to processional corridors leading to courts. Furthermore, Warren (2006) points out not only how frequent scenes of processions are on relief stone vases, sealstones and ring bezels, and frescos, but also how among the various objects carried in these processions it is containers that are the most frequent. And among the containers stone vessels feature prominently, including rhyta, of course. So rhyta therefore have contextual connections with other kinds of stone vases, and with processions.[9]

This link with processions allows us to draw yet another link. Processional corridors in elite buildings in Minoan Crete, notably the palace at Knossos, seem often to have been lined with frescos. These frescos depict scenes of procession, some featuring rhyta. Many of the earliest examples from Knossos are in relief and depict bull imagery, often life-size and seemingly in flying gallop, hence possibly in bull-leaping scenes (Blakolmer 2006, 11–12; cf. also Blakolmer, 2010). This creates two further connections with rhyta. First, there is a strong iconic connection, in that many rhyta are made in the shape of bull's heads, and relief rhyta bear images of bulls in flying gallop, such as on the Boxer Rhyton from Aghia Triadha (Koehl 2006, 164–5). Secondly, the fact that the earliest Knossian bull frescos are in relief is also significant, as this creates a connection with the relief depiction of bulls on stone vases and sealstones (Blakolmer 2006; 2010). Hood (2000) develops a convincing argument for the earliest bull relief frescos at Knossos to belong in MM IIIA, which is also the precise period when we see notable relief bulls depicted on a storage jar from Anemospilia (Sakellarakis and Sakellaraki 1997) and on a large lentoid flask from Akrotiri on Thera, an import from central Crete (Knappett and Nikolakopoulou 2008), not to mention a white-on-dark bull rhyton from Kommos (Koehl 2006, 127, cat. 350). Bull imagery continues to be important in subsequent periods, found across the Cyclades and indeed further afield in the Palatial periods, with perhaps the most striking in this regard being the dramatic bull-leaping frescoes from Tell el-Daba in Egypt, testifying to transmission of Cretan iconography and perhaps technique, albeit much later, in LM IB (Bietak, Marinatos, and Palyvou 2007; Brysbaert 2007; Shaw 2009). Yet it is this early combination of bull imagery, frescos, rhyta, and processions at the very beginning of the Neopalatial period, seemingly coming together first

[9] On relief stone vases and elite propaganda, see also Logue 2004.

at Knossos, that testifies to the strong networking possibilities of groups of cult artefacts and practices.[10] As well as rhyta and other kinds of containers, bull motifs also appear on sealings. This brings us to the domain of administration and objectifying practices.

In this MM IIIA period there is as yet no sign of an association between bull imagery and the bureaucracy of Minoan administration. However, in LM IB the distribution of sealings impressed by signet rings with bull imagery has been used as an argument for the dissemination of Knossian 'propaganda' across Crete (Hallager and Hallager 1995). Although this evidence comes largely from the end of the LM I period, this may be because of the preservation conditions needed for clay sealings, that is, fire destructions, such as those that occurred in LM IB. It could be that this iconography was similarly distributed in MM III and LM IA (especially bearing in mind the above-mentioned ceramic evidence for bull iconography). Some evidence for the existence of such 'propaganda' in LM IA comes from Akrotiri, where a cache of sealings was found in room Delta 18b; here the fourteen different seal impressions include various bull scenes, with one of bull-leaping (see Karnava 2008). Also apparent at Akrotiri is the use of Linear A, with fifteen inscribed objects known thus far, while five are also known from Ayia Irini on Kea and three from Phylakopi on Melos (Karnava 2008). This evidence links the Cyclades to the bureaucratic system on Crete, which sees Linear A come to the fore as the sole script in the Neopalatial period, at the expense of Cretan Hieroglyphic. This is further indication of the establishment of an 'objectifying' network of material culture in the southern Aegean, established across a range of forms (see Knappett 2008 for connections among media).[11]

We could extend this discussion to other categories of material culture too, such as stone vases, which see similar processes at work in the Neopalatial period (Bevan 2007, 125–33), and faience, the production of which also peaks at this time (Tite *et al.* 2009). We should not forget architecture either—particular architectural styles seem to emerge at Knossos at the beginning of the Neopalatial period, and spread across the island thereafter, with features such as pier-and-door partitions used in Minoan Halls, found from Chania in the west to Zakros and Palaikastro in the east (Driessen 1982; 1989/90). As with many of the other traits discussed above, there is also evidence off-island for the take-up of Cretan architectural practices, with the best current evidence from Akrotiri on Thera (Palyvou 2005), not to mention Trianda on Rhodes (Marketou 1998). These spaces were almost certainly used for particular kinds of ceremonial activities that would have incorporated conical cups, rhyta, and stone vases, and in some cases might even have had frescos adorning the walls.

---

[10] Another material icon one might include is the double axe—see Haysom 2010.

[11] See also Wengrow 2008 for parallel ideas for the Near East, with notion of 'commodity branding'.

These contiguities of different object networks in practice would have lent them still further strength. The architectural configurations of Minoan halls and similar spaces, built of carefully formed, repetitive ashlar blocks, would have structured interactions in particular ways, creating specific patterns of circulation, movement, and bodily gestures. Indeed, Letesson argues for a fundamental shift in architectural logic between the Protopalatial and Neopalatial periods, from an organic, agglutinative system to a more systematic, articulated one (Letesson 2007). Perhaps for the first time in the Aegean, various forms of material culture were brought together to have effects that were both immediate and bodily and far-reaching and iconic. They were able to create a kind of consciousness, or objecthood, that was politically expedient.

ACCUMULATING AND ENCHAINING ASSEMBLAGES

What is it about this combination of the proximate and non-proximate that is so powerful? There are many different ways of describing this, whether in social or semiotic terms, but at base it arguably derives from a tension between presence and absence. Proximate interactions at the bodily scale build on presences: the conical cups, rhyta, wall paintings, and fine masonry are all there, in the scene, together. But then at the same time, because of their iconic, far-reaching qualities, they are also referencing any number of other examples of the same or related categories that are absent from the scene. Some fascinating perspectives have been put forward on this relationship between presence and absence, in art history and archaeology for example. Hans Belting (e.g. 2005*a* and *b*) has written with reference to images of the simultaneity and opposition of absence and presence. One intriguing case he employs is itself archaeological: Pre-Pottery Neolithic B skulls, for example from Jericho, that are given a new 'skin' of clay and eyes of shells. Here the absent body is represented metonymically by the skull; and the clay and shells are added to make an image. In this way, which Belting likens to broader processes of making masks, an image creates a new life, sustaining the personhood of the deceased and creating a material presence substituting for absence. In Belting's words, 'iconic presence still maintains a body's absence and turns it into what must be called visible absence' (Belting 2005*a*, 312).

What is curious about this is that Belting uses an archaeological example to make a set of points that are, oddly and unwittingly, remarkably close to some recent arguments put forward by archaeologists. Chapman, for example, in developing what he dubs 'fragmentation theory', has distinguished between two social practices, accumulation and enchainment, that he sees as providing a new framework for understanding social life in later Eurasian prehistory (Chapman 2000; Chapman and Gaydarska 2006). Accumulation describes processes such as creating sets of artefacts in hoards or tombs that together form a 'set' (see also Gamble 2004; 2007). Enchainment is the means by which social groups are held together in networks or 'nets', possibly spread over distance. Chapman identifies deliberate processes of fragmentation in the archaeological record of the Neolithic and Chalcolithic of south-east Europe, and suggests that deliberate redistribution of artefact fragments served to create enchained relations. Knappett (2006) offered a slight modification to this scheme, describing processes of 'layering' and 'networking' to supplement Chapman's ideas of accumulation and enchainment respectively. Accumulation, for example, does not cover the range of proximate processes whereby meaning can be generated; it describes the processes of placing artefacts together in sets, whereas the modification and creation of artefact surfaces are also means whereby proximate and contiguous meaning arises. In order to show the potential breadth of examples in which this might apply, Knappett showed how in the work of both Marcel Duchamp and Antony Gormley 'layering' processes at the proximate scale were important to the creation of meaning (Knappett 2006). If we return by way of example to the PPNB skull discussed by Belting, then 'accumulation' does not portray the process of elaboration as fully as does 'layering', with the clay 'skin' layered over the bone and the shells laid into the eye-sockets.

Another point emerges from this intersection of ideas. Chapman had suggested that a tension existed between accumulation and enchainment, as if they were in opposition. However, layering and networking often look like they are complementary and work in tandem, at least in the cases of Gormley and Duchamp (Knappett 2006, 248). It is as if the more distancing processes of networking rely upon first the layering processes occurring at the proximate level. The PPNB skull can become an icon, a visible absence, thanks to the layering work that happens up close. Similarly, the effects of Gormley's far-flung iconic body shapes takes hold through the close-up processes of imprinting, moulding, and layering.

There are many ways we might try to draw in all kinds of different currents into this discussion. One such current is that of semiotics, particularly of the Peircean variety (Knappett 2005; Preucel 2006). With its pragmatic basis it is really very different from the Saussurean semiotics that is rooted in language and which has sustained considerable and merited critique in terms of its applicability to material culture. Indeed, Peircean semiotics proves to be particularly strong in describing bodily semiotic processes (Daniel 1984; Crossland 2009). If iconicity is that which allows the image to have a life beyond the body and to create visible absence, then it is the index which is rooted in causality, factorality, and contiguity (see also Sonesson 1989). In the terms above, if icons are the kinds of substitutions that allow enchainment and networking, then it is indexes that create accumulation and layering. Yet we do not need to be fully committed to the Peircean project, whatever its numerous strengths; the word 'semiotic' still gets many people thinking of language, and perhaps its denigration in the novels of David Lodge! Indeed, Gamble (2007)[12] seems uncomfortable with 'semiotics' preferring to use the terms from rhetoric of 'metaphor' and 'metonymy'.[13] Even if one prefers to use these terms, one can still make very useful connections between accumulation/enchainment and a wider literature. Gamble sees these as metaphoric and metonymic processes (Gamble 2007, 66–79, 136–7). But what is missing from these innovative archaeological approaches is the important dynamic of presence and absence; for this one can then come full circle back to Belting, who talks of presence and absence in relation to metaphor as a process of substitution (Belting 2005*a* and *b*). Although he may not specifically distinguish between metaphor and metonymy as different substitutions of absence/presence, in his discussion of the PPNB skull as first seeing a *pars pro toto* substitution of skull for body, he is implicitly describing a metonymic process (Belting 2005*b*, 46). This selection, which then sees the addition of layering, sets the ground for metaphoric substitution.[14] These are surely two kinds of substitution that work in tandem most powerfully. The micro-scale metonymic process frees up the broader-scale metaphoric one. For Gamble, it would be the proximate and then the release from the proximate.[15]

If we come back to our conical cups and other forms of Aegean material culture, we can see how icon and index, or metonymy and metaphor, may inform what we are observing. In each case we see a combination of micro-scale, proximate, indexical actions—let us say, the consumption of wine released from rhyta into conical cups, surrounded by wall paintings and fine masonry in a Minoan hall—with wider-scale, non-proximate, iconic process-es, such that these practices can be seen to be playing out at another level, in the knowledge that other protagonists in distant communities may be performing the exact same actions with the same kinds of artefacts. This is the sense in which conical cups are 'iconic'. Their readily recognizable form and hence easy transmission render them both bodily and transcendent. The same might also be said for monuments—again both capable of changing how one feels proximately, while having iconic properties too.[16] The iconic quali-ties of an artefact type, an image, or indeed a monument can of course be

---

[12] There is no need to follow Gamble's (2007, 90) hasty refutation of semiotics citing its linguistic basis—this fails to take due account of the fundamentally pragmatic and 'phanero-scopic' basis of Peirce's semiotic scheme.

[13] See discussion in Knappett 2005 for problems with how these have been developed in relation to material culture, as in Tilley 1999.

[14] Runia (2006) distinguishes between metaphor as the transfer of meaning and metonymy as the transfer of presence.

[15] And arguably this would tally with the distinction between 'real space' and 'virtual space' (Summers 2003).

[16] 'Monuments are powerful because they appear to be permanent markers of memory and history and because they do so both iconically and indexically, i.e. they can evoke feelings

deliberately manipulated. Here we might mention processes such as representing a particular class of artefact iconically in script, as happens in Aegean scripts such as Cretan Hieroglyphic, Linear A, and Linear B; or the miniaturization of particular forms can also serve to focus attention on their iconic rather than functional qualities (Knappett 2008; 2012). Another such process is fragmentation, also with the potential to accentuate form, as is seen in the destructive fragmentation of bull's-head rhyta (Rehak 1995).

WHY ASSEMBLAGES?

Layering, accumulation, enchainment, and networking, sets and nets, icon and index, metaphor and metonymy: all or some of these might be useful as means for understanding the 'how' of object networks. They are terms that can point us towards the multiple associations that particular artefact categories may accrue in the course of practice. But while they might be useful in answering 'how', they do not necessarily tell us 'why'. *Why* should human groups pursue such associations? Gamble's answer is simple: identity. Sets and nets give humans different possibilities for exploring their social selves through materiality, with nets in particular enabling human action across ever-expanding scales, the 'release from proximity' (Gamble 1998; 2007). The use of material metaphors to develop object networks thus fulfils the need for individuals and groups to explore and establish their identities across spatial and temporal scales. In that the body is the source of identity, and there have always been bodies situated in material worlds, Gamble does not see how one can identify revolutions in these metaphorical processes; he talks more in terms of gradients of change. Both instrument and container metaphors are fundamental and stem from the body, though the balance between the two does shift, over the very long term, from the former to the latter.

Belting offers an explanation that is compatible though more metaphysical in outlook. Furthermore, he is not looking to explain the use of objects in the release from proximity, but rather the history of the making of images. These images are, arguably, what allow for the release from proximity of which Gamble speaks. Belting sees the drive to avoid death as the ultimate explanation, or at least the drive to overcome the finality of absence that death represents. Hence the primeval death mask: in a sense the origin of the image, which all subsequent images somehow resemble. It is the mask as image that creates a visible absence, mitigating the finality of death's absence. And the greater its visibility over space and time, the more that death is

through their materiality and form as well as symbolize social narratives of events and sacrifices retold in public rituals' (Rowlands and Tilley 2006, 500).

mitigated. This could, in Gamble's terms, be seen as a search for identity, though it is perhaps for Belting posed at an individual level, rather than the community level which might concern Gamble.

THE EFFICIENCY OF NETWORKS?

It is perhaps implicit that these transformations are expressed through material metaphors because they are in some sense 'efficient', though Gamble does not use such a term. Materials are efficient because their durability means they can perpetuate identities over space and time (and arguably this is good for resilience of the group/individual). What also goes unstated is whether the dynamics responsible for the shift from instrument to container metaphors have anything to do with changing cost–benefits of these material metaphors in shifting conditions. Gamble seems to state that material metaphors permit a release from proximity (Gamble 2007, 211). Though not expressed as such, it would seem then that material metaphors bring benefits in their capacity to extend and express identity over space and time, in ways that social relationships alone cannot.

The above-mentioned 'metaphoric' processes have not been considered within the context of costs and benefits. Surely some such processes are more or less persistent because they constitute, at some level, effective material means of establishing relations, of extending human interactions beyond the proximate. How are sets and nets effective? We ought to be able to ask this question because, although Gamble may not consider metaphor from the perspective of cognitive efficiency, recent work by the likes of Hutchins on conceptual blends does appear to imply that metaphor ought to be or could be cognitively efficient. Perhaps certain kinds of associations across space and time, established iconically and/or indexically, such as enchainment or accumulation, offer differing degrees of cognitive efficiency. How do these processes employ cost-saving mechanisms such as scaffolding, blending, or piggybacking? Substitution—making the absent present through materiality—could surely be seen as cognitively cost-effective too, as might a material process like 'compression' (Stafford 2007), perhaps enacted through miniaturization.

But how is it that wider and wider networks bring 'economies of scale', so to speak? Why don't ever-increasing networks just spiral out of control, becoming more and more unwieldy and cognitively unmanageable? If we follow a line of argument taken from recent groundbreaking interdisciplinary work in the economics of innovation, then larger and larger object networks, or what is aptly dubbed 'agent–artefact space', can paradoxically create benefits by increasing the likelihood of the identification of new functionalities and new problem-solving capacities (Lane, Pumain, and van der Leeuw 2009). So an increase in the size of the space may actually be accompanied by cognitive reduction, if that space is appropriately structured. More and more benefits may accrue, but without much additional cost. Network effects may minimize costs and maximize benefits. That said, complex networks usually have non-linear dynamics, which can mean that small changes can create unpredictable results.

As cast here, the efficiency of object networks seems to be an accidental effect of human interactions, rather than a cause. But need there only be one 'cause', here identified as the human search for identity? In Gamble's case, he looks for very long-term processes in this 'release from proximity' in searching for identity; and in the case studies I have used, the scalar expansion of object networks is more to do with an expression of political identity. We should also entertain the possibility that there are other causes at work. One is that cognitive functional efficiency might also be driving the expansion of object networks. Another is that there might be more metaphysical drives at stake here, caught up in questions of human emotion and desire. In trying to come to terms with the ineffability of the material world, one set of responses could entail various means of 'objectifying', of condensing, of making sense. This could, conceivably, be contrasted with other responses that follow the flow of the material world, of phenomena, of 'things'. Though 'control' through objects can achieve many ends, physical and metaphysical, social and political, this control is precarious when it disregards the recalcitrance and indissolu-bility of the world of 'things'. In the simple terms laid out in this chapter, it can be construed as a balancing of the benefits and costs of certain kinds of interaction with and in the material world of phenomena.

CONCLUSIONS

This chapter has been about the benefits of object networks. In the next chapter I will consider some of the costs. Evidently there are always costs working against the benefits; sometimes these costs are recognized, and net-works simply fail for reasons that are understood but unavoidable. But sometimes the costs are invisible. One of the problems is that the explicit nature of objects as categories is always under pressure, as we incorporate objects into our action repertoires and literally stop thinking about them. In this process objects can slip from the world of ideas into the world of phenomena, and thus somewhat out of our control. I shall discuss this in the next chapter in terms of a tension between 'objecthood' and 'thingness'.

I will then in Chapter 9 examine the nature of this tension and how it has been implicitly addressed in different cultures past and present. One way in which objects can easily fall into thingness is when, in the course of object innovation for example, only the front-end of the problem is conceptualized, and the aftermath or back-end is not. At some scales in the human past we can see that groups did plan for the whole life-cycle of an object or monument—with processes of structured deposition or abandonment, for example. We also see vast networks of obsolescence too—and evidently humans do not always think through the end-stories of their material networks. In Chapter 9 I will therefore introduce the notion of 'biographical care' as a means of thinking through the convergent and divergent temporalities at play in object networks.

8

Meshworks of Things

There was no ordinariness to return to, no refuge from the blinding potency of things, an apple screaming its sweet juice. Every thing belonged to, had been retrieved from, impossibility—both the inorganic and the organic—shoes and socks, their own flesh.

(Anne Michaels, *Fugitive Pieces*)

INTRODUCTION

The previous chapter gave the impression that it is humans that elaborate and control multi-scale object networks. It can only be humans that generate the *intentionality* behind such networks, which is also often taken to mean that they lie in sole possession of agency in these networks. But agency need not be so closely coupled to intentionality. This is at least in part accepted in arguments positing that artefacts may possess secondary agency, such that a human agent delegates agency to an artefact—as with a speed-bump, or a landmine (Gell 1998). One problem with this idea of delegation is that artefacts do not always perform as designed: materials have properties that are not always fully understood by the human agent. An example we might use is the interaction of potter, wheel, and clay in the creation of a ceramic vessel. The potter may not always be in full control of either the equipment or the clay, sometimes being 'led' by the clay (Malafouris 2008b). And this also raises the point that human protagonists may have very variable skill levels, which has implications for the distribution of agency across a task. A very skilled potter may have the capacity to be in full control; but then switching clays may require some adjustment to the properties of the new clay; and the highly skilled potter may even choose to be led by the clay's properties, perhaps producing a vessel that was not initially intended. Thus, even with a relatively simple socio-technical complex—potter, wheel, and clay—it is not quite as simple as saying that the capacity to act lies entirely in the hands of the potter, or is in some instances delegated by the potter to the clay. The capacity to act would seem at least in part to be inherent in the materials in play; and the degree to which this is true probably varies with the skill of the protagonist.

If we start to consider more complex socio-technical assemblages, with both multiple artefacts and human actors (of differing skill levels), such as the design processes for missiles or metro systems studied by Bruno Latour and others in Actor-Network Theory (Latour and Lemonnier 1994), then the capacity to act would seem to be less and less in human hands alone. This is not to say that intentionality becomes distributed, with the machines taking over in the manner of any number of science-fiction films; but that the capacity to act (that is, agency) is very much affected by the diverse material properties and imbrications. It is perhaps no longer useful to search for who or what possesses agency, but to begin to investigate the manner in which agency is distributed across such complexes. Recent attention to 'material agency' is not really concerned with switching the locus of agency from humans to materials, but rather with underscoring the need to consider materials as critical in processes of agency (Knappett and Malafouris 2008). We need to rethink our tendency to assume that agency is a human attribute. While humans generate intentionality, the capacity to act is distributed across humans and non-humans in most real-world situations. And we should not restrict the 'non-human' to the artefactual and inorganic: it might very well also include plant life, as in the ways that trees can shape social landscapes (Jones and Cloke 2008), and animal life, with the agency of farm animals such as sheep in altering landscapes, and indeed in bringing entire agricultural economies crashing to a halt, as in the UK foot-and-mouth crisis of a decade ago (Law and Mol 2008).

While in many cases the extension of human capacities through networks may be a harmonious process, with the network serving human needs as designed, these networks may also be recalcitrant, providing unpleasant surprises. They resist. Connections fail. Artefacts break. Trees multiply. Sheep fall ill. We do not always fully understand the 'behaviour' of materials, organic and inorganic, no matter how hard we try to bring the unruly world of things within our conceptual frameworks. Indeed, our frameworks are frequently self-limiting in being oriented towards 'explicit and precise forms of wholeness' (Callon and Law 2004, 3), dubbed the 'romantic' paradigm by Kwa (2002). This is in contrast to a 'baroque' paradigm, which construes a messier world in which complexity does not necessarily have such order (Callon and Law 2004). If the previous chapter was aligned with the romantic, this chapter is much more concerned with the baroque: that component of human interaction seeking to broach the 'otherness' of the world of phenomena, which can appear strange, opaque, and impenetrable. I will draw on a range of approaches to 'things' past and present, before developing some thoughts on transparent objects and indissoluble things in connection with Aegean Bronze

Age examples. And in counterpoint to Chapter 7, in which the *benefits* of object networks were highlighted, here I focus on their *costs*.

RESISTING THINGS, RESISTING DEATH

There is arguably something frustrating, opaque, and intransigent about the inanimate world of things. Things are not like us. They do not grow or die. We might interact with another human being in building up a relationship, but such interaction is not possible with a thing. We may try nonetheless, in a futile effort to get under its skin. As Peter Schwenger (2006, 6–7) has noted, quoting Sartre:

> The in-itself has nothing secret; it is solid (*massif*). In a sense we can designate it as a synthesis. But it is the most indissoluble of all: the synthesis of itself with itself. The result is evidently that being (that is, the object's being) is isolated in its being and that it does not enter into any connection with what is not itself... It knows no otherness; it never posits itself as other-than-another-being. It can support no connection with the other. (Sartre 1957, lxvi, *Being and Nothingness*)

The opacity of things is akin to the opacity of death. And yet we react to this opacity not with indifference, but with continued efforts at interaction. The rift between us and them is thus thrown into ever sharper relief and is, according to Schwenger, an inevitable source of melancholy. And in recent cultural and literary studies Schwenger is not alone in exploring the ineffable qualities of the phenomenal world, and the efforts in various forms of cultural production to describe this ineffability without reducing it to the knowable human world. Frow (2003), for example, cites this fascinating poem 'Pebble' by Zbigniew Herbert:

> The pebble
> is a perfect creature
> equal to itself
> mindful of its limits
> filled exactly
> with a pebbly meaning
> with a scent which does not remind one of anything
> does not frighten anything away does not arouse desire
> its ardour and coldness
> are just and full of dignity
> I feel a heavy remorse
> when I hold it in my hand
> and its noble body
> is permeated by false warmth

—Pebbles cannot be tamed
to the end they will look at us
with a calm and very clear eye

Frow's paper goes on to examine other aspects of the strangeness of phenomena as captured (or not) in literature, as in the novel *Eucalyptus* by Murray Bail: a travelling salesman comes into town and, transfixed by a waitress in a café, decides to hide behind the café to watch her undress—but while doing so, he is transformed into a telegraph pole, forever rooted to the same spot. We might also consider Trachtenberg's (2003) treatment of the photography of Wright Morris; the focus is very much on everyday things, mostly in the midwest United States in the 1930s and 1940s: 'practical objects unmistakable, yes, but meanings ambiguous, imprecise, inciting the imagination to flights of memory, dreams, and wonder' (Trachtenberg 2003, 431). All three of these authors are contributors to a volume called simply *Things*: it is an edited work by Bill Brown, also in cultural/literary studies, who begins the book with an essay 'Thing Theory'. What is this theory?

THING THEORY

'Things' would appear to be as neutral a term as one might imagine, whether used in everyday speech or in academic discourse, as in a recent volume *Thinking Through Things* (Henare, Holbraad, and Wastell 2007). This judgement seems all the more valid when compared with roughly equivalent terms like 'artefacts' (implying human intervention) or 'objects' (implying a perceiving subject). Yet Bill Brown, as mentioned above, has set out to coin what he terms 'thing theory' (Brown 2001; 2003; 2006). While he playfully suggests that the last thing that things need is a theory, he succeeds in weaving together in his edited volume *Things* a series of contributions that all broach the opacity and indissolubility of the phenomenal world, in the approaches of Schwenger, Frow, and Trachtenberg mentioned already, as well as others such as Mitchell (2001/3; and further in 2005).

What, then, are the principal tenets of this 'thing theory'? Things are ambiguous and undefined; when you say 'pass me that green thing over there', the thing is unintelligible in some way. And things are to be understood in contrast to objects, which are named, understood, and transparent. Objects might be pulled out of the miasma of thingness (through naming, for example). It is important to note that objecthood and thingness are relational registers, in that the status of the material entity is partly contingent upon the perceiver: a thing to one onlooker might be an object to another. For example, imagine looking out of the window on a train journey: everything you see may just merge together, unnamed (especially in an unknown landscape). What you see is thingness, one thing running into another in a constant flow. Another traveller in the next seat, however, might pick out known, named features and landmarks—objects, in other words. Alternatively, you may switch back and forth between different modes, either letting the landscape flow over and past you, or consciously picking out specific features as they zip by.

With the above example, the shift from one register to another, from thingness to objecthood, may occur quite suddenly, through a change of mood or some external prompt. But there also exist various means by which this shift of register can be effected more consciously. I have already mentioned Schwenger and his citing of Sartre. Schwenger is interested in linguistic processes for transforming things into objects. Indeed, he argues that we 'murder' things in naming them with words, and links this back to Heidegger's observation that, while we bring the unknowable thingness of 'x' into our domain through naming and objectifying, we retain a sense of its unknowability (Schwenger 2006, 22–4). We can never fully grasp thingness.

Displaying things can also have a similar effect to naming them, as discussed by Gosden (2004a). In defining things and objects, he suggests that things are embedded in assemblages, and are inalienable and unquantifiable, whereas objects are disembedded, alienable, and quantifiable (ibid. 38–9). Thus, in the production and use of material culture there exist a whole series of interconnected processes that make it difficult to single out any individual item. In other words, we are habitually surrounded in our everyday lives by things. Yet, in certain circumstances, individual items may be singled out and displayed, whether in the museum, the shop, or the home—such items may qualify as objects, in Gosden's terms. Gosden is careful to point out that display is not necessarily a solely modern phenomenon, but may be identified in prehistoric contexts too, such as in the deliberate placement and display of bones and artefacts in British Neolithic tombs (ibid. 41).

THE THING IN HEIDEGGER

It may seem an odd coincidence that both Brown in literary/cultural studies and Gosden in archaeology have developed angles on 'things and objects' at virtually the same time, particularly with the lack of mutual citation (though in a later (2005) paper Gosden does cite the work of Mitchell). What is unstated in the paper by Gosden, and only mentioned sparingly in the work of Brown (e.g. Brown 2003; 2006, 7, n. 30), is the debt that the notion of 'things' owes to Heidegger, who wrote extensively on 'das Ding' (Heidegger 1971a; Brown 2003, 5, n. 15). Heidegger's focus is on everyday things, and how in our daily practice the equipment that surrounds us can recede from view. This mode of encounter between agent and world is described in Heidegger as *Zuhanden-heit*, or 'readiness-to-hand' (Wheeler 2005, 128 ff.; Harman 2010, 18). It is contrasted with *Vorhandenheit*, or 'presence-at-hand', a mode of encounter whereby things lose their everyday usefulness. Harman identifies at least three different kinds of situations in which 'presence-at-hand' obtains. The first is when objects are present in consciousness. The second concerns 'broken tools' that hence become obtrusive. The third example of objects being 'present-at-hand' is when they occupy a distinct point in space and time (Harman 2010, 19).

Let us use an example to think through these three situations. The example that Heidegger used was that of the hammer, which as a tool used in the hand is easily understandable in terms of equipment that may or may not be ready to or present at hand. When a hammer is being skilfully used, it is unobtrusive, well embedded in a situation, in harmony with the user and surrounding tools. As such it is a thing. However, a user could presumably stop in mid-swing, stand back, and start thinking about the shape of the hammer, its brand markings, or the smoothness of its wooden handle. Brought into conscious-ness in this way, the hammer becomes, perhaps even momentarily, an object. This is the shift in mode of encounter described above on the train, whereby someone may slip between different modes as things are brought in and out of consciousness. This 'object' mode can also occur when things break or go wrong, becoming obtrusive in the process. This is the second kind of situation Harman describes, and is one that Heidegger raises in relation to a hammer that breaks. Of course, as soon as it is repaired it can slip straight back into its previous mode of being ready-to-hand as a thing. The third kind of situation concerns formal categorizations whereby 'science' abstracts certain properties from the natural world, creating a distinct object fixed in space and time. This would in this scenario be the category 'hammer', which allows one to think about this entity even when not engaged in action. It is the epistemic quality of hammer, not its pragmatic quality. This too serves to objectify the thing, interrupting its 'readiness-to-hand'.

Not all things and objects are so obviously equipment held in the hand. We should try thinking this through with a different kind of thing/object. Imagine a window. Not something 'to hand' in the same way, or something that we obviously imagine as equipment or tool; yet still the window is equipment, and it can have as much presence-at-hand or readiness-to-hand as a hammer. When the window is functioning effectively, for example, in the sense that it is insulating from the cold and affording viewing, it is invisible even while we look. It is equipment that 'remains concealed from view insofar as it functions effectively' (Harman 2010, 18). But imagine then a crack developing, hinder-ing clear vision, and perhaps letting in the cold too. In this situation of the equipment no longer functioning effectively, the windowpane as such becomes obtrusive. We may begin to pay attention to its particular properties as an object. The mode of encounter has switched from thing to object, from *Zuhandenheit* to *Vorhandenheit*. Furthermore, as we saw with the above case of the hammer, the tool does not need to break for it to come into view in itself. It may simply be brought into consciousness through a process of attention, and thereby become an object, again perhaps only fleetingly. And the third situation is as applicable to the window as the hammer—the objectified category of window also serves to diminish the readiness-to-hand of actual windows in their everyday pragmatic functioning.[1]

Harman's identification of these three situations of presence-at-hand in Heidegger is an extremely useful clarification, and helps us grasp more completely the accounts of things/objects offered by Brown, Gosden, and others. But what of the question of opacity, which features prominently in Brown, and indeed Schwenger, though rather less in Gosden? One could imagine that the material world might reveal elements of its opacity in those very moments when things break, or when we bring things into our consciousness. These kinds of 'interruption' may sometimes appear to show to us the uncanny, indissoluble nature of the material world. However, Heidegger was adamant that it is in thingness, in the midst of readiness-to-hand, that the opacity lies. Even when the thing is embedded in equipment, and we see 'smooth coping' in human interactions with this equipment (Wheeler 2005), the material world always has surprises in store, exercising its recalcitrance when least expected. Being has mystery, indissolubility, and unknowability at its core, and for Heidegger this mystery is a positive feature; this is why we as humans should strive to engage ourselves in the world with *aletheia*, that is to say with a recognition of the need for 'unconcealment', for bringing forth being out of concealment (Heidegger 1971b; 1977; Harman 2007, 138–9). It is modern technology that 'marks the reign of boundless presence-at-hand, stripping all mystery from being' (Harman 2010, 20). In Heidegger, therefore, it is quite clear that the opacity of the world lies in that mode of encounter where things have readiness-to-hand, and not in those instances where things are brought to consciousness as objects. The more something comes into consciousness, the more it loses its strangeness.

Is there, then, nothing of the indissolubility of the phenomenal world that comes to the fore when objects are present-at-hand? For if humans are fully embedded in a world of things, pragmatically not epistemically engaged, then how would they even recognize mystery? Surely in some way mystery/opacity needs to be brought partially into consciousness to be recognized as such, and

---

[1] Perhaps these different modes are always present in some way, rather than oscillatory. Consider pragmatic/epistemic action distinction (Kirsh and Maglio 1995; Clark 1997), which suggests rather more seamless complementarity between embedded pragmatic 'thingly' understandings and the discursive, 'epistemic' actions.

for it to be embraced or reviled. Perhaps it is in these moments of transformation from thing to object and back again that opacity is encountered—those moments when something breaks, or is brought into consciousness, that the uncanny world appears to us. It is what Schwenger has described very fittingly as the 'uneasy flicker between two versions of worldhood, more disturbing than if either version prevailed' (Schwenger 2006, 54).

Heidegger believed that an attendance to mystery, and to the processes of revealing that which is concealed in being, had been lost in the modern world. With his notion of *Gestell* (literally a 'rack') or 'enframing', he argued that modern technology had no flicker, but saw only objects and not things: that 'all of nature and all of history are hung out to dry on this global rack, all perfectly arranged, stripped of all mystery' (Harman 2007, 137). In contrast, however, the ancient Greeks had a much more complete approach to technology, engendered in the Greek word *technē*, meaning both craft and art (Heidegger 1971b). *Technē* was capable of bringing forth entities out of their concealment—paying heed to the thingly qualities of phenomena while simultaneously creating humanized objects. Heidegger's romanticization of Greek artful craft is a rhetorical device to set apart modern technology from history, and as such ought not to be taken too literally. No doubt further detailed probing of Classical craftsmanship would find some divergences between some technologies that were indeed artful and others that were more instrumental. Indeed, by the same token, not all modern technology is hopelessly objectifying. One can find such divergences in many cultures, past and present, and we should perhaps expect to find gradients rather than the ultimate origins of one tendency or another (see Gamble 2007 on origins research). To demonstrate that one can find both object and thing modes in many times and places, I return now to the Aegean Bronze Age to show that artistic and technological traditions even more ancient than those raised by Heidegger saw tensions between thingness and objecthood, with some hints of the kinds of 'enframing' that Heidegger considered predominantly modern.

AEGEAN THINGS

In the previous chapter I argued that in the Neopalatial period on Crete, *c.*1700–1500 BC, various kinds of material culture—such as conical cups, rhyta, wall paintings, and ashlar masonry—were mobilized together as iconic markers in object networks. Though their iconic qualities facilitated transmission across distance, in effect colonializing the southern Aegean and spreading Minoan identity, these qualities were ultimately grounded in bodily, indexical, proximate interactions. Much as with the Pre-Pottery Neolithic B skull cited by Belting (2005*b*), the metaphorical substitutions in play built upon metonymic connections. Thus, whereas Belting may point up the lack of body in contemporary media icons (ibid.), and Summers the disarticulations of real and virtual space (2003), in the Aegean Bronze Age icons were certainly embodied. Rather than look, however, for a critical moment in human history when this all changed, a switch from premodern to modern so to speak, I would prefer to envisage a range of cultural responses to the object–thing challenge. One very important corollary of the groundedness of icons is that the objectifying qualities of these artefacts are not free and floating separate from their thingly properties. That is to say, there does appear to be some recognition of the uncanny, opaque, and indissoluble qualities of the phenomenal world.

Let us look at a few possible examples of this. Arguably, miniaturization (or in fact both micrographia and megalographia) can provoke this feeling. At the same time as something micrographic can serve to objectify and make an image of a canonical-scale object, it also brings out the tension between the modes of objecthood and thingness. Removing the functionality of an object can highlight the transformation from *Zuhandenheit* to *Vorhandenheit*, thereby acknowledging the existence of the former. When scale is reduced, or indeed enlarged, the pragmatic qualities of the artefact are removed while the epistemic features are brought to the fore (see Kirsh and Maglio 1995 on pragmatic and epistemic action). Clark (2010) suggests that small-scale models are effective in abstract reasoning because they tend to reduce the information load, through 'selective concretisation' and 'temporal relaxation'. Whereas in archaeology miniatures are often interpreted as either cult objects or toys, this cognitive approach allows us to see miniaturization in a wider context (Figure 8.1; Knappett 2012).

2 cm

Figure 8.1. Minoan miniatures

Figure 8.1. Continued

Another process discussed in the previous chapter in the context of object networks was fragmentation; this too can uncover some of the thingly qualities of artefacts in the same moment as it objectifies. The thing's ineffability is partially compromised by fragmentation, and so it ought to be done with care. The natural world fragments and destroys enough as it is without we humans joining in and adding to the processes of destruction and ruin. Thus a kind of controlled fragmentation can be a powerful means of recognizing the tension between thing and object. We can perhaps see examples of this in the attention devoted to very particular ways of fragmenting bull's head rhyta (Rehak 1995).

The bull's-head rhyton (Figure 8.2) is an interesting example in another sense, in that the rhyton is a particular artefactual form designed to control the flow of liquids quite carefully; and yet the association with the bull creates a link to powerful forces of nature that are not necessarily that well understood or readily controlled.

An interesting perspective on the depiction of animals and the deposition of animal remains of various kinds in Minoan Crete is found in recent work by Shapland (2009; 2010*a*, *b*). In his thesis Shapland highlights the particular processes whereby unfamiliar animal species were brought into familiar, controlled settings, while conversely, representations of familiar domesticated

Figure 8.2. Bull's-head rhyton, from Little Palace, Knossos

species were deposited in unfamiliar locales. As an example of the former, the famous Temple Repositories in the Palace at Knossos, excavated by Sir Arthur Evans included faience representations of flying fish and argonauts, as well as thousands of seashells, some of which were painted. These animals, particularly the argonauts and flying fish, were probably unfamiliar to most residents of Knossos.[2] As for the latter, thousands of animal figurines, the vast majority of which represented domesticated quadrupeds, either sheep/goat or cattle (Zeimbekis 2004), were deposited at the peak sanctuary of Mount Iuktas, some 10 km to the south. These 'familiar' animals were represented as simple clay figurines and in some form of cult practice were used in ceremonies in what must have been a rather 'unfamiliar' place, a peak some 800 m high. One might say the same for those cult practices that took place in even more distant and unfamiliar settings, such as the Psychro or Idaean caves, in the highlands to the east and west of Knossos.

Shapland also highlights the multiple representations of animals in a range of other media. At the very smallest scale, often just 1–2 cm, stone seals were decorated with intricate carved motifs that incorporated animal depictions (see also Krzyszkowska 2005). The animals on seals are predominantly connected with hunting, either the hunted (deer, wild goats) or the hunting, such as dogs. This activity is a form of engagement with the wild, the marginal, and unfamiliar (Shapland 2009; 2010*a*). A further marker of this interaction with the unfamiliar is the fact that lions are the second-most represented animal on seals—the lion can hardly have been a commonly encountered animal for the average Cretan (Shapland 2010*b*). Seals may have been small, with barely visible motifs, yet they were used to create seal impressions in bureaucratic practices, and hence would have been powerful status insignia as well as personal amulets. Their capacity for multiple impressions gave them a kind of 'promiscuity', meaning that the images they bore could be transmitted far and wide.

The dynamics of seal imagery were rather different to those of wall paintings, which by contrast were large-scale and visually arresting but at the same time, of course, immobile. In Minoan wall paintings too we see frequent animal depictions, and again the emphasis seems to fall on unfamiliar, undomesticated species. Some of the earliest figurative depictions in the palace at Knossos were probably of bulls (see also Chapter 7), and the bull can certainly be recalcitrant, as mentioned above in connection with the rhyton. Shapland further points out the partridges and hoopoes in the Caravanserai fresco, and the birds and monkeys in the House of the Frescos. Hoopoes are migrating birds that would only have been intermittently present in the area, and monkeys are not endemic to Crete. Both were unfamiliar, from 'over the

---

[2] Another powerful combination of the unfamiliar is seen in the stone triton from Malia bearing a representation of the Minoan genii (Baurain and Darcque 1983).

horizon' in some sense (Shapland 2009). Even more unfamiliar creatures are found depicted too, with fantastical hybrids such as the griffin (and in other media, sphinxes and Minoan genii). These depictions suggest an interest in phenomena not immediately within the objectifying grasp of human control. Is this evidence for an understanding of the need to attend to the opacity of things, the incredible potential of the phenomenal world to resist and remain opaque? If one thinks of the power of the natural world to pull objects back into the mire of thingness—in its most dramatic form, natural phenomena such as earthquakes, volcanic eruptions, floods, and tsunamis—then there is every reason to believe that the inhabitants of Crete in the Bronze Age were more than familiar with the unpredictable force of such events, given the awesome destructive power of the Theran eruption *c.*1530 BC (Driessen and Macdonald 1997).

Thus, one sees the applicability of Belting's ideas on the close relationship between death, ritual, and the creation of images. If things can get a hold on us and drag us towards an actual or metaphorical death, then it is through objectifying images that we can resist absence with presence. Put another way, 'warmth is ebbing from things . . . we must compensate for their coldness with our warmth if they are not to freeze us to death' (Brown 2006, 177, epigraph citing Walter Benjamin). If the death mask (or 'effigy'—see Summers 2003) is some primeval form of presencing, then in archaeological studies of material culture we can conceivably trace any number of further cases of this kind, not least the gold death masks uncovered by Schliemann in the Shaft Graves of Mycenae. Cult practice using art objects is therefore a particularly effective way of attending to the flicker or tension between objects and things—a means of recognizing the inevitable pull towards death in both the animate and the inanimate.

It is one thing to strive constantly to objectify the phenomenal world, either singly in objects or multiply in networks. It is another to attend to this process of conversion and transformation. Barbara Stafford states that 'art that encourages one to pay attention is the binding exercise that keeps consciousness functioning' (Stafford 2011). No doubt Heidegger would maintain that in Greek *technē*, which combined both artistic creativity and technical skill in artful craft, this process of paying attention would have been fully present. In the supposed absence of the artful in modern technology, it is arguably now the role of art to keep the tension between object and thing in play. The same function may also be described for cult, in that the flicker between object and thing mimics that between life and death. An object–thing dichotomy is not one we should persevere with other than as a means to get to a third state where material culture *is* this flicker.

FROM THINGS TO MESHWORKS

It is not just individual artefacts that work singly as things, although much analysis across different domains tends to take single things as a focus, whether Heidegger's hammer or jug, or Frow's pebble. Just as objects may be interconnected in wide-ranging networks, so also things are gathered together in collectives. Here we can return to the notion of the 'meshwork' to try to capture this different topology (Ingold 2007b; Knappett 2010). The tension between meshwork and network was described in earlier chapters. If human engagement in the everyday world is primarily embodied, pragmatic, and 'unthinking' in some sense, then perhaps we need to try to think of this kind of embodiment not in terms of discontinuous networks, but instead as a continuous flow of people and things enmeshed together and moving along paths and lines without stoppages (Ingold 2007b). In these everyday worlds there is no neatness, no hierarchy of form; it is the world of the baroque rather than the romantic (Callon and Law 2004). Other terms have been used to try to capture something of this topology, such as gel, or smooth space (e.g. Sheller 2004; Moreira 2004). There is unruliness in the world of things, such that whole meshworks of things may work on and disorient the human. It is as if things want something of us, imposing their own desires and needs (Mitchell 2005; Gosden 2005). It is not just the artwork in a gallery that stares back at us, but the unruly world of things *in toto* (Elkins 1997). Even the seemingly most ordered human collections of artefacts, in museums, can resist this order and turn it on its head; Gosden and colleagues have recently argued that museums and their artefacts collect people as much as the other way round (Gosden, Larson, and Petch 2007). Things make demands of us, demands that are hard to either fathom or avoid when we are so deeply intertwined with them in meshworks.

ART, CULT, AND THE EVERYDAY?

This sense of the potential opacity of things is also developed in the literature about 'the everyday' that, like thing theory, spans a wide range of disciplines (Certeau 1984; Lefebvre 1991; Highmore 2002; Shove *et al.* 2007). The everyday, one might presume, is everything that is familiar, the object world that we create for ourselves and then conveniently overlook as long as it is serving its purpose. But the burgeoning literature on the everyday also identifies the world of things that surrounds us in quite different terms: as ambiguous, indeterminate, and indissoluble. Many things are highly resistant to description and attention (Frow 2003, 353, citing Gadamer 1976, 71: we are not ready

Figure 8.3. The everyday in Place Saint Sulpice, March 2010

to hear things in their own being). How can we even begin to attend to the everyday? Sheringham (2000; 2006) looks at processes employed by writers such as Georges Perec and Jean Rolin, sociologists Henri Lefebvre and Michel de Certeau, and the philosopher Maurice Blanchot. In the case of Georges Perec, for example, simple experiments are employed in an attempt to get under the skin of the everyday. One of these, *Tentative d'épuisement d'un lieu parisien*, a text of some forty pages, records Perec's three-day trip to the Place Saint Sulpice in Paris (Figure 8.3; Sheringham 2000, 195). Sitting at different cafés or on benches for stints of two to three hours at a time, Perec logged the to-ings and fro-ings around him, in the following manner:

Un 70 passe
Un 63 passe
Il est deux heures cinq.
Un 87 passe.
Des gens par paquets, toujours et encore.
Un curé qui revient de voyage (il y a une etiquette de compagnie aérienne qui pend
à sa sacoche).
Un enfant fait passer un modèle réduit de voiture sur la vitre du café (petit bruit).
Un homme s'arrête une seconde pour dire bonjour au gros chien du café, paisible-
ment étendu devant la porte.
Un 86 passe.
Un 63 passe. (quoted in Sheringham 2000, 197)

With this kind of notation—short observations intermingling people and things—Perec establishes a certain rhythm. Mostly he is concerned in this passage with movement, not with the static features observable in the square. It may give the effect of the attempt at an objective description, but the aim is more to train attention in order to 'stay tuned to an elusive frequency' (ibid. 196). In this sense it may be described as ethnographic, in that the ethnographer must not simply assimilate another culture into his/her own, but maintain some sense of its difference, its otherness, while describing it in recognizable terms. The ethnographer's field-notes may in some part be a process of tuning attention to new frequencies rather than straightforward description. However, the ethnographic process is also one of 'participant observation'—of taking part in social actions and events as a member of the group. Perec's detached, asocial, non-participation is very different from ethnography in this regard.

Arguably, despite their differences, both the methods used in ethnography and by Perec (and one might also include Rolin; and note Sheringham does discuss the ethnographer Marc Augé too) consist of what could be described as an 'oblique' angle on the everyday. The everyday is so elusive that it cannot be apprehended directly. As soon as one tries to reveal the thingness of the thing, it evaporates under our objectifying gaze. If, however, one can avoid gazing by somehow looking askance, perhaps the thingness of the everyday will offer itself up unwittingly. Others, however, *have* adopted a more direct approach, tackling the everyday head-on. Surrealist art and writing confronts the status of the everyday (Sheringham 2006), a 'tradition' that continues in much contemporary art (Papastergiadis 2006; Saito 2007; Johnstone 2008). By taking everyday objects and placing them in settings and combinations in which their mundanity is very starkly challenged, various artists have produced works that bring out the uncanny and the opaque residing amidst what seems to be the ordinary and the transparent. Many examples suggest themselves: the urinals and snow-shovels of Marcel Duchamp, the megalographic everyday objects (e.g. clothes-pegs) of Claes Oldenburg, and the simulated everyday objects of Peter Fischli and David Weiss (not to mention many others). This does not even begin to skim the surface of photographic and video art, which also create particular processes of attention towards the everyday. One might, for example, consider the video pieces of Mark Lewis, which linger in a single shot of four minutes on a posed everyday setting—such as ice-skating on a public rink in Toronto—forcing a prolonged attention.

I could initiate here an extensive discussion of how different authors and artists through the twentieth and into the twenty-first century have found ways to reveal something of the indissolubility of the everyday. Some have used direct techniques, others more oblique. What is remarkable, however, is that such a discussion would be predicated on one fundamental point: that it is apparently only 'art' that can succeed in revealing the everyday for what it is.

We are so immersed in our daily lives in the constant flicker between object-hood and thingness that we cannot see it. Our everyday ways of viewing preclude us from seeing beyond. And yet whence does art derive if not from the everyday? Is not every artist, of whatever ilk, always part of an everyday life as well? There is scope for creativity in the midst of the everyday; it is perhaps a matter of taking those rare moments when we are briefly outside of ourselves in the midst of the everyday, and developing means for capturing or prolong-ing them. Thus while in the twentieth- and twenty-first-century West it falls to art to bring the object–thing flicker into the open, that art is not a separate domain inured to the everyday, but is integral to it.

What of other cultures, however, with a very different contextual setting for artistic practice? Are there not other ways to bring the flicker to the fore? It is perhaps 'cult' that plays this role. Indeed, some art historians and archaeolo-gists maintain that cult and art were primevally intertwined, as in the argu-ments for the shamanistic origins of the earliest cave art (Lewis-Williams 2002).[3] This is the kind of argument also made by art historian Hans Belting (2005a; b). With the Aegean Bronze Age examples discussed above, certainly cult and art practice seem to combine in dealing with the articulation of the familiar and the unfamiliar.

Are there other means of revealing the opacity of the everyday besides cult and art? One is a kind of careful looking that is akin to forensics or archaeolo-gy. One might think this sounds like quite the opposite: a means of 'taming' the opacity of the everyday and creating transparency and order, in the manner of Sherlock Holmes (Ginzburg 1980; Highmore 2002). However, there is a way of using this general sensibility to get at the everyday rather more obliquely—and that is to wait until the everyday is 'over', when it has been discarded, abandoned, or ruined. This is the technique of Walter Benja-min (cf. the idea of 'chiffonier'; see Olivier 2008), and has also been developed of late in approaches in geography, sociology, and archaeology, as we will now explore.

ABANDONMENT, WASTE, DESTRUCTION

The thingness of the everyday reveals itself not only through the lenses of art and cult but also through destruction and abandonment, processes that seem to go hand in hand with the modern industrial technologies that Heidegger critiqued. Given that the natural world is destructive enough, the intensity of destructive forces of its own making that modern culture unleashes on itself is

---

[3] Also bear in mind evidence from early Neolithic sites in Anatolia such as Çatalhöyük or Göbekli Tepe.

potentially very disturbing. These processes are explored in a range of fascinating recent accounts across disciplines such as human geography, archaeology, and sociology. DeSilvey actually looks at the intermingling of natural and cultural ruin in her examination of a Montana farmstead and how it has gradually fallen in to decay; how thingness works away at objecthood, and how vestiges and traces can reveal, in their very incompleteness, strangely seductive narratives (DeSilvey 2006; 2007). Wilford (2008) has also focused on the workings of nature on culture, but in rather more dramatic form, namely the case of Hurricane Katrina and the flooding of New Orleans. He looks at the unsettling effects of the putrid floodwater on houses, and how those houses were rendered unfamiliar and thingly by these destructive forces. Of course, the destruction wrought was socio-natural rather than purely natural, given that human decision-making had gone into the construction and maintenance of the levees. González-Ruibal (2008) looks at the destructive power of war, and indeed the excesses of supermodernity generally; the extreme level of ruin that results serves to foreground the thingly character of the everyday. Though excessive in the cases he uses, there is a common and fundamental problem that arises when we fail to conceptualize the 'back-end' of the everyday. The objects we create are somehow out of category, de-objectified as they fall back into thingness. In a similarly spectacular vein, archaeologists have also begun to think about the destruction surrounding 9/11, considering there to be something 'profoundly archaeological' about the experience (Shanks, Platt, and Rathje 2004, 61). And yet this too is linked to the everyday, and is a kind of contemporary archaeological sensibility that owes much to Rathje's rather more prosaic work on garbage and the contents of landfill (Rathje 1992). And in the discipline of geography, Kevin Hetherington has also questioned our disposal of things without working out a proper conceptual disposal (2004); Edensor (2005*a*) too says something similar about the debris of industrial ruins, and how their materiality challenges us and confronts us uncomfortably. Objects in the world of ideas are sucked back into the phenomenal, in the process losing their transparency. We often fail to anticipate changing meanings of objects as they move through their life-cycle into a disposal phase; many objects are left suspended, and we simply do not know what to do with them. This 'lack of care' contrasts with much of what we observed above for the Aegean Bronze Age, and we will come back to it in Chapter 9 when we turn to the different temporalities of objects and things.

CONCLUSION: CARING FOR THE UNEASY FLICKER

Yet the world is neither a network of objects nor a meshwork of things. It is both, and there is a tension between them, 'an uneasy flicker'. We seek to control the material world and bring it into our systems of understanding, but at the same time the phenomenal world resists this process. The 'thing' in and of itself is already complete and any single process can only partially succeed in cracking it open. We may objectify a thing to some extent by naming it, framing it, or fragmenting it, but each process only gets a partial grip on its subject. By applying multiple overlapping processes of objectification we may exert a tighter grip—hence the power of object *networks*—but it is never total, and eventually the thing always slips away back into the miasma of thingness. But faced with the impossibility of indifference, such processes nevertheless provide some small comfort. They fulfil some basic desire for interaction, even if also provoking melancholy. This psychological, metaphysical, and emotional component of multi-scale interaction has been little explored.

It is perhaps in this light that we can recast much of the above discussion in this and the previous chapter. Whether we cast the debate in terms of metaphor and metonymy, index and icon, accumulation and enchainment, sets and nets, or layering and networking, it is the tension between objects and things that is fundamental. Just as it does not make much sense to only consider one or the other of the phenomena in these pairs, so we fool ourselves if we think that either objects or things can tell the whole story. We need to find ways of attending to the 'flicker', the uneasy tension, and ways of understanding how past societies attended to this flicker too.

In the next chapter I argue that one particular way of attending to this flicker is through biographical care. There are innumerable examples of such care from traditional and ancient societies, and indeed from contemporary Western society, although the latter may risk losing some of its means for exercising such care. Museums remain one means, as do forms of contemporary art. What we risk by disregarding biographical care is disconnect and disorientation, as discussed implicitly by Heidegger (1971) and more explicitly by Bernard Stiegler (2009). If we recall the quote from Sartre cited earlier in this chapter, things are powerful, indissoluble, and opaque; we place our relations with the world and thus ourselves at risk if we forget or deny this. The idea of 'care' means that our interactions with objects and things have to be not only networked spatially but also longitudinally and in the long-term, otherwise we risk reaping short-term benefits while overlooking long-term costs. Without such long-term balancing of the costs and benefits of investing in objects, things will get a hold on us and run amok. Things have a different temporality, which needs to be kept in mind when thinking through the costs and benefits of certain kinds of object–thing actions.

9

Temporalities and Biographical Care

INTRODUCTION

In this, the third and final chapter of Part III, I broaden the scope of my enquiry concerning the 'why' of human interaction. In the two previous chapters we considered the benefits and costs of increasing interactions across scales. On the one hand, object networks bring benefits, in that they facilitate both a more stable expression of identity, as well as the exploration of new dimensions for identity. On the other, these benefits are counteracted by costs, in that object networks are always under pressure from the destabilizing effects of the world of things. Work needs to be invested in maintaining networks of interaction across ever larger scales, and we considered the ways in which artefacts are an efficient means of facilitating such interactions. However, my discussion of scale has thus far been biased towards the spatial, with limited attention given to the temporal dimension (though the simple networks of Chapter 4 do incorporate time evolution). 'Work' implies an unfolding over time, both at the micro-scale of daily investment and the macro-scale of maintaining and extending networks across generations. Networks of objects will unravel over time if not receiving investment, as the forces of the world of things operate upon them, whether silently and gradually or dramatically and cataclysmically. Here I explore how and why human groups invest 'care' in both human and non-human biographies, ensuring continuity and memory from one generation to the next.

ARTEFACT BIOGRAPHIES

It is a truism to say that in archaeology there is no shortage of approaches to artefacts that emphasize their temporal dimension. Aside from the endless typological studies that place artefacts in temporal sequences, an essential, albeit under-utilized resource in the discipline, there is a now well-established literature on artefact biographies (Skeates 1995; Gosden and Marshall 1999;

Meskell 2004; Joy 2009). This overlaps with and is in part inspired by an ethnographic literature on artefact biographies and life-histories that deals with materials and their temporalities (e.g. Hoskins 1998; Bonnot 2002). However, the focus is generally limited to the life-history of a particular artefact through the course of a single human life-cycle. One might take the case from a scenario in the film *Amélie* in which the eponymous character finds a child's trinket box hidden behind a wall in her apartment. A neighbour remembers a previous occupant from forty years earlier as a child named Dominique Bredoteau, and Amélie tracks him down. Learning of his daily routine, she leaves the box in a phone booth on the route of his daily walk, then calls the phone just as he is passing, so that he steps in to answer and miraculously comes across the long-lost trinket box. He opens the box and its childhood contents bring powerful personal memories flooding back (Jeunet 2001). In the case of Bredoteau, his childhood, or part of it, is encapsulated in a small rusty box and its meagre contents. In ethnographic studies too, we may see a good deal of selectivity in the stages of a life-history that receive attention. The 'death' or disposal stage in a life-history, for example, is often overlooked, as Hetherington remarks (2004). Artefacts may be 'lost' if not attended to when the individual to which they are tied dies. To avoid this, in some cases artefacts may be buried with the deceased individual, signifying their loss. They may be destroyed, or taken out of circulation in other ways. Or they may be passed on to the next generation. By paying more attention to the *inter-generational* connections between artefacts and people, we give ourselves some interesting opportunities. First, it enables us to interrogate the different temporal trajectories of objects and things, how thingness works away at object-hood *over time* and how societies develop strategies to attend to this tension. Secondly, we are able to broach the issue of *why* humans interact with objects/things over time. What is the point of biographical care? One might imagine that such investment over the long term would be costly, and so would need to provide notable benefits. The answer may lie in the same territory as that to the question of why humans distribute their agency across networks: it is an exploration of the limits of identity.

INTER-GENERATIONALITY

There has, of course, been some consideration of the inter-generationality of artefact biographies. We can see this in the work on heirlooms and curated artefacts (Lillios 1999; Joyce 2000; Kristiansen 2008; Caple 2010; Driessen 2010). In many cases it is difficult distinguishing between an object that has been consciously passed on from one generation to the next, and one that has more straightforwardly endured over generations. Examples of the latter may be storage jars which continue in use over many generations simply because they do not break and go on being useful. Returning to some of the Aegean Bronze Age examples used in previous chapters, the extensive ceramic assemblages from Quartier Mu at Malia include large storage jars (pithoi) that must have been manufactured in the late Prepalatial period, and yet which are found in late Protopalatial contexts—which means they were in use some 400–500 years after they were first made (Poursat and Knappett 2005). Examples of the longevity of ceramic storage jars are actually rather commonplace, if not always readily recognized. Among the decorated storage jars (pitharakia) from the Late Minoan IB destruction of the palace at Zakros are many that were in all likelihood made in the preceding ceramic phase, LM IA, some 50–100 years earlier (Platon 1971). And the abundant ceramic finds from the volcanic destruction horizon of Akrotiri on Thera, which occurred at a time coeval with LM IA on Crete, include vessels from the Middle Minoan III period (Figure 9.1).

Although such storage vessels may simply have held continuing utility, Caple suggests that artefacts such as these are 'venerable' by virtue of the fact that they have been retained in their original form (Caple 2010, 307). We might be more inclined to think in terms of venerable artefacts and heirlooms with more personal items, such as individualized drinking-vessels; but we rarely see such cases, perhaps because of their greater fragility and hence more regular breakage. Yet we do occasionally see evidence for repair of fine wares, as in the example from Akrotiri shown in Figure 9.2 below. In this case the vase in question is an import from Crete to Thera, and so may have been particularly prized. This is what Caple dubs 'veneration through restoration' (ibid. 308). We can see other examples where imported pottery might be more valued and hence curated, such as the Middle Bronze Age Cycladic jugs found in an LM IB context at Myrtos Pyrgos (Cadogan 1978; see also Driessen 2010), though here we are perhaps seeing veneration through display (Caple 2010, 308).

When we see inter-generationality in more valuable vessels, then the notion that they might have been deliberately and consciously transmitted from one generation to the next seems much more plausible. Stone vases in the Aegean Bronze Age fall into this category. While various kinds of locally made stone vessels on Crete may well have been widely curated, particular categories imported from Egypt appear to be subject to complex curation strategies that see them reused often many centuries later (Bevan 2007, 124–5). And if we adopt the idea that 'rituals are highly charged moments of memory work' (Mills and Walker 2008, 7), then we might well imagine that these strategies of curation (and veneration) probably included a ritual component. A ritual transfer of an object from one generation to the next would have served to consolidate and sustain particular memories connected with the object; or perhaps to transform the nature of those memories. With the stone vases in

Figure 9.1. Middle Minoan III pithos in Late Cycladic I context at Akrotiri Thera

question often deposited in tombs, it is likely that these moments of transformation went hand in hand with mortuary rituals that served to manage the passage from the living to the dead. These rites of passage not only bring artefacts such as stone vases into play, but also invariably involve the manipulation of the dead body in various ways, with the body treated as an artefact of

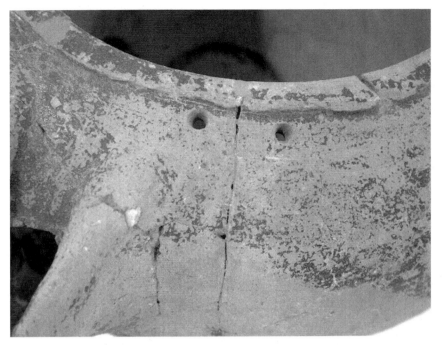

Figure 9.2. Mending-holes on bridge-spouted jar from Akrotiri, Thera

sorts (Sofaer 2007). We might cite numerous examples from prehistory, but here let us look briefly at one set of examples from the Neolithic Near East.

BODIES AS CURATED OBJECTS

Kuijt (2008) draws attention to a fascinating suite of practices from the Neolithic Near East involving the transformations of bodies at death, with the plastering of skulls particularly iconic. In what is known as the Middle Pre-Pottery Neolithic B Period (MPPNB), *c.*10,500–9,500 BP, a set of secondary mortuary practices involving skull removal is observed at sites like Ain Ghazal and Jericho. Following a period of some months or years after initial burial, an individual grave would have been re-excavated in order to remove the skull. This was then plastered and painted to provide rudimentary facial features; in some cases seashells were placed to re-create the eyes. Evidence pointing to further modification of the skulls suggests they remained in circulation for some time, before eventually being reburied in caches of multiple skulls. Kuijt argues that this sequence of modifications was a form of commemoration that helped enact a transformation from individual experience to collective

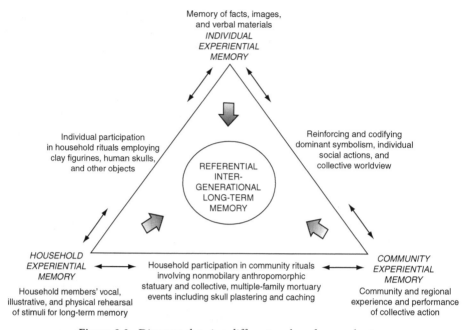

Memory of facts, images, and verbal materials
INDIVIDUAL EXPERIENTIAL MEMORY

REFERENTIAL INTER-GENERATIONAL LONG-TERM MEMORY

Individual participation in household rituals employing clay figurines, human skulls, and other objects

Reinforcing and codifying dominant symbolism, individual social actions, and collective worldview

HOUSEHOLD EXPERIENTIAL MEMORY
Household members' vocal, illustrative, and physical rehearsal of stimuli for long-term memory

Household participation in community rituals involving nonmobilary anthropomorphic statuary and collective, multiple-family mortuary events including skull plastering and caching

COMMUNITY EXPERIENTIAL MEMORY
Community and regional experience and performance of collective action

Figure 9.3. Diagram showing different scales of remembering

reference. That is to say, rather than a known individual being commemorated over the long term, the individual is subsumed into 'an ancestral memory that is anonymous, homogenised, and collective' (Kuijt 2008, 174).

Kuijt also describes this in terms of a dialectic between remembering and forgetting (Figure 9.3): the individual is in a sense 'forgotten', but this process is a transformative one that is managed with care. Forgetting, in this case, is a staged process that is really a 're-membering'. We shall revisit this question of forgetting in the context of contemporary commemoration. It is also important to consider those cases of accidental, 'careless' forgetting.

FROM INDIVIDUAL TO GROUP

The focus on individual skulls and their biographies is in a sense typical of an overwhelming pattern that sees the focus in archaeological and ethnographic investigation fall on *individual* pieces. Kuijt (2008) does also, to be fair, place these individual objects within wider assemblages too, notably in terms of the skull caches that are their final destination. While in previous chapters this individual fetishism has been critiqued, with a call for attention to object networks, it is noteworthy that in work on structured deposition in archaeology there does seem to be a distinct focus on assemblages. This can be traced back to a study of depositional activity at Durrington Walls, a Neolithic henge monument close to Stonehenge, which seemed to indicate that patterns of discard were not easily accounted for functionally, but were instead arranged formally and symbolically (Richards and Thomas 1984; Pollard 2008). Since then, as Pollard notes, 'structured deposits' have been identified in a number of prehistoric contexts, and Pollard goes on to develop a case study from a Neolithic causewayed enclosure, Etton in Cambridgeshire, where, he argues, deposition was 'a mechanism for exploring the materiality of the world and negotiating the complex and deeply embedded nature of relationships between people, animals, and things' (Pollard 2008, 59). An example he uses is a deposit that juxtaposes a human skull, a red-deer-antler baton, and animal bone, citing, he argues, human ancestors, the wild, and 'subsistence success' respectively. Interpretation of assemblages in this manner is part of a much broader trend in the study of later British prehistory, from the work of Richards and Thomas mentioned above to that of Bradley (1990) on hoards deposited in bogs and rivers in the British Bronze Age, to Jones's treatment of late Neolithic and early Bronze Age artefacts as 'nodes in indexical networks or fields' (Jones 2007, 140).

However effective this set of approaches may be in offering interpretations of ritual deposits, a focus on groups of objects-things should also be applicable in domestic contexts too; though of course this distinction between ritual and domestic does not hold up too well in many prehistoric contexts. Nonetheless, it is worthwhile switching focus to consider work on the 'house' as an inter-generational socio-material form. There are fascinating examples with what have been dubbed the 'history houses' of Çatalhöyük (Hodder and Pels 2010). Not all houses in this extensive early Neolithic village show a commitment to 'history', but certain among them appear to have done so, with building sequences pointing to four-to-six rebuilds on the same spot, with each building lasting for between seventy and 100 years. This seems to be a particular strategy that in all likelihood had metaphorical as well as practical significance. A similar process can be seen in Neolithic villages in northern Greece too, with some houses seeing multiple rebuilds, while others are simply abandoned and replacements built nearby—this appears to be the case for the famous site of Sesklo (Kotsakis 2006). But whereas there is no burial evidence to speak of in connection with the rebuilding episodes at Sesklo, at Çatalhöyük the houses with multiple rebuilds also tend to include human remains within their fabric. Hodder and Pels note one such house that had sixty-two human burials beneath the floors, 'including parts of bodies interred as secondary burials—perhaps initially buried in other or earlier buildings'. They further suggest that wall installations were curated from one building to another, with features such as bull-horns and other wild-animal parts. Furthermore, there is some evidence for the reuse and re-burial of human skulls, sometimes indeed plastered (Meskell 2008), which serves as a connection to the earlier Near Eastern tradition discussed by Kuijt (2008).

Hodder and Pels link their evidence for inter-generationality to the notion of 'house societies', an ethnographic concept derived from Lévi-Strauss that has seen something of a resurgence in the last few years (e.g. Carsten and Hugh-Jones 1995; Joyce and Gillespie 2000; Beck 2007). In a house society the 'house' is a major organizational form, here house meaning neither an individual building nor the household as productive unit. The house is both a social and material form that endures beyond the individual dwelling—it is a kind of corporate group that is grounded in a particular dwelling site. Hence one should expect to find heirlooms playing an important role in the inter-generational maintenance of the house as a unit (Joyce 2000), and an investment in its enduring character and symbolism over time, phenomena that the Çatalhöyük evidence would appear to support, at least for some houses.

Archaeologists working in a wide variety of contexts are seeing elements of house societies in their data, as evidenced in the recent edited volume by Beck (2007). As more and more scholars pay increasing attention to the interconnections between different classes of evidence in everyday houses, so such patterns might be expected to emerge. At some stage we will need to ask the question whether there is really a distinctive category of 'house societies', or whether this inter-generational socio-material form and process is really a widespread feature in many different kinds of society. This is brought to the fore by another study in the east Mediterranean that identifies 'the house' as a key organizational form, here in the context of Bronze Age Crete. Driessen (2010) makes a convincing argument that many houses see a clear commitment to inter-generationality in social and material expression. We will look at this evidence shortly, but if we have Neolithic societies in Anatolia and Bronze Age 'palatial' societies on Crete both seemingly organized around the concept of the 'house', then we may need to look at the implications of such a broad range of scenarios for house societies more closely.

Driessen (2010) argues that Minoan Crete sees numerous examples of multi-generational structures in the same places spanning many centuries. He takes as his starting-point the considerable size of many Minoan houses that seem to go beyond what one would expect of the household of a nuclear family, and perhaps suggesting some higher order of organization. Further to this, Driessen notes that much of the Minoan mortuary evidence indicates some sort of group status larger than that of the nuclear family, though scholars are vague as to what the groups may be. When the enduring character of both Minoan houses and tombs is then considered, Driessen sees the particular inter-generational qualities of 'the house' as worth exploring as a social organizational form that can account for certain features of the Minoan material evidence (more effectively than can notions such as 'factions' or 'corporate groups'). He underlines the 'continuity of place' of many Cretan

Bronze Age buildings, best encapsulated in the site of Knossos with its incredible continuous occupation of the palace area for millennia, from the Early Neolithic through to the Bronze Age. While Driessen then also mentions buildings at the sites of Palaikastro and Tylissos, there are many other examples of multiple rebuilds across many centuries.

Indications that this is more than just a functional reaction to the many seismic events on the island necessitating reconstruction are found in 'foundation' or 'building' deposits that often include heirlooms. Herva (2005) has drawn attention to this phenomenon, though his mention of only twenty examples from Minoan Crete overlooks much published evidence (e.g. six unmentioned from Palaikastro alone, see MacGillivray, Sackett, and Driessen 1999). One of these Palaikastro examples shows the use of an heirloom, though not a particularly 'ancient' one: a bridge-spouted jug from the MM IIB period used in the construction of an MM IIIA building, Building 6. That the practice is not confined to the Palatial periods, but goes back much further, into the Prepalatial, is seen in an example from Malia involving Early Minoan IIB Vasiliki ware (Driessen 2007). Foundation deposits like these do not particularly involve the deposition of 'antique' heirloom items though (and note the particular connection Joyce 2000 makes between the use of heirlooms and the inter-generationality in house societies). Indeed, Herva opens up the definition beyond what Minoan scholars typically refer to as 'foundation deposits' so as to include those building deposits that are not necessarily parts of foundations. In this way he is able to include deposits from the Temple Repositories and the Vat Room (both at Knossos) in his discussion. The former contained the famous faience 'snake goddesses', not to mention thousands of shells, other faience objects, and numerous storage jars (see Figure 9.4; also Panagiotaki 1999; Shapland 2009). The Temple Repositories do not contain objects that might be considered heirlooms, however. The Vat Room deposit consists of far fewer objects, but among them is one object that would certainly appear to be 'antique', an incised clay pyxis that is difficult to date but would seem to be much earlier than the latest pottery in the deposit, which is MM IB (Panagiotaki 1999).

A fuller exploration of the 'structured deposition' represented in the Temple Repositories has recently been undertaken by Hatzaki (2009). She demonstrates deliberate fragmentation and argues for an elaborate ritual involving large numbers of participants. If the Temple Repositories can be identified as an exceptional form of foundation deposit, fitting for the exceptional nature of the building in question, the palace of Knossos, then it may be that this deposit was connected with a substantial rebuild in the LM IA period following the massive seismic destruction of MM IIIB. If so, then we are observing a pronounced preoccupation with the enduring symbolism of the palace structure over time, as if from one generation to another. The burial of such ritually charged items in deep stone-lined cists in the heart of the palace would have

Figure 9.4. Some of the contents of the Temple Repositories

removed them from view permanently, while keeping them close by and controlled. This is precisely the kind of phenomenon described by Mills (2008) in her description of dedicatory offerings seen in the great kivas of Chaco Canyon. She suggests that items that are 'secreted' out of sight, perhaps permanently, 'may be remembered for long periods of time' (Ibid. 82). She describes this as 'remembering while forgetting', which relates also to notions of 'absent presences' (cf. Runia 2006). The Near Eastern and Anatolian Neolithic examples discussed in Kuijt (2008), Meskell (2008), and Hodder and Pels (2010) also invoke a kind of 'present absence' through intra-mural burial.

CAREFUL AND CARELESS FORGETTING

This notion of 'remembering while forgetting' implies a structured absencing of particular material forms. Care is taken over disposal, almost as if there is a realization that 'the absent is only ever moved along, and is never fully gotten rid of' (Hetherington 2004, 162). This careful forgetting may be contrasted with more careless forgetting, whereby artefacts and buildings are abandoned materially without an accompanying 'conceptual' abandonment. The literature on forgetting, which is minimal in comparison to that on memory

(Connerton 2006, 319; 2009; Della Sala 2010), seems to be principally concerned with the careful form (Forty and Kuechler 1999; Kuijt 2008; Mills 2008). In terms of approaching this distinction in ancient cultures, there is evidently abundant evidence for abandonment that could fall into the category of 'careless' forgetting, though such evidence has not been considered from such a perspective. We need first to explore further these issues of care in relation to remembering and forgetting in contemporary settings, as there are a number of lines of inquiry we can pursue. What I shall be working towards are a couple of related ideas. One is that careful forgetting is part of a broader process of what we might call 'biographical care', itself connected to inter-generationality. And secondly, biographical care has an important function, in its capacity to balance the tension between objects and things, and to ward off the 'disorientation' that can result when this relationship is skewed.

First, though, let us devote some attention to issues of care and forgetting in contemporary settings, starting with examples where considerable care has been invested in the biographies of things and places. Laurent Olivier (2008, 90–5) recounts what is perhaps one of the most striking examples imaginable. It concerns the French village of Oradour-sur-Glane, destroyed on 10 June 1944 by soldiers of a Waffen SS regiment. These soldiers killed 642 men, women, and children, seemingly without reason, and burned the village to the ground. After the war the French government decided to make a memorial at the site by freezing Oradour in historical time, in 1944, as if in the immediate aftermath of its destruction. However, the maintenance of memory through physical form requires a lot of work and investment, perhaps unanticipated: the creation of lawns to keep weeds at bay, the replacement of rotting roof-beams. Fewer and fewer of the original components remain. The case of Dr Desourteaux's car is especially poignant (see Figure 9.5). This has been left *in situ* since the moment he pulled up into the village on 10 June 1944, only to be immediately apprehended and killed by the SS. However, the car is only very partially frozen in historical time, having largely succumbed to archaeological time: all the paint has disappeared, the wipers, the tires. This is no longer a car of the 1940s—it is a fossil of a 1940s car such as it might appear in the 2000s (ibid. 93). How are we to interpret Oradour in terms of inter-generational memory and the investment of biographical care? Is it possible to invest too much care? Or does Oradour point to a misdirected care? It is as if the authorities have not recognized that forgetting is a part of remembering; and that, indeed, remembering can occur even when some features have become absent. If the process of forgetting is managed with care, it should be possible to allow some element of decay at Oradour. As presently preserved, memory is comprised only of remembering and not of forgetting, and this is achieved by staunching the flow of decay, thereby negating archaeological time (ibid.).

A second example concerns an equally traumatic destructive episode: the bringing down of the World Trade Centre in New York City, the events of

Figure 9.5. The car of Dr Desourteaux, Oradour-sur-Glane

9/11. And here too the authorities have been faced with difficult issues as to how to mark this calamity in the collective memory for future generations. This process has been described as something profoundly archaeological (Shanks, Platt, and Rathje 2004), with these same authors highlighting the role played by New York and Washington museums in the aftermath of 9/11. An exhibition mounted by the Smithsonian, for example, displayed artefacts from the World Trade Centre site, such as a battered wallet, torn clothing, or parts of the World Trade Centre structure itself (ibid. 61). Yet many such objects were not recovered *in situ* but rather from the massive landfill site at Staten Island to which much of the debris was removed. This is perhaps the most strikingly archaeological dimension of this process, as it is with debris and 'garbage' that archaeologists primarily deal (ibid. 65; see also Rathje *et al.* 1992). And here we see the tension between remembering and forgetting too: certain artefacts that are deemed capable of anchoring a narrative are re-trieved, while others are left to oblivion in the landfill. But it is perhaps the sense of careful retrieval that is important here—that the garbage was carefully sifted, given attention, before being 'forgotten'. The debris was not abandoned to ruin immediately. Some forgetting needs to take place in the course of

Figure 9.6. Overgrown trenches

remembrance, but it has to be careful, structured forgetting. Absence is managed.

Some traumatic events are not carefully forgotten, however. Examples of unstructured abandonment are abundantly present in the remains of twentieth-century conflicts: the remains of an ambush in the Ethiopian civil war, consisting of four trucks and an anti-aircraft gun by the side of the road (González-Ruibal 2008, 249), or overgrown trenches from the Spanish Civil War (González-Ruibal 2008, fig. 7; see Figure 9.6). González-Ruibal (ibid. 258) notes that this form of 'oblivion' is one of the enemies of memory; the other is an overabundance of recollections, for which Oradour and perhaps 9/11 might be examples.[1]

Though writing from an archaeological perspective, there is something lyrical in the way that González-Ruibal uses photography to support his arguments concerning memory and oblivion. This kind of lyrical documentation is used in contemporary art too, and here we might consider the work of

---

[1] Connerton (2006, 319–22) differentiates between different forms of forgetting: structural amnesia, forgetting that is constitutive in the formation of a new identity, repressive erasure, politically expedient forgetting, and humiliated silence.

Figure 9.7. *Classroom in Kindergarten #7, Golden Key, Pripyat, 2001*

Canadian photographic artist Robert Polidori.[2] Again, these feature traumatic scenes of twentieth-century destruction, or more accurately, their aftermath. One series of images are from Chernobyl, photographs taken some fifteen years after the disaster at the nuclear power plant. We see (as in Figure 9.7) scenes of oblivion, of unstructured abandonment, though this classroom, a scene from everyday life, does not depict the ruin of the nuclear facility itself. Here there has been no careful forgetting to facilitate remembrance, although Polidori's images may mark a step in that direction.

Polidori has also photographed the aftermath of another catastrophe, in New Orleans following Hurricane Katrina, though in this case just weeks rather than many years afterwards. We see in Figure 9.8 a familiar everyday household scene, albeit eerily transformed, with its peeling walls. How is this

---

[2] I would like to thank Elena Soboleva for bringing the work of Robert Polidori to my attention.

Figure 9.8. *6539 Canal Street, New Orleans, September, 2005*

traumatic event to be remembered? What kinds of careful forgetting are necessary to avoid an excess of memory?

The effects wrought on New Orleans homes by Katrina is also discussed by a cultural geographer, Justin Wilford (2008), who remarks on the conceptual importance of the house as a mediator between the natural and cultural worlds. As such, the signs of the work of nature on the interiors of houses seems to have been particularly unsettling when residents returned to find their homes in the grip of toxic slime, mould, and wood-rot (ibid. 659). These material indexes of the disaster need to be made absent for conceptual order to be restored, though this requires considerable care and effort as the sense of despair created by these natural signs of chaos is profound. Wilford also describes the salvaging of objects from homes, however mundane, as another means of overcoming despair; in the terms expressed in this chapter, one might say that this is a form of 'care', however cursory. A rather more sustained form of 'care' in this context is seen in the work of artist Jana Napoli.[3] For her piece 'Floodwall', Napoli assembled 700 drawers salvaged

---

[3] I thank Katherine Jackson for alerting me to the work of Jana Napoli.

from homes in New Orleans post-Katrina, arranging them on a memorial wall. These drawers preserve some of the traces of flood damage, such as mould. By taking just these household fragments, selected with 'care' over the course of four months of wandering around ruined neighbourhoods, Napoli has negotiated this tension mentioned above between memory oblivion on the one hand and memory excess on the other. Through her process of selection, which entails necessarily rejection and deliberate abandonment, Napoli forgets some pieces in order to facilitate remembrance.

Although many of these examples we have been discussing do deal with everyday scenarios, they do so in the context of trauma and catastrophe— World War II, 9/11, Chernobyl, Katrina. However, we might also look at more prosaic cases of unstructured abandonment where houses are simply abandoned, left to a gradual ruin. DeSilvey (2006; 2007) brings such a process to our attention very effectively in her study of a Montana homestead (see also Chapter 8). First settled in 1889 and abandoned in 1995, the homestead became the property of the City of Missoula in 1996, which turned it into a public heritage site in 1998 (DeSilvey 2007, 403–4). DeSilvey encounters this derelict set of structures as a volunteer caretaker and curator for the community organization entrusted with managing the property (see Figure 9.9). She confronts the decayed traces of past lives contained in the ruins and works on retelling stories from these fragments alone. The final residents may not have seen to the final abandonment of the homestead in a structured manner, foregoing the opportunity for 'careful forgetting'. However, sedimented within the ruins are clues as to the ongoing attention to memory of previous generations, with traces from its occupation in the 1890s and 1930s, for example, part of the fabric of the house. In a sense it is DeSilvey who comes in and completes the process, with a level of careful attention that she dubs 'cultural memory-work' (ibid. 404).

DeSilvey draws on important work by other cultural geographers in interpreting her scene, particularly that of Tim Edensor (2005*a*) and Kevin Hetherington (2004). Edensor studies waste and ruin, highlighting the 'disordering effects of ruination', which in other words may be thought of as the way in which chaotic 'thingness' gets a hold of 'objecthood'. Hetherington comments on the need to move things along conceptually as well as physically, because 'disposal' is not so much a complete removal as a transformation or partial absencing. This we might link back to the point made earlier, whereby Mills has argued that items may be 'secreted' and made absent, creating a particular kind of memory that is a partial forgetting (Mills 2008).

Interestingly, both Edensor (see also 2005*b*) and Hetherington refer to ruins as potentially the sites of haunting. When something that is conceptually and physically present is made physically absent but not conceptually absent, then we are in the domain of the ruin. Absence needs to be taken care of, through a process of 'careful' forgetting: when it is not, then this uncertain spatial and

Figure 9.9. Decay on a Montana homestead

temporal territory is there for the haunting. As Hetherington puts it, 'the representational figure of unfinished or unmanaged disposal is the ghost and its agency is expressed in the idea of haunting' (Hetherington 2004, 170; also citing Gordon 1997). We can trace connections in this line of thinking to the work on 'things' that we discussed in the last chapter. For example, thingness is always lurking in the background ready to undermine objecthood—and as soon as humans are careless and stop working at their object categories, even in the process of disposal and abandonment, then the uncertainty and opacity of thingness can begin to gain purchase on the cultural world. It is what Schwenger (2006) seems to have in mind when he talks of how words may murder things, but nonetheless the shadow of the thing still lurks in the background, a kind of haunting. And in the same vein, as we saw in Chapter 8, Walter Benjamin stated that 'warmth is ebbing from things ... we must compensate for their coldness with our warmth if they are not to freeze us to death' (cited in Brown 2006, 177). Indeed, thingness is a little like death: unfamiliar, unknowable, threatening, opaque. Death is always working away at life just as thingness gnaws away at objecthood. Turning this back to the specific topic of memory, one can also see how such notions of haunting might apply equally well to humans as well as objects. A lack of biographical care—a lack of inter-generational remembering of ancestral spirits—might very conceivably threaten individual and collective identity. This is a theme aptly developed by Inge Daniels (2009) in her study of the social life and 'death' of unused gifts in Japan. Gifts that are not properly 'disposed' of in Hetherington's sense, which in this case essentially means trying to pass on gifts to a 'good home' rather than a process of cynical re-gifting, are dangerous. It is better, it appears, to hang on to a gift for some time until it can be put to good use, rather than offload it too quickly. A gift that ends up in the wrong hands is one that can haunt: 'many [participants] entertained the possibility that domestic things that are not treated with care might have a negative effect on the well-being of all those living under the same roof' (ibid. 402).[4]

CARE, DEATH, AND CULT

We can, through these approaches, and the use of the metaphor of 'haunting', draw a connection to death and the human body. The loss that comes with death is an absence that needs to be carefully managed, and when it is not, the

---

[4] Other recent papers on related issues of waste, disposal, and loss in relation to material culture include Wirtz 2009 and Miller and Parrott 2009.

risk of haunting looms.[5] There are two points that we can develop from this in different directions, and to do so we need to turn to the groundbreaking work of Hans Belting in art history and visual studies (e.g. Belting 2001; 2005a; b). Belting makes the radical point that the *raison d'être* for images is death. The ideal and primeval substitution that the image performs is when it stands in for the absent body. Though the body may only be temporarily absent, that is, spatially removed, in the most extreme form it is the permanent absence of death. The image creates an 'iconic presence' that substitutes for the body, which has an absence which is made visible by the image (Belting 2005a, 312). What Belting has in mind as the purest substitutions are tomb effigies and death masks, stating that 'the mask is the most brilliant invention that ever occurred in the making of images' (2005b, 47). He returns repeatedly to the MPPNB plastered skulls from Jericho, and the limestone mask from Nehal Hamar (e.g. ibid., figs. 3–5). While many kinds of image might act as an 'iconic presence' substituting for the absent body, the mask does so particularly ingeniously as it bears the indexical imprint of the absence which it makes present. The mask as a presentation of the absent body is thus particularly powerful as it testifies to the 'care' that has been afforded to the body and its absencing: it required contiguity to the body for its generation. The power and danger of the dead body has been treated, and the risk of haunting minimized through the control exerted by the imprinted image.

There is a wider critique that Belting has in mind, concerning the overemphasis on the iconic in much art history at the expense of the indexical; or in other words, representation over presentation (see also Gumbrecht 2004; Moxey 2008). This opens up the subject to a broader debate that we cannot enter here. However, a second important component of Belting's approach is more relevant to my current argument, and concerns the role of *cult*. Belting makes the valid observation that much of the earliest human interaction with images would have been in connection with not just the dead, but cults of the dead: 'The experience of images in those times was linked to rituals such as the cult of the dead, through which the dead were reintegrated into the community of the living' (Belting 2005a, 307). Though he is far too sweeping and monolithic in his treatment of prehistoric times, and chooses to focus predominantly on the Neolithic plaster skulls already mentioned—why not the stunning finds from Göbekli Tepe or Çatalhöyük, not to mention Lascaux?— the triple connection of image (or arguably 'art'), death, and cult seems worthwhile. In the context of my present argument concerning the need for 'care' in processes of remembering and forgetting across generations, then we might well remind ourselves of the observation made earlier that 'rituals are highly charged moments of memory work' (Mills and Walker 2008, 7).

---

[5] Note Hetherington's (2004, 171) comment about how disposal in two stages can be a useful means of stabilizing social relations through material means.

Though we should be aware that rituals need not be cultic (that is, they may be sacred or profane), it is reasonable to suggest that the kind of care required to ensure inter-generational memory, and to keep 'haunting' at bay, is demanding, and worthy of a special kind of attention—the kind of heightened attention we may understand as either cult/ritual action or art practice, or indeed in many contexts, both together. And if we turn our attention back to prehistory for a moment, to the kinds of context that Belting has in mind, we might see that there is more often than not a very close relationship between images, death, and cult.

BIOGRAPHICAL CARE IN PREHISTORY

In a lot of cases we *can* see such a close relationship. It would be hard to argue against the notions of biographical care and careful forgetting in the examples from Çatalhöyük discussed earlier. The material strategies seen here and elsewhere (e.g. Bronze Age Crete) are means for promulgating object networks over time in order to ward off 'ghostly' things. Some strategies involve tensions between living and dead, for example in the 'history houses' of Çatalhöyük, where 'death' is kept close, integrated into the texture of the house (Hodder and Pels 2010; also note patterns of structured abandonment for houses, Marciniak, pers. comm.). Other examples can be found from far and wide, as in the case of Cladh Hallan, a Bronze Age settlement on the island of South Uist in western Scotland, where 'mummified' burials beneath the floors of roundhouses suggest that the cycle of life and death was tied to daily practices that also had their own cycle that played out in different parts of the house (Parker Pearson, Sharples, and Symonds 2004). And we may also see how Minoan 'houses' incorporate recognition of the tension between life and death, objecthood and thingness, with concern for genealogy and biography, though burials within houses do not generally occur (Driessen 2010).

The insights of Belting could certainly benefit from more concerted archaeological investigation: archaeologists are largely ignorant of his work. It is also dangerous to essentialize the prehistoric past to such an extent that we are unable to locate any examples at all of *careless* forgetting. It would surely be a mistake to argue that this is solely a twentieth-century Western failing. Though this is beyond the scope of this book, it may be worthwhile examining the variable commitment to inter-generational memory in different prehistoric settings, for example through the long course of the Aegean Bronze Age. What this means is that we cannot yet develop any sense from prehistory of the costs of careless forgetting and what fallout there may be of a lack of biographical care. For this, we return briefly to the contemporary world.

WHY CARE? COUNTERING DISORIENTATION

If care is not given to person and thing biographies, there is risk of biographical disconnect. This entails the loss of understanding of the tension between objects and things, life and death. Arguably there has been a loss of care in contemporary Western life, with insufficient attention devoted to human and artefact biographies alike. This may be observed in a range of processes from production through to consumption. In terms of production, one might cite the helter-skelter hurtling towards multiple material inventions, seemingly in the absence of any developed sense of how those materials might be consumed (Küchler 2008). We inhabit a world of incredible numbers of patents, with innovation arguably 'super-linear' (Bettencourt *et al.* 2007). And as for consumption, a lack of forethought as to the future biographies of many of the things we consume is very widely prevalent—one need only mention the millions of paper coffee-cups disposed of (e.g. 1 million daily in Toronto alone), or the growth of self-storage facilities for personal clutter, with 40,000 self-storage depots in the United States (Naish 2008, 93). This lack of attention to biographies is surely part of the 'cultural amnesia' that Connerton (2009, 125) argues is an intrinsic and necessary condition of modernity.

Though we may give some thought to individual moments in artefact biographies, we do not connect these different moments together—hence the idea proposed here of biographical disconnect. It is not that we do not consider the present, or the future, or the past, but that we do not join them up. Indeed, it would be hard to sustain an argument for the contemporary West not looking to the future: the problem is more that it does not bear in mind the past when doing so. An interesting idea that is salient here is that of 'dorsality' (Wills 2008). From a philosophical standpoint that draws substantially on Heidegger, Wills argues that in moving forward with new technologies we fail to acknowledge our 'backs'—where we have come from, and how we are already substantially technologized. Without watching our backs, so to speak, we make mistakes moving forward. This can be linked also to remarks made by van der Leeuw (2008) concerning the ways in which we approach innovation: if we look at innovation after the fact, a posteriori, we see a successful innovation as a *fait accompli*, yet invention often occurs a priori, in the moment; to understand innovation, van der Leeuw argues, we really need to be looking both forwards and backwards.

So if there is a lack of care, it may be due to biographical disconnect: a failure to look both forwards and backwards. What might be the cause of this in the contemporary West? There are many possible answers to this, and this is not the place to explore them exhaustively. But one very interesting possibility is raised by Laurent Olivier in his recent book on archaeology and memory (2008). Following Walter Benjamin, he argues that the losses of the

Great War, and also of World War II, were so profound that they were literally unspeakable. From the impossibility of expression follows the loss of collective memory, or at least memory that can be transmitted inter-generationally—how can one generation explain such wars to those that have not experienced them? So there is a kind of unravelling of genealogy that eats away at the capacity for memory and perhaps for 'dorsality'. Olivier is careful to note that other forms of destructive excess can have a silencing effect, illustrating the point with the example of the Chernobyl nuclear disaster of 1986 (ibid. 126–9). This too was so unspeakable as to work against inter-generational memory. The photography of Robert Polidori, described above, is understood in a new light in its character of silent witness, finding a presentational rather than representational means of testimony.

If this mass destruction is potentially a cause, then what is the effect? If this erodes dorsality, then what does a lack of dorsality create? According to philosopher Bernard Stiegler, the outcome is disorientation (see Heidegger 1971a; Stiegler 2009). Stiegler is careful to point out that the technologized human always is at risk of disorientation, and since humankind is technological from its very origins, this risk has been ever-present. Thus disorientation is not an artefact only of the twentieth century, though it has seen an acceleration with the industrialization of memory. Stiegler gives memory a central role in his rethinking of Heidegger, stating that the human limits to memory—what he calls 'retentional finitude'—is what gives meaning to the artefactual and technical. It is material culture that provides support to the 'essentially failing, radically forgetful' human memory (Stiegler 2009, 8), and allows it to endure over space and time. This is, arguably, the same process as the 'release from proximity', an idea we encountered in the very first chapter (Quiatt and Reynolds 1993, 141). Yet this extension of human practice and identity across space and time, facilitated by ever-expanding object networks, is double-edged. For, as Stiegler maintains, 'spatiotemporalization, as exteriorization (as "conquest of space and time"), is always already also detemporalization and deterritorialization' (2009, 65). And it is this process that is experienced as disorientation, he argues. The new possibilities for countering retentional finitude that are opened up by object networks, expanding across space and time, also bring with them costs. If care is not given—and the accelerating speed of spatio-temporalization runs against care—then the disorienting 'thing' will destabilize the object.

How can care be re-established? Religion and cult can establish care by casting light on the thing–object relation. Art can also do this. Museums too are a means of countering disorientation, with curation of objects as biographical care. They serve to re-temporalize and re-territorialize. Archaeologies of the contemporary past can also fill this role: 'both archaeology and heritage are involved in a therapeutic process of retrieval and memorialisation of the past' (Harrison and Schofield 2010, 8). Without such attention devoted to the full biographies of objects, and to their uneasy flicker with things, the result may be to live in a world haunted by artefactual ghosts (Hetherington 2004; Edensor 2005a; b). We can see in many prehistoric cultures the degree of care that was exercised, as with the history houses of Çatalhöyük or the heirlooms of Minoan Crete. Biographical care may appear costly—the complications of cult practices, the considerable time needed to learn artful crafting—considering the intangible nature of the benefits. Moreover, there is a long delay in the investment being rewarded: the thwarting of haunting may play out over long time-scales. But it is arguably the balancing of these benefits and costs that is critical to a resilient society. What can seem like conservative practices rooted in arcane traditions, with complete disregard for innovation and 'progress', may actually turn out to be of profound importance in establishing 'dorsality' (Wills 2008), the need to retain what lies behind you while moving forward. Inter-generational memory thus becomes an indispensable factor in sustaining community far into the future.

CONCLUDING REMARKS: ATTENDING TO THINGS

Networks of objects—with both spatial and temporal extension, as we have seen in this chapter—bring all kinds of benefits for human interaction. But seeing just the world of objects and ignoring the world of things—and failing to give due attention to the 'uneasy flicker' between these two versions of worldhood—can have unsettling consequences and considerable 'cost'. Things/objects have a dynamic that humans share in, taking us along unexpected paths with varying temporalities and topologies. If we are to understand our networked/meshworked pasts, presents, and futures, we need to realize our deep entanglement, the significance of different kinds of links as well as nodes, and the trans-scale nature of human–non-human interactions.

Epilogue: Future Challenges

Individuals act, interact, and think through their bodies and the objects around them. Though some argue that this is still a novel perspective in the humanities (Slingerland 2008), it is now with some regularity expressed within archaeology (e.g. Gamble 2007; Malafouris 2008*a*), social anthropology (Ingold 2007*a*; Henare, Holbraad, and Wastell 2007), art history (Stafford 2007; Moxey 2008), sociology (Cerulo 2009), and psychology (Costall 1995; 2006). But the focus often, understandably, falls on the mediating role of *individual* objects in human interaction. Where I hope this book goes further is to argue that it is not just individual objects, but whole *assemblages* of objects that are critical to human thought and interaction. These are often arranged as networks spanning time and space. Indeed, it is these very networks that allow humans to harness time and space to their advantage, across ever-expanding scales. Yet balanced against the benefits of these networks are their costs. The desire to 'colonize' space and time with objects is risky if the uncanny recalcitrance of the material world is overlooked. Things do not always act as they are meant to. As argued in the preceding chapter, failure to attend to and 'care for' this tension between objects and things can lead to social disorientation. Thinking about material culture in terms of its costs and benefits over space and time thus provides, I hope, a different angle on the nature of human interactions.

My approach is generated, in part, from readings in other disciplines. This is always as risky as it is rewarding, since the likelihood of missing major debates and omitting key works is high. Still, I firmly believe in this approach for material culture studies, and I think it can be seen even more persuasively in works of scholars such as Ingold (2007*a*), Miller (2005), Meskell (2005), and Olsen (2010), to name but a few, and recently exemplified in the thoroughly interdisciplinary scope of the recent *Oxford Handbook of Material Culture Studies* (Hicks and Beaudry 2010). If one considers that the foregrounding of material culture, such that objects do not just sit in the background, is a relatively new position, taking as a somewhat artificial starting-point Appadurai's (1986) *The Social Life of Things*, then the level of maturity already reached in the domain of material culture studies is impressive. Nevertheless, significant challenges remain, and in my opinion there are substantial gaps in the area of methodology that, unless filled, jeopardize the field's capacity to develop more concerted interdisciplinary ventures over the long term.

Perhaps it is the pragmatic side of the archaeologist that always raises the question, often impatiently and too quickly: 'But how can I apply this?' So what I have tried to do in this book is show how network ideas have associated methods, and how they in turn may be applied to data to bring out new patterns and interpretations. Often such efforts do fall short and are almost always a little frustrating in this regard. This book, I am sure, is no exception. There is still something of a mismatch between the theory and the data. The full working through of techniques for elaborating and visualizing object networks is still underdeveloped, as is the issue of how to illustrate the articulations of different network scales. Still, I hope I have travelled far enough along in the direction of a network archaeology for readers to see where I am headed, to realize the possibilities, and, hopefully, to see enough potential to take up the thread themselves and think more explicitly about interactions, whether using formal network models or not.

I am also mindful of the fate that can befall works of this kind—that a reader may find the case studies satisfactory at a certain level, in terms of an explanation of the particular patterns in hand, but that the relevance to his or her own archaeological material appears slim at best. And so we end up with as many separate methods and approaches as we do case studies. Not that I am against diversity, but sometimes the differences are such that there is little communication between domains that ought to be communicating. One case in point is the recent growth in the use of ideas from social network analysis in archaeology (for a review, see Brughmans 2010). This is very welcome and exciting in many ways, yet there are some basic differences that might undermine further growth. The nodes in some of these studies are sites, in other cases they are entire cultures. This kind of incommensurability is not always even immediately apparent, and more dialogue is required even among those taking up network analysis, let alone between these scholars and those who remain sceptical of its merits. This is a largely surmountable problem, however. There are much deeper divides developing, such as that between those who apply biological models for understanding cultural transmission and those who strongly resist the basic assumptions of such models. Due to the way the lines appear to have been drawn up, this division looks like developing into a deep one, even though there is certainly a dialogue to be had as more overlap exists than one might expect (see Slingerland 2008).

Given such difficulties of communication that can sometimes arise within a field, what hope is there for useful communication across fields? I have argued here that not only can archaeology very usefully take on board lessons from recent complexity science and network analysis, but that in fact archaeology can feed back and influence the very direction of that science. In this area, my experience in an interdisciplinary project with theoretical physicists Ray Rivers and Tim Evans has been extremely useful and encouraging; our working with archaeological datasets, inherently patchy in nature, has forced us to be explicit about the nature of our models (Knappett, Evans, and Rivers 2008; Evans, Knappett, and Rivers 2009). This collaboration was but one part of a much larger EU-funded project—ISCOM, The Information Society as a Complex System—that sought to develop a whole series of insights into modelling in the social sciences by bringing together very different disciplines in a concerted manner (Lane *et al.* 2009), using to a large extent the example of the Santa Fe Institute.[1] Archaeologist Sander van der Leeuw was a co-director on ISCOM, and has used his experience on this project in developing the new interdisciplinary directions taken by the School of Human Evolution and Social Change at Arizona State University, with a particular focus on issues of long-term resilience in socio-natural systems (e.g. van der Leeuw and Redman 2002; van der Leeuw and Kohler 2007).

A second interdisciplinary area in which archaeology is also beginning to have some impact is that of cognitive science. The work of archaeologists such as Lambros Malafouris and Dietrich Stout is showing how the distinctively archaeological perspective on the active role of material culture in cognition is slowly making its mark on cognitive philosophers and neuroscientists (Stout *et al.* 2008; Malafouris 2008*a*; 2010; Malafouris and Renfrew 2010). Although this work has thus far been largely targeted on questions in human evolution, it does have the potential for much wider applicability in trans-disciplinary studies of material (and visual) culture.[2]

A third interdisciplinary area now benefiting from an archaeological perspective, though this within the humanities, is the study of the contemporary past, perhaps normally considered the domain of history, geography, or sociology. What archaeology brings to this domain is a starting-point in material culture, a recognition of long-term processes, and, as a result, an acceptance that change is the norm (Harrison and Schofield 2010, 6). Some of the insights brought by an archaeology of the contemporary past were highlighted in Chapter 9, such as in the work of González-Ruibal (2008) and Olivier (2008), where it was also noted that such approaches are quite compatible with literary and cultural studies and contemporary art practice. Thus archaeology has been reaching out in very different directions, towards complexity science, neuroscience, and the humanities. This characteristic feature of archaeology actually makes it an interesting model for the kind of dialogue between the sciences and the humanities envisaged by Slingerland (2008).

---

[1] Note that the Santa Fe Institute has as its current director an archaeologist, Jerry Sabloff—the first time this post has been held by a scholar from this field.
[2] Here one could mention work at the interface of art and neuroscience, such as Stafford 2007; Freedberg and Gallese 2007.

Arguably in each of the above areas it is the 'pragmatism' of archaeology as a discipline that brings something distinctive to the table. In a recent new edition of a well-known textbook, *Contemporary Archaeology in Theory*, the editors add a subtitle, *The New Pragmatism* (Preucel and Mrozowski 2010). Their objective in the use of this term is to convey the growing feeling that archaeology needs to show a fuller integration with its social context, 'in ways that serve contemporary needs' (ibid. 3). The authors view archaeology as a social practice rather than an objective science; and as a social practice it should and does engage diverse interest-groups. They also draw on the work of philosopher Patrick Baert (2005), who sees archaeology and anthropology as two disciplines that have adopted a pragmatic spirit, perhaps in the case of archaeology 'due to the increasing prominence of heritage in contemporary society' (Preucel and Mrozowski 2010, 32). This feel for the importance of recognizing the contemporary production of archaeological knowledge as an embedded social practice is also central to a recent critique of 'material culture studies' (Hicks 2010). Hicks does not talk of 'pragmatism' per se, but his sense of a 'material-cultural turn' conveys the same spirit as that evoked by Preucel and Mrozowski. Hicks is at pains to point out that, as an archaeologist, his take on material culture studies is different to that of anthropologists such as Tim Ingold or Danny Miller. In order to stress how we *enact* knowledge through what we do as scholars, he reminds us that 'the archaeological process yields not just fragments of abraded and residual ceramic sherds, but mud on the boots and dirt under the fingernails' (ibid. 95).[3] It is not that this is new to archaeologists—but perhaps we are only now realizing the significant distinctiveness of our daily practices. To return to the question with which I ended Chapter 1, I may still not be able to explain why I return year after year to study ancient Greek vases; but this embedded social practice is as responsible for the form and content of this book as is any amount of interdisciplinary reading.

Pragmatism does have an epistemological component too, and can be traced back to the American philosophers William James and Charles Sanders Peirce (Preucel and Mrozowski 2010, 28–9). Its basic tenet is that the 'truth' or validity of an idea is judged by how useful it is in practice. This inseparability of idea and practice helps us overcome the Cartesian separation of mind and body in our analysis of ancient material culture. The archaeologist does not have to choose between either a practice-based, functional explanation or an ideational, symbolic explanation, because these two dimensions are bound together. This is made clear in the pragmatic-semiotic approach put forward by Preucel, largely inspired by Peirce (e.g. Preucel and Bauer 2001;

---

[3] Note too the 'empirical' approach advocated by Gosselain and colleagues, as a particular reaction to the model-building (non-pragmatic) Darwinian approach to cultural dynamics: Gosselain, Zeebroek, and Decroly 2008.

Preucel 2006).[4] It is not only in our understanding of the ancient world that this combination is relevant, but also in how we approach theory-building within and between disciplines. Slingerland (2008, 239) argues that pragmatism helps us avoid the polarized objectivist–relativist debate that impedes dialogue between the humanities and natural sciences. From a pragmatist viewpoint, theory, of whatever derivation, should be useful: it should work. I hope that the network approach I develop in this book fulfils this criterion. It should offer a way to do archaeological analysis, not just to think about it. Furthermore, it ought to be able to facilitate the kinds of archaeological analysis that have relevance to contemporary concerns. Charting both the costs and the benefits of interaction with artefact assemblages across multiple scales qualifies, I would argue, as a pressing contemporary concern.

---

[4] See also Knappett 2005, combining Peircean semiotics with Gibsonian ecological psychology.

References

Aiello, L., and R. Dunbar, 1993. 'Neocortex size, group size and the evolution of language', *Current Anthropology*, 34, 184–93.

Amin, A., and P. Cohendet, 2004. *Architectures of Knowledge: Firms, Capabilities and Communities*. Oxford: Oxford University Press.

Appadurai, A. (ed.), 1986. *The Social Life of Things: Commodities in Cultural Perspective*. Cambridge: Cambridge University Press.

Arafat, K., and C. Morgan, 1994. 'Athens, Etruria and the Heuneburg: mutual misconceptions in the study of Greek–barbarian relations', in I. Morris (ed.), *Classical Greece: Ancient Histories and Modern Archaeologies*, 108–34. Cambridge: Cambridge University Press.

Arthur, W. B., 2009. *The Nature of Technology: What it Is and How it Evolves*. New York: Free Press.

Ashmore, M., Wooffitt, R., and S. Harding, 1994. 'Humans and others, agents and things', *American Behavioral Scientist*, 37(6), 733–40.

Bachelard, G., 1964. *The Poetics of Space*. New York: Orion Press.

Baert, P., 2005. *Philosophy of the Social Sciences: Towards Pragmatism*. Cambridge: Polity Press.

Banning, E. B., 1996. 'Houses, compounds and mansions in the prehistoric Near East', in G. Coupland and E. B. Banning (eds.), *People Who Lived in Big Houses: Archaeological Perspectives on Large Domestic Structures*, 165–85. Monographs in World Archaeology No. 27. Madison, Wisc.: Prehistory Press.

Bapty, I., and T. Yates (eds.), 1990. *Archaeology After Structuralism*. London: Routledge.

Barabási, A.-L., 2002. *Linked: The New Science of Networks*. Cambridge, Mass.: Perseus Publishing.

——and R. Albert, 1999. 'Emergence of scaling in random networks', *Science*, 286, 509–12.

Barnes, J. A., 1954. 'Class and committees in a Norwegian island parish', *Human Relations*, 7, 39–58.

——1972. *Social Networks*. Reading, Mass.: Addison-Wesley.

Bar-Yosef, O., and P. van Peer, 2009. 'The *chaîne opératoire* approach in Middle Palaeolithic technology', *Current Anthropology*, 50(1), 103–31.

Batty, M., 2004. 'Distance in space syntax', *CASA Working Papers, no. 80*. ISSN 14671298 Working paper. London: Centre for Advanced Spatial Analysis (UCL).

Baurain, C., and P. Darcque, 1983. 'Un triton en pierre à Malia', *BCH* 107(1), 3–73.

Beck, R. A. (ed.), 2007. *The Durable House: House Society Models in Archaeology*. Occasional Paper 35, Centre for Archaeological Investigations, Southern Illinois University Carbondale.

Bell, T. L., and R. L. Church, 1985. 'Location-allocation modeling in archaeological settlement pattern research: some preliminary applications', *World Archaeology*, 16(3), 354–71.

Belting, H., 2001. *Bild-Anthropologie: Entwürfe für eine Bildwissenschaft.* Munich: Wilhelm Fink.

——2005*a*. 'Image, medium, body: a new approach to iconology', *Critical Inquiry*, 31, 302–19.

——2005*b*. 'Toward an anthropology of the image', in M. Westermann (ed.), *Anthropologies of Art*, 41–58. New Haven and London: Yale University Press.

Bentley, R. A., Hahn, M. W., and S. J. Shennan, 2004. 'Random drift and culture change', *Proc. R. Soc. Lond. B* 271, 1443–50.

Berg, I., 1999. 'The southern Aegean system', *Journal of World-Systems Research*, 5(3), 475–84.

——2004. 'The meanings of standardisation: conical cups in the late Bronze Age Aegean', *Antiquity*, 78, 74–85.

——2007. 'Meaning in the making: the potter's wheel at Phylakopi, Melos (Greece)', *Journal of Anthropological Archaeology*, 26, 234–52.

Berthoz, A., 1997. *Le Sens du mouvement.* Paris: Odile Jacob.

Bettencourt, L. M. A., 2002 [in preprint archive]. 'From boom to bust and back again: the complex dynamics of trends and fashions', *cond-mat/0212267.*

——Cintron-Arias, A., Kaiser, D. I., and C. C. Chavez, 2006. 'The power of a good idea: quantitative modeling of the spread of ideas from epidemiological models', *Physica A*, 364, 513–36.

——Lobo, J., Helbing, D., Kühnert, C. and G. West, 2007. 'Growth, innovation, scaling and the pace of life in cities', *Proceedings of the National Academy of Sciences*, 104, 7301–6.

Bevan, A., 2007. *Stone Vessels and Value in the Bronze Age Mediterranean.* Cambridge: Cambridge University Press.

——Kiriatzi, E., Knappett, C., Kappa, E., and S. Papachristou, 2002. 'Excavation of neopalatial deposits at Tholos (Kastri), Kythera', *Annual of the British School at Athens*, 97, 55–96.

Bietak, M., Marinatos, N., and C. Palyvou, 2007. *Taureador Scenes in Tell El-Dab'a (Avaris) and Knossos.* Vienna: ÖAW, Verlag der Österreichischen Akademie der Wissenschaften.

Binford, L. R., 1978. 'Dimensional analysis of behavior and site structure: learning from an Eskimo hunting stand', *American Antiquity*, 43(3), 330–61.

Blake, E., 2002. 'Spatiality past and present: an interview with Edward Soja, Los Angeles, 12 April 2001', *Journal of Social Archaeology*, 2(2), 139–58.

——2004. 'Space, spatiality, and archaeology', in L. Meskell and R. W. Preucel (eds.), *A Companion to Social Archaeology*, 230–54. Oxford: Blackwell.

Blakolmer, F., 2006. 'The Minoan stucco relief: a palatial art form in context', *Proceedings of the 10th International Cretological Conference, Elounda 1–6 October 2001*, Vol A3, 9–25. Heraklion: Cretan Historical Society.

Blakolmer, F., 2010. 'La Peinture murale dans le monde minoen et mycénien: distribution, fonctions des espaces, déclinaison du repertoire iconographique', in I. Boehm and S. Müller (eds.), *Espace religieux et espace civil en Grèce à l'époque mycénienne. Actes des Journées d'archéologie et de philologie mycénienne, 1er février 2006 et 1er mars 2007*, 147–70. Lyon: Travaux de la Maison de l'Orient et de la Méditerranée 54.

Blier, S. P., 1987. *The Anatomy of Architecture: Ontology and Metaphor in Batamma-liba Architectural Expression*. Cambridge: Cambridge University Press.

Blondel, V. D., Guillaume, J.-L., Lambiotte, R., and E. Lefebvre, 2008. 'Fast unfolding of communities in large networks', *Journal of Statistical Mechanics*, 1742-5468/2008/10/P10008.

Boivin, N., 2008. *Material Cultures, Material Minds: The Impact of Things on Human Thought, Society and Evolution*. Cambridge: Cambridge University Press.

Bonnot, T., 2002. *La vie des objets: d'ustensiles banals à objets de collection*. Paris: Editions MSH.

Borgatti, S. P., Mehra, A., Brass, D. J., and G. Labianca, 2009. 'Network analysis in the social sciences', *Science*, 323, 892–5.

Bott, E., 1971. *Family and Social Network*, 2nd edn., New York: Free Press.

Boyd, M. J., Whitbread, I. K., and J. A. MacGillivray, 2006. 'Geophysical investigations at Palaikastro', *BSA* 101, 89–134.

Bradley, R., 1990. *The Passage of Arms: An Archaeological Analysis of Prehistoric Hoards and Votive Deposits*. Cambridge: Cambridge University Press.

Brandt, L. and P. A. Brandt, 2005. 'Making sense of a blend—a cognitive-semiotic approach to metaphor', *Annual Review of Cognitive Linguistics*, 3(1), 216–49.

Branigan, K., 1981. 'Minoan colonialism', *BSA* 76, 23–33.

Broodbank, C., 1993. 'Ulysses without sails: trade, distance, knowledge and power in the Early Cyclades', *World Archaeology*, 24(3), 315–31.

——2000. *An Island Archaeology of the Early Cyclades*. Cambridge: Cambridge University Press.

——2004. 'Minoanisation', *Proceedings of the Cambridge Philological Society*, 50, 46–91.

Brooks, R. A., 1991. 'Intelligence without representation', *Artificial Intelligence Journal*, 47, 139–59.

Brown, B., 2001. 'Thing theory', *Critical Inquiry*, 28(1), 1–22.

——(ed.), 2003. *Things*. Chicago: University of Chicago Press.

——2006. *A Sense of Things: The Object Matter of American Literature*. Chicago: University of Chicago Press.

Brück, J., 2005. 'Experiencing the past? The development of a phenomenological archaeology in British prehistory', *Archaeological Dialogues*, 12(1), 45–72.

Brughmans, T., 2010. 'Connecting the dots: towards archaeological network analysis', *Oxford Journal of Archaeology*, 29(3), 277–303.

Brusasco, P., 2004. 'Theory and practice in the study of Mesopotamian domestic space', *Antiquity*, 78, 142–57.

Brysaert, A., 2007. *The Power of Technology in the Bronze Age Eastern Mediterranean: The Case of the Painted Plaster*. London: Equinox.

Buchanan, M., 2002. *Nexus: Small Worlds and the Groundbreaking Science of Networks*. London: W. W. Norton.

Buchli, V., 2000. *An Archaeology of Socialism*. London: Berg.

——(ed.), 2002. *The Material Culture Reader*. London: Berg.

Burt, R. S., 1980. 'Models of network structure', *Annual Review of Sociology*, 6, 79–141.

Butts, C. T., 2009. 'Revisiting the foundations of network analysis', *Science*, 325, 414–16.

Cadogan, G., 1978. 'Pyrgos, Crete, 1970–77', *Archaeological Reports, 1977–8*, 70–84.

—— 1990. 'Lasithi in the Old Palace Period', *BICS* 37, 172–4.

Cadogan, G., and C. Knappett, in prep. *Myrtos Pyrgos: The Period III pottery*. British School at Athens.

Callon, M., 1986. 'Some elements for a sociology of translation: domestication of the scallops and the fishermen of St-Brieuc Bay', in J. Law (ed.), *Power, Action and Belief: A New Sociology of Knowledge?*, 196–223. Sociological Review Monograph. London: Routledge & Kegan Paul.

—— and J. Law, 2004. 'Guest editorial', *Environment and Planning D: Society and Space*, 22, 3–11.

Caple, C., 2010. 'Ancestor artefacts—ancestor materials', *Oxford Journal of Archaeology*, 29(3), 305–18.

Carraher, T. N., Carraher, D. W., and A. D. Schliemann, 1985. 'Mathematics in the streets and in the schools', *British Journal of Developmental Psychology*, 3, 21–9.

Carrington, P. J., Scott, J., and S. Wasserman (eds.), 2005. *Models and Methods in Social Network Analysis*. Cambridge: Cambridge University Press.

Carsten, J., and S. Hugh-Jones (eds.), 1995. *About the House: Lévi-Strauss and Beyond*. Cambridge: Cambridge University Press.

Carter, T., 2004. 'Transformative processes in liminal spaces: craft as ritual action in the Throne Room area', in G. Cadogan, E. Hatzaki, and A. Vasilakis (eds.), *Knossos: Palace, City, State*, 273–82. London: British School at Athens Studies 12.

—— 2007. 'The theatrics of technology: consuming obsidian in the Early Cycladic burial arena', in Z. X. Hruby, R. K. Flad, and G. P. Bennett (eds.), *Rethinking Craft Specialization in Complex Societies: Archaeological Analyses of the Social Meaning of Production*. Archaeological Papers of the American Anthropological Association, 17 (1), 88–107.

Certeau, M. de, 1984. *The Practice of Everyday Life*, trans. S. Rendall. Berkeley: University of California Press.

Cerulo, K. A., 2009. 'Nonhumans in social interaction', *Annual Review of Sociology*, 35, 531–52.

Chapman, J., 2000. *Fragmentation in Archaeology: People, Places and Broken Objects in the Prehistory of South Eastern Europe*. London: Routledge.

—— and B. Gaydarska, 2006. *Parts and Wholes: Fragmentation in Prehistoric Context*. Oxford: Oxbow Books.

Cheney, D., and R. M. Seyfarth, 1990. *How Monkeys See the World: Inside the Mind of Another Species*. Chicago: University of Chicago Press.

Chevalier, S., 1998. 'From woollen carpet to grass carpet: bridging house and garden in an English suburb', in D. Miller (ed.), *Material Cultures: Why Some Things Matter*, 47–71. Chicago: University of Chicago Press.

Childs, S. T., 1991. 'Style, technology, and iron smelting furnaces in Bantu-speaking Africa', *Journal of Anthropological Archaeology*, 10, 332–59.

Chorley, R. J., and P. Haggett (eds.), 1967. *Models in Geography*. London: Methuen.

Christakis, K., 2005. *Cretan Bronze Age Pithoi: Traditions and Trends in the Production and Consumption of Storage Containers in Bronze Age Crete.* Prehistory Monographs, 18. Philadelphia: INSTAP Academic Press.

——2008. *The Politics of Storage: Storage and Sociopolitical Complexity in Neopalatial Crete.* Philadelphia: INSTAP Academic Press.

Christakis, N., and J. H. Fowler, 2007. 'The spread of obesity in a large social network over 32 years', *New England Medical Journal*, 357, 370–9.

——— 2009. *Connected: The Surprising Power of Our Social Networks and How They Shape Our Lives.* New York: Little Brown.

Clark, A., 1997. *Being There: Putting Brain, Body, and World Together Again.* Cambridge, Mass.: MIT Press.

——2008. *Supersizing the Mind: Embodiment, Action and Cognitive Extension.* Oxford: Oxford University Press.

——2010. 'Material surrogacy and the supernatural: reflections on the role of artefacts in "off-line" cognition', in L. Malafouris and C. Renfrew (eds.), *The Cognitive Life of Things: Recasting the Boundaries of the Mind*, 23–8. Cambridge: McDonald Institute Monographs.

——and D. Chalmers, 1998. 'The Extended Mind', *Analysis*, 58(1): 7–19.

Clarke, D. L., 1968. *Analytical Archaeology.* London: Methuen.

——1972. 'Models and paradigms in contemporary archaeology', in D.L. Clarke (ed.), *Models in Archaeology*, 1–60. London: Methuen.

——(ed.), 1977. *Spatial Archaeology.* London: Academic Press.

Coldstream, J. N., and G. L. Huxley (eds.), 1972. *Kythera.* London: Faber & Faber.

Cole, M., 1996. *Cultural Psychology: A Once and Future Discipline.* Cambridge, Mass.: Harvard University Press.

Collar, A., 2007. 'Network theory and religious innovation', *Mediterranean Historical Review*, 22(1), 149–62.

Conneller, C., 2007. 'Inhabiting new landscapes: settlement and mobility in Britain after the Last Glacial Maximum', *Oxford Journal of Archaeology*, 26(3), 215–37.

Connerton, P., 1989. *How Societies Remember.* Cambridge: Cambridge University Press.

——2006. 'Cultural memory', in C. Tilley *et al.* (eds.), *Handbook of Material Culture*, 315–24. London: Sage.

——2009. *How Modernity Forgets.* Cambridge: Cambridge University Press.

Conolly, J., and M. Lake, 2006. *Geographical Information Systems in Archaeology.* Cambridge: Cambridge University Press.

Costall, A., 1995. 'Socialising affordances', *Theory and Psychology*, 5, 467–82.

——2006. 'On being the right size: affordances and the meaning of scale', in G. Lock and B. L. Molyneaux (eds.), *Confronting Scale in Archaeology: Issues of Theory and Practice*, 15–26. New York: Springer.

Coudart, A., 2007. 'Is archaeology a science, an art or a collection of individual experiments . . .?' *Archaeological Dialogues*, 13(2), 132–8.

Coward, F., 2008. 'Standing on the shoulders of giants', *Science*, 319, 1493–5.

——2010. 'Small worlds, material culture and ancient Near Eastern social networks', *Proceedings of the British Academy*, 158, 449–79.

Coward, F. and C. Gamble, 2008. 'Big brains, small worlds: material culture and human evolution', *Philosophical Transactions of the Royal Society, Series B*, 363, 1969–79.

Crawford, O. G. S., 1912. 'The distribution of Early Bronze Age settlements in Britain', *Geographical Journal*, 40, 184–203.

—— 1922. 'Prehistoric geography', *Geographical Review*, 12(2), 257–63.

Crewe, L., 2007. 'Sophistication in simplicity: the first production of wheelmade pottery on Late Bronze Age Cyprus', *Journal of Mediterranean Archaeology*, 20(2), 209–38.

—— *Early Enkomi. Regionalism, Trade and Society at the Beginning of the Late Bronze Age on Cyprus*, BAR International Series 1706. Oxford: Archaeopress.

Crossland, Z., 2009. 'Of clues and signs: the dead body and its evidential traces', *American Anthropologist*, 111, 69–80.

Cutting, M., 2003. 'The use of spatial analysis to study prehistoric settlement architecture', *Oxford Journal of Archaeology*, 22(1), 1–21.

Damasio, A. R., 2000. The Feeling of What Happens: Body and Emotion in the Making of Consciousness. New York: Harcourt Brace.

Daniel, V., 1984. *Fluid Signs: Being a Person the Tamil Way*. Berkeley: University of California Press.

Daniels, I. M., 2001. 'The "untidy" Japanese house', in D. Miller (ed.), *Home Possessions: Material Culture Behind Closed Doors*, 201–29. Oxford: Berg.

—— 2009. 'The "social death" of unused gifts: surplus and value in contemporary Japan', *Journal of Material Culture*, 14(3), 385–408.

Dant, T., 2005. *Materiality and Society*. Buckingham: Open University Press.

Davis, J. L., 1982. 'Thoughts on Prehistoric and Archaic Delos', *Temple University Aegean Symposium*, 7, 23–33.

Day, P. M., and D. E. Wilson, 1998. 'Consuming power: Kamares Ware in Protopalatial Crete', *Antiquity*, 72, 350–8.

—— —— 2002. 'Landscapes of memory, craft and power in Prepalatial and Protopalatial Knossos', in Y. Hamilakis (ed.), *Labyrinth Revisited: Rethinking 'Minoan' Archaeology*, 143–66. Oxford: Oxbow.

—— Relaki, M., and E. Faber, 2006. 'Pottery making and social reproduction in the Bronze Age Mesara', in M. H. Wiener, J. L. Warner, J. Polonsky, and E. E. Hayes (eds.), *Pottery and Society: The Impact of Recent Studies in Minoan Pottery. Gold Medal Colloquium in Honor of Philip P. Betancourt*. Boston: Archaeological Institute of America.

Deetz, J., 1977. *In Small Things Forgotten: The Archaeology of Early American Life*. New York: Doubleday.

Deleuze, G., and F. Guattari. 1988. *A Thousand Plateaus: Capitalism and Schizophrenia*. London: The Athlone Press.

Della Sala, S. (ed.), 2010. *Forgetting*. Hove: Psychology Press.

DeMarrais, E., Castillo, L. J., and T. Earle, 1996. 'Ideology, materialization, and power strategies', *Current Anthropology*, 37(1), 15–31.

DeSilvey, C., 2006. 'Observed decay: telling stories with mutable things', *Journal of Material Culture*, 11, 318–38.

—— 2007. 'Salvage memory: constellating material histories on a hardscrabble homestead', *Cultural Geographies*, 14, 401–24.

Dickens, P., 1977. 'An analysis of historical house-plans: a study at the structural level', in D. L. Clarke (ed.), *Spatial Archaeology*, 33–45. London: Academic Press.

Doonan, R. C. P., Day, P. M., and N. Dimopoulou-Rethemiotaki, 2007. 'Lame excuses for emerging complexity in Early Bronze Age Crete', in P. M. Day and R. C. P. Doonan (eds.), *Metallurgy in the Early Bronze Age*, 98–122. Sheffield Studies in Aegean Archaeology, 7. Oxford: Oxbow.

Doreian, P., Batagelj, V., and A. Ferligoj, 2005. 'Positional analyses of sociometric data', in P. J. Carrington, J. Scott, and S. Wasserman (eds.), *Models and Methods in Social Network Analysis*, 77–97. Cambridge: Cambridge University Press.

Driessen, J., 1982. 'The Minoan Hall in domestic architecture on Crete: to be in vogue in Late Minoan IA?' *Acta Archaeologica Loveniansa*, 21, 27–92.

——1989/90. 'The proliferation of Minoan palatial architectural style: (I) Crete', *Acta Archaeologica Lovaniensa*, 28–9, 3–23.

——1999. 'The dismantling of a Minoan Hall at Palaikastro (Knossians go home?)', in P. P. Betancourt, V. Karageorghis, R. Laffineur, and W.-D. Niemeier (eds.), *Meletemata: Studies in Aegean Archaeology presented to Malcolm H. Wiener as he Enters his 65th Year*, 227–36. Liège and Austin: Aegaeum 20.

——2007. 'IIb or not IIb: on the beginnings of Minoan monument building', in J. Bretschneider, J. Driessen, and K. van Lerberghe (eds.), *Power and Architecture: Monumental Public Building in the Bronze Age Near East and Aegean*, 73–92. Leuven: Peeters.

——2010. 'Spirit of place: Minoan houses as major actors', in D. Pullen (ed.), *Political Economies of the Aegean Bronze Age: Papers from the Langford Conference, Florida State University, Tallahassee, 22–24 February 2007*, 35–65. Oxford: Oxbow Books.

——and C. F. Macdonald, 1997. *The Troubled Island: Minoan Crete Before and After the Santorini Eruption*. Liège: Aegaeum 17.

——and D. Frankel, 2012. 'Minds and mines: settlement networks and the diachronic use of space on Crete and Cyprus', in *Parallel Lives: Ancient Island Societies in Crete and Cyprus. Proceedings of the Conference held at Nicosia 1–3 December 2006 (BSA Supplement)*, eds. G. Cadogan, M. Iacovou, K. Kopaka, and J. Whitley, 61–84.

Dunbar, R. I. M., 1996. *Grooming, Gossip and the Evolution of Language*. London: Faber & Faber.

——and S. Shultz, 2007. 'Evolution in the social brain', *Science*, 317, 1344–7.

——Gamble, C., and J. Gowlett (eds.), 2010. *Social Brain, Distributed Mind*. London: British Academy.

Durkheim, E., and M. Mauss [1903], 1963. *Primitive Classification*. London: Cohen & West.

Earle, T. K., and R. W. Preucel, 1987. 'Processual archaeology and the radical critique', *Current Anthropology*, 28(4), 501–38.

Edensor, T., 2005a. 'Waste matter—the debris of industrial ruins and the disordering of the material world', *Journal of Material Culture*, 10(3), 311–32.

——2005b. 'The ghosts of industrial ruins: ordering and disordering memory in excessive space', *Environment and Planning D: Society and Space*, 23, 829–49.

Eerkens, J. W., and C. P. Lipo, 2005. 'Cultural transmission, copying errors and the generation of variation in material culture in the archaeological record', *Journal of Anthropological Archaeology*, 24, 316–34.

Eliopoulos, T., 2000. 'A Minoan potter's wheel with "marine" decoration from Skhinias, Mirabello District', *Annual of the British School at Athens*, 95, 107–14.

Elkins, J., 1997. *The Object Stares Back: On the Nature of Seeing*. New York: Harcourt Brace.

Emirbayer, M., 1997. 'Manifesto for a relational sociology', *American Journal of Sociology*, 103(2), 281–317.

——and J. Goodwin, 1994. 'Network analysis, culture and the problem of agency', *American Journal of Sociology*, 99(6), 1411–54.

Empson, R., 2007. 'Separating and containing people and things in Mongolia', in A. Henare, M. Holbraad, and S. Wastell (eds.), *Thinking Through Things: Theorising Artefacts Ethnographically*, 113–40. London: Routledge.

Euler, L., 1953. 'The Königsberg bridges', *Scientific American*, July 1953, 66–70.

Evans, A. J., 1921. *The Palace of Minos at Knossos*, Vol. 1. London: Macmillan.

——1930. *The Palace of Minos at Knossos*, Vol. 3. London: Macmillan.

Evans, T., 2004. 'Complex networks', *Contemporary Physics*, 45, 455–74.

——Knappett, C., and R. Rivers, 2009. 'Using statistical physics to understand relational space: a case study from Mediterranean prehistory', in D. Lane, D. Pumain, S. van der Leeuw and G. West (eds.), *Complexity Perspectives on Innovation and Social Change*, 451–79. Berlin: Springer Methodos series.

Faber, E., Kilikoglou, V., and P. M. Day, 2002. 'Technologies of Middle Minoan polychrome pottery: traditions of paste, decoration and firing', in V. Kilikoglou, Y. Maniatis, and A. Hein (eds.) *Modern Trends in Scientific Studies on Ancient Ceramics. Papers Presented at the Fifth European Meeting on Ancient Ceramics, Athens 1999*, 129–41. Oxford: BAR International Series 1011.

Fauconnier, G., and Turner, M., 2008. 'Rethinking metaphor', in R. Gibbs (ed.), *Cambridge Handbook of Metaphor and Thought*, 53–66. Cambridge: Cambridge University Press.

Faust, K., 1997. 'Centrality in affiliation networks', *Social Networks*, 19, 157–91.

——2005. 'Using correspondence analysis for joint displays of affiliation networks', in P. J. Carrington, J. Scott, and S. Wasserman (eds.), *Models and Methods in Social Network Analysis*, 117–47. Cambridge: Cambridge University Press.

Ferme, M. C., 2001. *The Underneath of Things: Violence, History, and the Everyday in Sierra Leone*. Berkeley: University of California Press.

Finnegan, R., 2002. *Communicating: The Multiple Modes of Human Interconnection*. London: Routledge.

Flannery, K. V., 1972. 'The cultural evolution of civilizations', *Annual Review of Ecology and Systematics*, 3, 399–426.

Forty, A., and S. Kuechler (eds.), 1999. *The Art of Forgetting*. Oxford: Berg.

Foster, S., 1989. 'Analysis of spatial patterns in buildings (access analysis) as an insight into social structure: examples from the Scottish Atlantic Iron Age', *Antiquity*, 63, 40–50.

Freedberg, D., and V. Gallese, 2007. 'Motion, emotion and empathy in esthetic experience', *Trends in Cognitive Science*, 11(5), 197–203.

Frow, J., 2003. 'A pebble, a camera, a man who turns into a telegraph pole', in B. Brown (ed.), *Things*, 346–61. Chicago: University of Chicago Press.

Gadamer, H.-G., 1976. 'The nature of things and the language of things', in *Philosophical Hermeneutics*, trans. and ed. D. E. Linge. Berkeley: University of California Press.

Gallay, A., 2007. 'The decorated marriage jars of the inner delta of the Niger (Mali): essay of archaeological demarcation of an ethnic territory', *The Arkeotek Journal*, 1 (1) (http://www.thearkeotekjournal.org).

Gamble, C., 1998. 'Palaeolithic society and the release from proximity: a network approach to intimate relations', *World Archaeology*, 29(3), 426–49.

——1999. *The Palaeolithic Societies of Europe*. Cambridge: Cambridge University Press.

——2007. *Origins and Revolutions: Human Identity in Earliest Prehistory*. Cambridge: Cambridge University Press.

Gastner, M. T., and M. E. J. Newman, 2006. 'The spatial structure of networks', *Eur. Phys. J. B*, 49, 247–52.

Gelbert, A., 2003. *Traditions céramiques et emprunts techniques dans la Vallée du Fleuve Sénégal*. Editions de la MSH, Editions Epistèmes, Paris. (English CD ROM, demonstration chapter on http://www.arkeotek.org).

Gell, A., 1998. *Art and Agency: Towards a New Anthropological Theory*. Oxford: Clarendon Press.

Gibson, J. J., 1979. *The Ecological Approach to Visual Perception*. Boston, MA: Houghton Mifflin.

Ginzburg, C., 1980. 'Morelli, Freud and Sherlock Holmes: clues and scientific method', *History Workshop Journal*, 9(1), 5–36.

Girvan, M., and M. E. J. Newman, 2002. 'Community structure in social and biological networks', *PNAS* 99(12), 7821–6.

Glassie, H., 1975. *Folk Housing in Middle Virginia: A Structural Analysis of Historic Artifacts*. Knoxville, Tenn.: University of Tennessee Press.

——1999. *Material Culture*. Bloomington, Ind.: Indiana University Press.

Godart, L., and J.-P. Olivier, 1976–85. *Recueil des inscriptions en linéaire A*, vols. I–V. Paris: Etudes Crétoises 21.

Goffman, E., 1959. *The Presentation of Self in Everyday Life*. New York: Doubleday.

——1967. *Interaction Ritual: Essays on Face-to-Face Behavior*. New York: Doubleday.

——1974. *Frame Analysis: An Essay on the Organisation of Experience*. New York: Harper & Row.

González-Ruibal, A., 2008. 'Time to destroy: an archaeology of supermodernity', *Current Anthropology*, 49(2), 247–79.

Goodwin, C., 1994. 'Professional vision', *American Anthropologist*, 96(3), 606–33.

——2010. 'Things and their embodied environments', in L. Malafouris and C. Renfrew (eds.), *The Cognitive Life of Things: Recasting the Boundaries of the Mind*, 103–20. Cambridge: McDonald Institute Monographs.

Gordon, A., 1997. *Ghostly Matters: Haunting and the Sociological Imagination*. Minneapolis: University of Minnesota Press.

Gorenflo, L. J., and T. L. Bell, 1991. 'Network analysis and the study of past regional organisation', in C.D. Trombold (ed.), *Ancient Road Networks and Settlement Hierarchies in the New World*, 80–98. Cambridge: Cambridge University Press.

Gosden, C, 1994. *Social Being and Time*. Oxford: Blackwell.

——2004a. 'Making and display: our aesthetic appreciation of things and objects', in C. Renfrew, C. Gosden, and E. DeMarrais (eds.), *Substance, Memory, Display: Archaeology and Art*, 35–45. Cambridge: McDonald Institute Monographs.

——2004b. *Archaeology and Colonialism: Cultural Contact from 5000 BC to the Present*. Cambridge: Cambridge University Press.

——2005. 'What do objects want?' *Journal of Archaeological Method and Theory*, 12(3), 193–211.

——and Y. Marshall, 1999. 'The cultural biography of objects', *World Archaeology*, 31(2), 169–78.

——Larson, F., and A. Petch, 2007. *Knowing Things: Exploring the Collections at the Pitt Rivers Museum 1884–1945*. Oxford: Oxford University Press.

Gosselain, O. P., 2000. 'Materialising identities: an African perspective', *Journal of Archaeological Method and Theory*, 7(3),187–217.

——Zeebroek, R. and J.-M. Decroly, 2008. 'Introduction: des babioles, des bricoles', in O. Gosselain, R. Zeebroek, and J.-M. Decroly (eds.), *Des choses, des gestes, des mots: repenser les dynamiques culturelles*, 10–17. *Techniques et Culture* 51. Paris: Editions MSH.

Grady, J. E., Oakley, T., and Coulson, S. 1999. 'Blending and metaphor', in G. Steen and R. Gibbs (eds.), *Metaphor in Cognitive Linguistics*. Philadelphia: John Benjamins.

Graham, S., 2006. 'Networks, agent-based models and the Antonine itineraries: implications for Roman archaeology', *Journal of Mediterranean Archaeology*, 19(1), 45–64.

Granovetter, M. S., 1973. 'The strength of weak ties', *American Journal of Sociology*, 78 (6), 1360–80.

——1983. 'The strength of weak ties: a network theory revisited', *Sociological Theory*, 1, 201–33.

Grassé, P.-P., 1959. 'La reconstruction du nid et les coordinations inter-individuelles chez *Bellicositermes natalensis* et *Cubitermes* sp. La théorie de la stigmergie: Essai d'interprétation du comportement des termites constructeurs', *Insectes Sociaux*, 6, 41–81.

Gray, W.-D., and W.-T. Fu, 2004. 'Soft constraints in interactive behavior: the case of ignoring perfect knowledge in the world for imperfect knowledge in the head', *Cognitive Science*, 28(3), 359–82.

Green, D., and C. Haselgrove, 1978. 'Some problems in cross-disciplinary communication as viewed from archaeology and geography', in D. Green, C. Haselgrove, and M. Spriggs (eds.), *Social Organisation and Settlement: Contributions from Anthropology, Archaeology and Geography*, Pt I, vii–xxxvi. BAR International Series (Supplement) 47.

Guillaume, J.-L., and M. Lapaty, 2006. 'Bipartite graphs as models of complex networks', *Physica A*, 371, 795–813.

Guimera, R., Sales-Pardo, M., and L. A. N. Amaral, 2007. 'Module identification in bipartite and directed networks', *Physical Review E*, 76, 036102.

Gumbrecht, H.-U., 2004. *Production of Presence: What Meaning Cannot Convey.* Stanford: Stanford University Press.

Hacigüzeller, P. (n.d.), 'Spatial distribution analysis of the Middle Minoan II pottery at Quartier Mu', paper presented at the *110th Annual Meeting of the Archaeological Institute of America*, Philadelphia, 9 January 2009.

Hage, P., and F. Harary, 1991. *Exchange in Oceania: A Graph Theoretic Analysis.* Oxford: Clarendon Press.

——— 1996. *Island Networks: Communication, Kinship and Classification Structures in Oceania.* Cambridge: Cambridge University Press.

Hägerstrand, T., 1967. *Innovation Diffusion as a Spatial Process.* Chicago: University of Chicago Press.

Hägg, R., 1995. '"The East Hall." A forgotten cult room in the palace of Knossos', *Pepragmena Z Diethnous Kritilogikou Sinedriou*, Tomos A1, 359–67. Rethymno.

——— and N. Marinatos (eds.), 1984. *The Minoan Thalassocracy: Myth and Reality.* Stockholm: Skrifter Utgivna av Svenska Institutet i Athen. (distributed by Paul Åström).

Haggett, P., and R. J. Chorley, 1969. *Network Analysis in Geography.* London: Edward Arnold.

Hahn, H.-P., 2005. *Materielle Kultur. Eine Einführung.* Berlin: Reimer.

Hall, E. T., 1966. *The Hidden Dimension.* New York: Doubleday.

——— 1968. 'Proxemics', *Current Anthropology*, 9, 83–108.

Hallager, E., 1996. *The Minoan Roundel and Other Sealed Documents in the Neopalatial Linear A Administration.* Liège: Aegaeum 14.

Hallager, B.P., and E. Hallager. 1995. 'The Knossian bull: political propaganda in Neo-Palatial Crete', in R. Laffineur and W.-D. Niemeier (eds.), *Politeia: Society and State in the Bronze Age. Proceedings of the 5th International Aegean Conference, University of Heidelberg, Archäologisches Institut, 10–13 April 1994*, 547–55. Aegaeum 12. Liège: Université de Liège.

Halstead, P., and J. Barrett (eds.), 2005. *Food, Cuisine and Society in Prehistoric Greece.* Oxford: Oxbow.

Hamilakis, Y., 1996. 'Wine, oil and the dialectics of power in Bronze Age Crete: a review of the evidence', *Oxford Journal of Archaeology*, 15(1), 1–32.

——— 1999. 'Food technologies/technologies of the body: the social context of wine and oil production and consumption in Bronze Age Crete', *World Archaeology*, 31, 38–54.

——— 2008. 'Time, performance, and the production of a mnemonic record: from feasting to an archaeology of eating and drinking', in L. Hitchcock, R. Laffineur, and J. Crowley (eds.), *Dais: The Aegean Feast. Proceedings of the 12th International Aegean Conference, University of Melbourne, Centre for Classics and Archaeology, 25–29 March 2008*, 3–19. Liège: Aegaeum 29.

Hammond, N., 1972. 'Locational models and the site of Lubaantun: a Classic Maya centre', in D. L. Clarke (ed.), *Models in Archaeology*, 757–800. London: Methuen.

Harary, F., 1960. 'Some historical and intuitive aspects of graph theory', *SIAM Review*, 2, 123–31.

Harman, G., 2002. *Tool-being: Heidegger and the Metaphysics of Objects*. Chicago and La Salle: Open Court.

——2007. *Heidegger Explained: From Phenomenon to Thing*. Chicago and La Salle: Open Court.

——2010. 'Technology, objects and things in Heidegger', *Cambridge Journal of Economics*, 34, 17–25.

Harper, R., Taylor, A., and M. Molloy, 2008. 'Intelligent artefacts at home in the 21st Century', in C. Knappett and L. Malafouris (eds.), *Material Agency: Towards a Non-Anthropocentric Approach*, 97–119. New York: Springer.

Harrison, R., and J. Schofield, 2010. *After Modernity: Archaeological Approaches to the Contemporary Past*. Oxford: Oxford University Press.

Harvey, D. W., 1969. *Explanation in Geography*. London: Arnold.

——1973. *Social Justice and the City*. London: Arnold.

——1996. *Justice, Nature and the Geography of Difference*. Oxford: Blackwell.

Hatzaki, E., 2009. 'Structured deposition as ritual action at Knossos', in A.-L. D'Agata and A. van de Moortel (eds.), *Archaeologies of Cult: Essays on Ritual and Cult in Crete in Honor of Geraldine C. Gesell*, 19–30. Hesperia Supplement 42. Athens: American School of Classical Studies in Athens.

Haysom, M., 2010. 'The double-axe: a contextual approach to the understanding of a Cretan symbol in the Neopalatial period', *Oxford Journal of Archaeology*, 29(1), 35–55.

Heidegger, M., 1971a. 'The Thing', in *Poetry, Language, Thought*, trans. A. Hofstadter. New York: Harper.

——1971b. 'The Origin of the Work of Art', in *Poetry, Language, Thought*, trans. A. Hofstadter. New York: Harper.

——1977. *The Question Concerning Technology, and Other Essays*. New York: Harper & Row.

Helbing, D., Johansson, A., and H. Z. Al-Abideen, 2007. 'The dynamics of crowd disasters: an empirical study', *Physical Review E*, 75, 046109.

Henare, A., Holbraad, M., and Wastell, S. (eds.), 2007. *Thinking Through Things: Theorising Artefacts Ethnographically*. London: Routledge

Herva, V.-P., 2005. 'The life of buildings: Minoan building deposits in an ecological perspective', *Oxford Journal of Archaeology*, 24(3), 215–27.

Hetherington, K., 1997. 'In place of geometry: the materiality of place', in K. Hetherington and R. Munro (eds.) *Ideas of Difference: Social Spaces and the Labour of Division*, 183–99. Oxford: Blackwell.

——2004. 'Secondhandedness: consumption, disposal, and absent presence', *Environment and Planning D: Society and Space*, 22, 157–73.

Hicks, D., 2010. 'The material-cultural turn: event and effect', in D. Hicks and M. Beaudry (eds.), *The Oxford Handbook of Material Culture Studies*, 25–98. Oxford: Oxford University Press.

——and M. Beaudry (eds.), 2010. *The Oxford Handbook of Material Culture Studies*. Oxford: Oxford University Press.

Highmore, B., 2002. *Everyday Life and Cultural Theory: An Introduction*. London: Routledge.

Hillier, B., 1996. *Space is the Machine: A Configurational Theory of Architecture.* Cambridge: Cambridge University Press.

—— 2005. 'Between social physics and phenomenology', in *Fifth Space Syntax Symposium, 13–17 June 2005.* Delft, The Netherlands.

—— and J. Hanson, 1984. *The Social Logic of Space.* Cambridge: Cambridge University Press.

—— Leaman, A., Stansall, P., and M. Bedford, 1978. 'Space syntax', in D. Green, C. Haselgrove, and M. Spriggs (eds.), *Social Organisation and Settlement: Contributions from Anthropology, Archaeology and Geography*, Pt. I, 343–81. BAR International Series (Supplement) 47.

Hinde, R.A., 1976. 'Interactions, relationships and social structure', *Man*, 11, 1–17.

Hirose, N., 2002. 'An ecological approach to embodiment and cognition', *Cognitive Systems Research*, 3, 289–99.

Hirth, K. G., 1978. 'Interregional trade and the formation of prehistoric gateway communities', *American Antiquity*, 43(1), 35–45.

Hitchcock, L., Laffineur, R., and J. Crowley (eds.), 2008. *Dais: The Aegean Feast. Proceedings of the 12th International Aegean Conference, University of Melbourne, Centre for Classics and Archaeology, 25–29 March 2008.* Liège: Aegaeum 29.

Hodder, I., 1974a. 'Regression analysis of some trade and marketing patterns', *World Archaeology*, 6(2), 172–89.

—— 1974b. 'Some marketing models for Romano-British coarse pottery', *Britannia*, 5, 340–59.

—— (ed.), 1978. *Simulation Studies in Archaeology.* Cambridge: Cambridge University Press.

—— 1982. *Symbols in Action: Ethnoarchaeological Studies of Material Culture.* Cambridge: Cambridge University Press.

—— (ed.), 1982. *Symbolic and Structural Archaeology.* Cambridge: Cambridge University Press.

—— and C. Orton, 1976. *Spatial Analysis in Archaeology.* Cambridge: Cambridge University Press.

—— and P. Pels, 2010. 'History houses: a new interpretation of architectural elaboration at Çatalhöyük', in I. Hodder (ed.) *Religion in the Emergence of Civilization: Çatalhöyük as a Case Study*, 163–86. Cambridge: Cambridge University Press.

Hood, M. S. F., 1996. 'Back to basics with Middle Minoan IIIB', in D. Evely, I. S. Lemos, and S. Sherratt (eds.), *Minotaur and Centaur: Studies in the Archaeology of Crete and Euboea Presented to Mervyn Popham*, 10–16. Oxford: BAR International Series 638.

Hood, M. S. F., 2000. 'Cretan fresco dates,' in S. Sherratt (ed.), *The Wall Paintings of Thera: Proceedings of the First International Symposium*, Athens, 191–208.

Horst, H., and D. Miller, 2006. *The Cell Phone: An Anthropology of Communication.* London: Berg.

Hoskins, J., 1998. *Biographical Objects: How Things Tell the Stories of People's Lives.* London: Routledge.

Howes, D., 2006. 'Scent, sound and synaesthesia: intersensoriality and material culture theory', in C. Tilley, W. Keane, S. Küchler, M. Rowlands, and P. Spyer (eds.), *Handbook of Material Culture*, 161–72. London: Sage.

Hunt, T. L., 1988. 'Graph theoretic network models for Lapita exchange: a trial application', in P. V. Kirch and T. L. Hunt (eds.), *Archaeology of the Lapita Cultural Complex: A Critical Review*, 135–55. Burke Museum Research Report, No. 5. Seattle: Burke Museum.

Hutchins, E., 1995. *Cognition in the Wild*. Cambridge, Mass.: MIT Press.

—— 2005. 'Material anchors for conceptual blends', *Journal of Pragmatics*, 37, 1555–77.

Ingold, T., 2000. *The Perception of the Environment: Essays on Livelihood, Dwelling and Skill*. London: Routledge.

——2004. 'Culture on the ground: the world perceived through the feet', *Journal of Material Culture*, 9, 315–40.

——2007*a*. 'Materials against materiality', *Archaeological Dialogues*, 14(1), 1–16.

——2007*b*. *Lines: A Brief History*. London: Routledge.

Ingold, T., 2008. 'When ANT meets SPIDER: social theory for arthropods', in C. Knappett and L. Malafouris (eds.), *Material Agency: Towards a Non-Anthropocentric Approach*, 209–15. New York: Springer.

Irwin, G., 1992. *The Prehistoric Exploration and Colonisation of the Pacific*. Cambridge: Cambridge University Press.

Irwin-Williams, C., 1977. 'A network model for the analysis of prehistoric trade', in T. K. Earle and J. E. Ericson (eds.), *Exchange Systems in Prehistory*, 141–51. London: Academic Press.

Isaakidou, V., 2007. 'Cooking in the labyrinth: exploring "cuisine" at Bronze Age Knossos', in C. Mee and J. Renard (eds.), *Cooking Up the Past: Food and Culinary Practices in the Neolithic and Bronze Age Aegean*, 5–24. Oxford: Oxbow Books.

Isaksen, L., 2008. 'The application of network analysis to ancient transport geography: a case study of Roman Baetica', *Digital Medievalist*, 4.

Jackson, M. O., 2008. *Social and Economic Networks*. Princeton: Princeton University Press.

Jenkins, D., 2001. 'A network analysis of Inka roads, administrative centers, and storage facilities', *Ethnohistory*, 48(4), 655–87.

Jennings, J., 2006. 'Core, peripheries, and regional realities in Middle Horizon Peru', *Journal of Anthropological Archaeology*, 25, 346–70.

Jeunet, J.-P., 2001. *Le Fabuleux Destin d'Amélie Poulain*.

Johansen, K. L., Laursen, S. T., and M. K. Holst, 2004. 'Spatial patterns of social organization in the Early Bronze Age of South Scandinavia', *Journal of Anthropological Archaeology*, 23, 33–55.

Johnson, G. A., 1977. 'Aspects of regional analysis in archaeology', *Annual Review of Anthropology*, 6, 479–508.

Johnson, M., 2006. 'On the nature of theoretical archaeology and archaeological theory', *Archaeological Dialogues*, 13(2), 117–32.

Johnstone, S. (ed.), 2008. *The Everyday*. Cambridge, Mass.: MIT Press.

Jones, A., 2007. *Memory and Material Culture*. Cambridge: Cambridge University Press.

Jones, O., and P. Cloke, 2008. 'Non-human agencies: trees in place and time', in C. Knappett and L. Malafouris (eds.), *Material Agency: Towards a Non-Anthropocentric Approach*, 79–96. New York: Springer.

Joy, J., 2009. 'Reinvigorating object biography: reproducing the drama of object lives', *World Archaeology*, 41(4), 540–56.

Joyce, R. A., 2000. 'Heirlooms and houses: materiality and social memory', in R. A. Joyce and S. D. Gillespie (eds.), *Beyond Kinship: Social and Material Reproduction in House Societies*, 189–212. Philadelphia: University of Pennsylvania Press.

Joyce, R. A., and S. D. Gillespie (eds.), 2000. *Beyond Kinship: Social and Material Reproduction in House Societies*. Philadelphia: University of Pennsylvania Press.

Kardulias, P. N., and T. D. Hall, 2008. 'Archaeology and world systems analysis', *World Archaeology*, 40(4), 572–83.

Karnava, A., 2008. 'Written and stamped records in the Late Bronze Age Cyclades: the sea journeys of an administration', in N. Brodie, J. Doole, G. Gavalas, and C. Renfrew (eds.), *Horizon: A Colloquium on the Prehistory of the Cyclades*, 377–86. Cambridge: McDonald Institute Monographs.

——and I. Nikolakopoulou, 2005. 'A pithos fragment with a Linear A inscription from Akrotiri, Thera', *Studi Micenei ed Egeo-Anatolici*, 47, 213–25.

Keane, W., 1997. *Signs of Recognition: Powers and Hazards of Representation in an Indonesian Society*. Berkeley: University of California Press.

——2003. 'Semiotics and the social analysis of material things'. *Language and Communication*, 23, 409–25.

Kirch, P. V., 1997. *The Lapita Peoples: Ancestors of the Oceanic World*. Oxford: Blackwell.

Kirsh, D., 1995. 'The intelligent use of space', *Artificial Intelligence*, 73, 31–68.

——2009. 'Problem solving and situated cognition', in P. Robbins and M. Aydede (eds.), *The Cambridge Handbook of Situated Cognition*, 264–306. Cambridge: Cambridge University Press.

——and P. Maglio, 1995. 'On distinguishing epistemic from pragmatic action', *Cognitive Science*, 18, 513–49.

Kleinberg, J. M., 2000. 'Navigation in a small world', *Nature*, 406, 845.

Knappett, C., 1999a. 'Tradition and innovation in pottery forming technology; wheel-throwing at Middle Minoan Knossos', *Annual of the British School at Athens*, 94, 101–29.

——1999b. 'Assessing a polity in protopalatial Crete: the Malia-Lasithi state', *American Journal of Archaeology*, 103, 615–39.

——1999c. 'Can't live without them—producing and consuming Minoan conical cups', in P. P. Betancourt *et al.* (eds.), *Meletemata: Studies in Aegean Archaeology Presented to Malcolm H. Wiener as he Enters his 65th Year*, Aegaeum 20, 415–20. Liège and Austin.

——2002. 'Photographs, skeuomorphs and marionettes: some thoughts on mind, agency and object', *Journal of Material Culture*, 7(1), 97–117.

——2005. *Thinking Through Material Culture: An Interdisciplinary Perspective*. Philadelphia: University of Pennsylvania Press.

——2006. 'Beyond skin: layering and networking in art and archaeology', *Cambridge Archaeological Journal*, 16(2), 239–51.

——2007. 'Materials *with* materiality?', response to Ingold's 'Materials against materiality', *Archaeological Dialogues*, 14(1), 20–3.

——2008. 'The neglected networks of material agency: artifacts, pictures and texts', in C. Knappett and L. Malafouris (eds.), *Material Agency: Towards a Non-Anthropocentric Approach*, 139–56. New York: Springer.

——2010. 'Communities of things and objects: a spatial perspective', in L. Malafouris and C. Renfrew (eds.), *The Cognitive Life of Things: Recasting the Boundaries of the Mind*, 81–90. Cambridge: McDonald Institute Monographs.

——2012. 'Meaning in miniature: semiotic networks in material culture', in M. Jensen, N. Johanssen, and H. J. Jensen (eds.), *Excavating the Mind: Cross-sections Through Culture, Cognition and Materiality*, 87–109. Aarhus: Aarhus University Press.

——and I. Schoep, 2000. 'Continuity and change in Minoan palatial power', *Antiquity* 74, 365–71.

——and T. Cunningham, 2003. 'Three Neopalatial deposits from Palaikastro, East Crete', *Annual of the British School at Athens*, 98, 107–87.

——— 2012. *Block M at Palaikastro: The Proto- and Neopalatial Town. Excavations 1986–2003.* British School at Athens Supplementary Volume 47, London.

——and Nikolakopoulou, I., 2005. 'Exchange and affiliation networks in the MBA southern Aegean: Crete, Akrotiri and Miletus', in R. Laffineur and E. Greco (eds.), *Emporia: Aegeans in East and West Mediterranean*, 175–84. Liège: Aegaeum 25.

——and L. Malafouris (eds.), 2008. *Material Agency: Towards a Non-Anthropocentric Perspective.* New York: Springer Press.

——Evans, T., and R. Rivers, 2008. 'Modelling maritime interaction in the Aegean Bronze Age', *Antiquity*, 82, 1009–24.

——Malafouris, L., and P. Tomkins, 2010. 'Ceramics as containers', in D. Hicks and M. Beaudry (eds.), *The Oxford Handbook of Material Culture Studies*, 588–612. Oxford: Oxford University Press.

Knoblich, G., and N. Sebanz, 2006. 'The social nature of perception and action', *Current Directions in Psychological Science*, 15(3), 99–104.

Knox, H., Savage, M., and P. Harvey, 2006. 'Social networks and the study of relations: networks as method, metaphor and form', *Economy and Society*, 35(1), 113–40.

Koehl, R. B., 2006. *Aegean Bronze Age Rhyta.* Prehistory Monographs 19. Philadelphia: INSTAP Academic Press.

Koh, A., 2008. *Wreathed in a Fragrant Cloud: Reconstructing a Late Bronze Age Aegean Workshop of Aromata.* Saarbrücken: VDM Verlag.

Kohl, P. L., 1975. 'The archaeology of trade', *Dialectical Anthropology*, 1, 43–50.

Kohler, T., and G. Gumerman (eds.), 2000. *Dynamics in Human and Primate Societies: Agent-based Modeling of Social and Spatial Processes.* Oxford: Oxford University Press.

——and S. E. van der Leeuw (eds.), 2007. *The Model-Based Archaeology of Socio-Natural Systems.* Santa Fe, N. Mex.: School of Advanced Research.

Kotsakis, K., 2006. 'Settlement of discord: Sesklo and the emerging household', in N. Tasic and C. Grozdanov (eds.), *Homage to Milutin Garasanin*, 207–20. Belgrade: Serbian Academy of Sciences and Arts.

Kristiansen, K., 2008. 'From memory to monument: the construction of time in the Bronze Age', in A. Lehoërff (ed.), *Construire le temps. Histoire et methods des chronologies et calendriers des derniers millénaires avant notre ère en Europe occidentale*, 41–50. Glux-en-Glenne: Bibracte.

——and T. B. Larsson, 2005. *The Rise of Bronze Age Society: Travels, Transmissions and Transformations.* Cambridge: Cambridge University Press.

Krzyszkowska, O., 2005. *Aegean Seals: An Introduction.* London: BICS Supplement 85.

Kubler, G., 1962. *The Shape of Time: Remarks on the History of Things.* New Haven and London: Yale University Press.

Küchler, S., 2008. 'Technological materiality: beyond the dualist paradigm', *Theory, Culture and Society*, 25(1), 101–20.

——and D. Miller (eds.), 2005. *Clothing as Material Culture.* London: Berg.

Kuijt, I., 2008. 'The regeneration of life: Neolithic structures of symbolic remembering and forgetting', *Current Anthropology*, 49(2), 171–97.

Kwa, C., 2002. 'Romantic and Baroque conceptions of complex wholes in the sciences', in J. Law and A. Mol (eds.), *Complexities: Social Studies of Knowledge Practices*, 23–52. Durham, NC: Duke University Press.

Lakoff, G., and Johnson, M. 1980. *Metaphors We Live By.* Chicago: University of Chicago Press.

Lane, D. A., Pumain, D., van der Leeuw, S. E., and G. West (eds.), 2009. *Complexity Perspectives on Innovation and Social Change.* New York: Springer.

Larson, F., Petch, A., and D. Zeitlyn, 2007. 'Social networks and the creation of the Pitt Rivers Museum', *Journal of Material Culture*, 12(3), 211–39.

Latour, B., 1999. 'On Recalling ANT', in J. Law and J. Hassard (eds.), *Actor Network Theory and After*, 15–25. Oxford: Blackwell.

——2005. *Reassembling the Social: An Introduction to Actor-Network-Theory.* Oxford: Oxford University Press.

——and P. Lemonnier (eds.), 1994. *De la préhistoire aux missiles balistiques: l'intelligence sociale des techniques.* Paris: La Découverte.

Lave, J., 1977. 'Cognitive consequences of traditional apprenticeship training in West Africa', *Anthropology and Education Quarterly*, 8(3), 177–80.

——1988. *Cognition in Practice: Mind, Mathematics and Culture in Everyday Life.* Cambridge: Cambridge University Press.

——and E. Wenger, 1991. *Situated Learning: Legitimate Peripheral Participation.* Cambridge: Cambridge University Press.

Law, J. (ed.), 1992. *A Sociology of Monsters: Essays on Power, Technology and Domination.* Routledge Sociological Review Monograph, London.

——2002. 'Objects and Spaces', *Theory, Culture and Society*, 19(5/6), 91–105.

——2004. *After Method: Mess in Social Science Research.* London: Routledge.

——and A. Mol, 2008. 'The actor-enacted: Cumbrian sheep in 2001', in C. Knappett and L. Malafouris (eds.), *Material Agency: Towards a Non-Anthropocentric Approach.* 57–77. New York: Springer.

Layton, R., 1989. 'Pellaport', in S. E. van der Leeuw and R. Torrence (eds.), *What's New? A Closer Look at the Process of Innovation*, 33–53. London: Unwin Hyman.

Leach, E., 1978. 'Does space syntax really "constitute the social"?', in D. Green, C. Haselgrove, and M. Spriggs (eds.), *Social Organisation and Settlement: Contributions from Anthropology, Archaeology and Geography*, Pt I, 385–401. BAR International Series (Supplement) 47.

Lee, N., and S. Brown. 1994. 'Otherness and the actor network: the undiscovered continent', *American Behavioral Scientist*, 37(6), 772–90.

Lefebvre, H., 1991. *The Production of Space*. Oxford: Blackwell.

Lesser, A., 1961. 'Social fields and the evolution of society', *Southwestern Journal of Anthropology*, 17, 40–8.

Letesson, Q., 2007. *Du phénotype au génotype: analyse de la syntaxe spatiale en architecture minoenne (MM IIIB–MR IB)*, Ph.D dissertation, Université Catholique de Louvain.

Levi, D., and F. Carinci, 1988. *Festos e la civilta minoica*. Rome: Incunabula Graeca.

Lewis-Williams, D., 2002. *The Mind in the Cave: Consciousness and the Origins of Art*. London: Thames & Hudson.

Lightfoot, K.G., Martinez, A., and A. M. Schiff, 1998. 'Daily practice and material culture in pluralistic social settings: an archaeological study of culture change and persistence from Fort Ross, California,' *American Antiquity*, 63 (2), 199–222.

Lillios, K., 1999. 'Objects of memory: the ethnography and archaeology of heirlooms', *Journal of Archaeological Method and Theory*, 6, 235–62.

Lock, G., and B. L. Molyneaux (eds.), 2006. Confronting Scale in Archaeology: Issues of Theory and Practice. New York: Springer.

Logue, W., 2004. 'Set in stone: the role of relief-carved stone vessels in Neopalatial Minoan elite propaganda', *Annual of the British School at Athens*, 99, 149–72.

Macdonald, C. F., and C. Knappett, 2007. *Knossos: Protopalatial deposits in Early Magazine A and the South-west Houses*. London: British School at Athens Supplementary Volume no. 41.

MacGillivray, J. A., 1998. *Knossos: Pottery Groups of the Old Palace Period*. London: BSA Studies 5.

——Sackett, L. H., and J. Driessen, 1999. '"Aspro Pato." A lasting liquid toast from the master-builders of Palaikastro to their patron', in P. P. Betancourt, V. Karageorghis, R. Laffineur, and W.-D. Niemeier (eds.), *Meletemata: Studies in Aegean Archaeology Presented to Malcolm H. Wiener as he Enters his 65th Year*. Liège: Aegaeum 20, 465–8.

————2000. *The Palaikastro Kouros*. London: BSA Studies 6.

————2007. *Palaikastro: Two Late Minoan Wells*. London: BSA Supplementary Volume 43.

——*et al.*, 1989. 'Excavations at Palaikastro, 1988', *Annual of the British School at Athens*, 84, 417–45.

——*et al.*, 1991. 'Excavations at Palaikastro, 1990', *Annual of the British School at Athens*, 86, 121–47.

Mackie, Q., 2001. *Settlement Archaeology in a Fjordland Archipelago: Network Analysis, Social Practice and the Built Environment of Western Vancouver Island, British Columbia, Canada, Since 2000 BP*. BAR International Series 926. Oxford: Archaeopress.

McPherson, M., Smith-Lovin, L., and J. M. Cook, 2001. 'Birds of a feather: Homophily in social networks', *Annual Review of Sociology*, 27, 415–44.

Malafouris, L., 2004. 'The cognitive basis of material engagement: where brain, body and culture conflate', in E. DeMarrais, C. Gosden, and C. Renfrew (eds.), *Rethinking Materiality: The Engagement of Mind with the Material World*, 53–62. Cambridge: McDonald Institute for Archaeological Research.

——2008*a*. 'Between brains, bodies and things: tectonoetic awareness and the extended self', *Philosophical Transactions of the Royal Society B*, 363, 1993–2002.

——2008*b*. 'At the potter's wheel: an argument for material agency', in C. Knappett and L. Malafouris (eds.), *Material Agency: Towards a Non-Anthropocentric Approach*, 19–36. New York: Springer.

——2010. 'The brain–artefact interface (BAI): a challenge for archaeology and cultural neuroscience', *Social Cognitive and Affective Neuroscience*, 5(2–3): 264–73.

——and C. Renfrew (eds.), 2010. *The Cognitive Life of Things: Recasting the Boundaries of the Mind*. Cambridge: McDonald Institute Monographs.

Malinowski, B., 1922. *Argonauts of the Western Pacific*. London: Routledge & Sons.

Marketou, T., 1998. 'Excavations at Trianda (Ialysos) on Rhodes: new evidence for the Late Bronze Age I Period', *Rendiconti, Atti della Accademia Nazionale dei Lincei IX* (1), 39–82.

Martlew, H., Tzedakis, Y., and M. K. Jones (eds.), 2008. *Archaeology Meets Science: Biomolecular Investigations in Bronze Age Greece: The Primary Scientific Evidence 1997–2003*. Oxford: Oxbow.

Maryanski, A., and J. H. Turner, 1991. 'The offspring of functionalism: French and British structuralism', *Sociological Theory*, 9(1), 106–15.

Massey, D., 2005. *For Space*. London: Sage.

——Allen, J., and S. Pile, 1998. *City Worlds*. London: Routledge.

Meskell, L., 2004. *Object Worlds in Ancient Egypt: Material Biographies Past and Present*. London: Berg.

——(ed.), 2005. *Archaeologies of Materiality*. Oxford: Blackwell.

——2008. 'The nature of the beast: curating animals and ancestors at Çatalhöyük', *World Archaeology*, 40(3), 373–89.

Mesoudi, A., Whiten, A., and K. N. Laland, 2006. 'Towards a unified science of cultural evolution', *Behavioral and Brain Sciences*, 29, 329–83.

Milardo, R. M., 1992. 'Comparative methods for delineating social networks', *Journal of Social and Personal Relationships*, 9, 447–61.

Milgram, S., 1967. 'The small world problem', *Psychology Today*, 2, 60–7.

Militello, P., 2012. 'Emerging authority: a functional analysis of the MM II settlement of Festos', in I. Schoep, P. Tomkins, and J. Driessen (eds.), *Back to the Beginning: Reassessing Social, Economic and Political Complexity in the Early and Middle Bronze Age on Crete. Proceedings of the Conference held in Leuven, 1–2 February 2008*, 236–72.

Miller, D., 1985. *Artefacts as Categories*. Cambridge: Cambridge University Press.

——1987. *Material Culture and Mass Consumption*. London: Blackwell.

——1988. 'Appropriating the state on the council estate', *Man*, 23(2), 353–72.

——1998. *A Theory of Shopping*. Cambridge: Polity Press.

——(ed.), 2001. *Home Possessions: Material Culture Behind Closed Doors*. London: Berg.

——(ed.), 2005. *Materiality*. Durham, NC: Duke University Press.

——2007. 'Stone age or plastic age?' *Archaeological Dialogues*, 14(1), 23–27.

——and F. Parrott, 2009. 'Loss and material culture in South London', *JRAI* ns 15, 502–19.

Mills, B., 2008. 'Remembering while forgetting: depositional practices and social memory at Chaco', in B. Mills and W. Walker (eds.), *Memory Work: Archaeologies of Material Practices*, 81–108. Santa Fe, N.Mex.: School for Advanced Research Press.

Mills, B. J., and W. H. Walker, 2008. 'Introduction: memory, materiality, and depositional practice', in B. J. Mills and W. H. Walker (eds.), *Memory Work: Archaeologies of Material Practices*, 3–23. Santa Fe: SAR Press.

Mitchell, J. C., 1974. 'Social networks', *Annual Review of Anthropology*, 3, 279–99.

Mitchell, W. J. T., 2005. *What Do Pictures Want? The Lives and Loves of Images.* Chicago: Chicago University Press.

Mizoguchi, K., 2009. 'Nodes and edges: a network approach to hierarchization and state formation in Japan', *Journal of Anthropological Archaeology*, 28, 14–26.

Mol, A., and J. Law, 1994. 'Regions, networks and fluids: anaemia and social topology', *Social Studies of Science*, 24, 641–71.

Molotch, H., 2003. *Where Stuff Comes From: How Toasters, Toilets, Cars, Computers and Many Other Things Come to Be as They Are.* London: Routledge.

Moody, J., and D. R. White, 2003. 'Structural cohesion and embeddedness: a hierarchical concept of social groups', *American Sociological Review*, 68(1), 103–27.

Moore, J. D., 1996. 'The archaeology of plazas and the proxemics of ritual: three Andean traditions', *American Anthropologist*, 98(4), 789–802.

Moreira, T., 2004. 'Surgical monads: a social topology of the operating room', *Society and Space*, 22, 53–69.

Moxey, K., 2008. 'Visual studies and the iconic turn', *Journal of Visual Culture*, 7(2), 131–46.

Munson, K., 1972. *Airliners Between the Wars, 1919–39.* London: MacMillan.

Munson, J. L., and M. J. Macri, 2009. 'Sociopolitical network interactions: a case study of the Classic Maya', *Journal of Anthropological Archaeology*, 28, 424–38.

Murdoch, J., 1998. 'The spaces of Actor-Network Theory', *Geoforum*, 29(4), 357–74.

——2005. *Post-Structuralist Geography: A Guide to Relational Space.* London: Sage.

Musso, P., 2003. *Critique des réseaux.* Paris: PUF.

Naish, J., 2008. *Enough: Breaking Free from the World of More.* London: Hodder & Stoughton.

Nakou, G., 2007. 'Absent presences: metal vessels in the Aegean at the end of the third millennium', in P. M. Day and R. C. P. Doonan (eds.), *Metallurgy in the Early Bronze Age*, 224–44. Sheffield Studies in Aegean Archaeology, 7. Oxford: Oxbow.

Neich, R., 1996. *Painted Histories: Early Maori Figurative Painting.* Auckland: Auckland University Press.

Newman, M. E. J., 2002. 'Assortative mixing in networks', *Phys. Rev. Lett.* 89(20), 208701: 1–4.

——2003a. 'The structure and function of complex networks', *SIAM Review*, 45, 167–256.

——2003b. 'Mixing patterns in networks', *Phys. Rev. E* 67, 026126: 1–13.

——2006. 'Modularity and community structure in networks', *PNAS* 103, 8577–82.

——and J. Park, 2003. 'Why social networks are different from other types of networks', *Phys. Rev. E* 68, 036122.

——Barabási, A.-L., and D. J. Watts (eds.), 2006. *The Structure and Dynamics of Networks*. Princeton: Princeton University Press.

Nikolakopoulou, I., 2002. 'Storage, storage facilities and island economy: the evidence from LC I Akrotiri, Thera', unpublished Ph.D thesis, University of Bristol.

Nilsson, B., 2007. 'An archaeology of material stories: dioramas as illustration and the desire of a thingless archaeology', response to Ingold's 'Materials against materiality', *Archaeological Dialogues*, 14(1), 27–30.

Noë, A., 2004. *Action in Perception*. Cambridge, Mass.: MIT Press.

Norman, D., 1998. *The Design of Everyday Things*. Cambridge, Mass.: MIT Press.

Odling-Smee, F. J., Laland, K. N., and M. W. Feldman, 2003. *Niche Construction: The Neglected Process in Evolution*. Monographs in Population Biology 37, Princeton: Princeton University Press.

Olivier, L., 2008. *Le Sombre Abîme du temps: mémoire et archéologie*. Paris: Seuil.

Olivier, J.-P., and L. Godart, 1996. *Corpus Hieroglyphicarum Inscriptionum Cretae*. Paris: Études Crétoises 31.

Olsen, B., 2007. 'Keeping things at arm's length: a genealogy of asymmetry', *World Archaeology*, 39(4), 579–88.

——2010. *In Defense of Things: Archaeology and the Ontology of Objects*. Lanham, Md.: AltaMira Press.

Olsson, G., 1974. 'The dialectics of spatial analysis', *Antipode*, 6: 50–62.

Onnela, J.-P., Saramäki, J., Hyvönen, J., Szabó, G., Lazer, D., Kaski, K., Kertész, J., and A.-L. Barabási, 2007. 'Structure and tie strengths in mobile communication networks', *PNAS* 104(18), 7332–6.

Orser, C. E., 2005. 'Network theory and the archaeology of modern history', in P. P. Funari, A. Zarankin, and E. Stovel (eds.), *Global Archaeological Theory: Contextual Voices and Contemporary Thoughts*, 77–95. New York: Springer.

Ortman, S., 2000. 'Conceptual metaphor in the archaeological record: methods and an example from the American Southwest', *American Antiquity*, 65, 613–45.

Padgett, J. F., and C. K. Ansell, 1993. 'Robust action and the rise of the Medici, 1400–1434', *American Journal of Sociology*, 98, 1259–319.

Palla, G., Barabási, A.-L., and T. Vicsek, 2007. 'Quantifying social group evolution', *Nature*, 446, 664–7.

Palyvou, C., 2005. *Akrotiri Thera: An Architecture of Affluence 3500 Years Old*. Philadelphia: INSTAP Press.

Panagiotaki, M., 1999. *The Central Palace Sanctuary at Knossos*. London: British School at Athens Supplementary Volume 31.

Papastergiadis, N., 2006. *Spatial Aesthetics: Art, Place and the Everyday*. London: Rivers Oram Press.

Parker Pearson, M., Sharples, N., and J. Symonds, 2004. *South Uist: Archaeology and History of a Hebridean Island*. Stroud: Tempus.

Parrochia, D., 1993. *Philosophies des réseaux*. Paris: PUF.

——2005. 'Quelques aspects historiques de la notion du réseau', *Flux* 4 (n 62), 10–20.

Patton, M., 1996. *Islands in Time: Island Sociogeography and Mediterranean Prehistory*. London: Routledge.

Peregrine, P., 1991. 'A graph-theoretic approach to the evolution of Cahokia', *American Antiquity*, 56(1), 66–75.

Pigeot, N., 1990. 'Technical and social actors: flintknapping specialists and apprentices at Magdalenian Étiolles', *Archaeological Review from Cambridge*, 9(1), 126–41.

Platon, N., 1971. *Zakros: The Discovery of a Lost Palace of Ancient Crete*. New York: Charles Scribner's Sons.

Platon, L., 1993. 'Ateliers palatiaux minoens: une nouvelle image', *BCH* 117(1), 103–22.

Pollard, J., 2008. 'Deposition and material agency in the early Neolithic of southern Britain', in B. Mills and W. Walker (eds.), *Memory Work: Archaeologies of Material Practices*, 41–59. Santa Fe, N. Mex.: School for Advanced Research Press.

Poursat, J.-C., 1988. 'La ville minoenne de Malia: Recherches et publications récentes', *Revue Archéologique*, 61–82.

——1992. *Guide de Malia au temps des premiers palais: le Quartier Mu*. École Française d'Athènes, sites et monuments VIII. Paris.

——1996. *Artisans minoens: les maisons-ateliers du Quartier Mu. Fouilles exécutées à Malia: le Quartier Mu III*. Paris: Études Cretoises 32.

——and Papatsarouha, E., 2000. 'Les sceaux de l'atelier de Malia. Questions de style,' in W. Muller (ed.), *Minoisch-Mykenische Glyptik. Stil, Ikonographie, Funktion. V. Internationales Siegel-Symposium Marburg, 23–25. September 1999*: 257–68. Berlin: CMS, Beiheft 6.

——and C. Knappett, 2005. *Le Quartier Mu IV. La poterie du Minoen Moyen II: production et utilisation*. Paris: Études Crétoises 33.

——— 2006. 'Minoan amphoras and inter-regional exchange: evidence from Malia', in *Proceedings of the Ninth International Congress of Cretan Studies*, vol. A1, 153–63. Heraklion: Historical Society of Crete.

Preucel, R., 2006. *Archaeological Semiotics*. Oxford: Blackwell.

Preucel, R., and A. A. Bauer, 2001. 'Archaeological pragmatics', *Norwegian Archaeological Review*, 34, 85–96.

——and S. Mrozowski (eds.), 2010. *Contemporary Archaeology in Theory: The New Pragmatism*, 2nd edition. Oxford: Wiley-Blackwell.

Quiatt, D., and V. Reynolds, 1993. *Primate Behaviour: Information, Social Knowledge and the Evolution of Culture*. Cambridge: Cambridge University Press.

Radcliffe-Brown, A. R., 1940. 'On social structure', *Journal of the Royal Anthropological Institute of Great Britain and Ireland*, 70(1), 1–12.

Radicchi, F., Castellano, C., Cecconi, F., Loreto, V., and D. Parisi, 2004. 'Defining and identifying communities in networks', *Proceedings of the National Academy of Sciences*, 101(9), 2658–63.

Rambusch, J., Susi, T., and T. Ziemke, 2004. 'Artefacts as mediators of distributed social cognition: a case study', in K. Forbus, D. Gentner, and T. Regier (eds.), *Proceedings of the 26th Annual Conference of the Cognitive Science Society*, 1113–18. Mahwah, NJ: Lawrence Erlbaum.

Rathje, W. L., *et al.*, 1992. 'The archaeology of contemporary landfills', *American Antiquity*, 57(3), 437–47.

Raymond, A., 2001. 'Kamares Ware (and Minoans?) at Miletus', *Aegean Archaeology*, 5, 19–26.

Read, D., 2010. 'From experiential-based to relational-based forms of social organization: a major transition in the evolution of *Homo sapiens*', in R. Dunbar, C. Gamble, and J. Gowlett (eds.), *Social Brain, Distributed Mind*, 199–229. London: British Academy.

——and S. E. van der Leeuw, 2008. 'Biology is only part of the story', *Phil. Trans. R. Soc. B*, 363, 1959–68.

——Lane, D., and S. E. van der Leeuw, 2009. 'The innovation innovation', in D. Lane, D. Pumain, S. van der Leeuw, and G. West (eds.), *Complexity Perspectives on Innovation and Social Change*, 43–84. Berlin: Springer Verlag.

Reed, E., 1988. *James J. Gibson and the Psychology of Perception*. New Haven: Yale University Press.

——1991. 'James Gibson's ecological approach to cognition', in A. Still and A. Costall (eds.), *Against Cognitivism: Alternative Foundations for Cognitive Psychology*, 171–97. London: Harvester Wheatsheaf.

Rehak, P., 1995. 'The use and destruction of Minoan stone bull's head rhyta', in R. Laffineur and W.-D. Niemeier (eds.) *Politeia: Society and State in the Aegean Bronze Age. Proceedings of the 5th International Aegean Conference*, 435–60. Liège: Aegaeum 12.

Renfrew, C., 1969. 'Trade and culture process in European prehistory', *Current Anthropology*, 10, 151–69.

——1975. 'Trade as action at a distance: questions of interaction and communication', in J. A. Sabloff, and C. C. Lamberg-Karlovsky (eds.), *Ancient Civilization and Trade*, 3–59. Albuquerque, N. Mex.: University of New Mexico Press.

——2004. 'Towards a theory of material engagement', in E. DeMarrais, C. Gosden, and C. Renfrew (eds.), *Rethinking Materiality: The Engagement of Mind with the Material World*, 23–31. Cambridge: McDonald Institute for Archaeological Research.

——2007. *Excavations at Phylakopi in Melos, 1974–7*. London: British School at Athens Suppl. Vol. 42.

——and J. Cherry (eds.), 1986. *Peer-Polity Interaction and Socio-Political Change*. Cambridge: Cambridge University Press.

——Frith, C., and L. Malafouris (eds.), 2009. *The Sapient Mind: Archaeology Meets Neuroscience*. Oxford: Oxford University Press.

Richards, C., and J. Thomas, 1984. 'Ritual activity and structured deposition in later Neolithic Wessex', in R. Bradley and J. Gardiner (eds.), *Neolithic Studies: A Review of Current Research*, 189–218. Oxford: British Archaeological Reports 133.

Riggins, S. H., 1994. 'Fieldwork in the living room: an autoethnographic essay', in S. H. Riggins (ed.), *The Socialness of Things: Essays on the Socio-Semiotics of Objects*, 101–48. Berlin: Mouton de Gruyter.

Rihll, T. E., and A. G. Wilson, 1991. 'Modelling settlement structures in ancient Greece: new approaches to the polis', in J. Rich and A. Wallace-Hadrill (eds.), *City and Country in the Ancient World*, 59–95. London: Routledge.

Rodseth, L., Wrangham, R. W., Harrigan, A., and B. B. Smuts, 1991. 'The human community as a primate society', *Current Anthropology*, 32, 221–54.

Rogers, D. S., and P. R. Ehrlich, 2008. 'Natural selection and cultural rates of change', *PNAS* 105(9), 3416–20.

Rogers, E. M., 2003. *Diffusion of Innovations*. 5th edn., New York: Free Press.

Roux, V., 2007. 'Ethnoarchaeology: a non-historical science of reference necessary for interpreting the past', *Journal of Archaeological Method and Theory*, 14(2), 153–78.

——and D. Corbetta,1990. *The Potter's Wheel: Craft Specialisation and Technical Competence.* New Delhi: Oxford and IBH Publishing.

——and B. Bril (eds.), 2005. *Stone Knapping: The Necessary Conditions for a Uniquely Hominin Behaviour.* Cambridge: McDonald Institute Monographs.

————and G. Dietrich, 1995. 'Skills and learning difficulties involved in stone knapping: the case of stone-bead knapping in Khambhat, India', *World Archaeology*, 27(1), 63–87.

Rowlands, M., 1993. 'The role of memory in the transmission of culture,' *World Archaeology*, 25(2), 141–51.

——and C. Tilley, 2006. 'Monuments and Memorials', in C. Tilley, W. Keane, S. Küchler, M. Rowlands, and P. Spyer (eds.), *Handbook of Material Culture*. 500–15. London: Sage.

Runia, E., 2006. 'Presence', *History and Theory*, 45(1), 1–29.

Rupp, D., and M. Tsipopoulou, 1999. 'Conical cup concentrations at Neopalatial Petras: a case for a ritualised reception ceremony with token hospitality', in P. P. Betancourt, V. Karageorghis, R. Laffineur, and W.-D. Niemeier (eds.), *Meletemata: Studies in Aegean Archaeology Presented to Malcolm H. Wiener as he Enters his 65th Year*, Aegaeum 20, 729–39. Liège.

Sackett, L. H., and M. R. Popham, 1965. 'Excavations at Palaikastro,VI', *Annual of the British School at Athens* 60, 248–315.

Saito, Y., 2007. *Everyday Aesthetics.* Oxford: Oxford University Press.

Sakellarakis, Y., and E. Sakellaraki, 1997. *Archanes: Minoan Crete in a New Light.* Athens: Ammos.

Sarpaki, A., 1987. 'The palaeoethnobotany of the West House, Akrotiri, Thera: a case study', unpublished Ph.D thesis, University of Sheffield.

Sarpaki, A., 1992. 'A palaeobotanical study of the West House, Akrotiri, Thera', *BSA* 87, 219–30.

Sarpaki, A., 2001. 'Processed cereals and pulses from the Late Bronze Age site of Akrotiri, Thera; preparations prior to consumption: a preliminary approach to their study', *BSA* 96, 27–40.

Schiffer, M. B., and A. R. Miller, 1999. *The Material Life of Human Beings: Artifacts, Behavior, and Communication.* London: Routledge.

Schoep, I., 1999a. 'The origins of writing and administration in Minoan Crete', *Oxford Journal of Archaeology*, 18(3), 265–76.

——1999b. 'Tablets and territories? Reconstructing Late Minoan IB political geography through undeciphered documents', *American Journal of Archaeology*, 103, 201–21.

Schwenger, P., 2006. *The Tears of Things: Melancholy and Physical Objects.* Minneapolis: University of Minnesota Press.

Scott, J., 2000. *Social Network Analysis: A Handbook.* London: Sage.

Sebanz, N., Bekkering, H., and G. Knoblich, 2006. 'Joint action: bodies and minds moving together', *Trends in Cognitive Science*, 10(2), 70–6.

Sellen, A. J., and R. H. R. Harper, 2002. *The Myth of the Paperless Office.* Cambridge, Mass.: MIT Press.

Shanks, M., 2007. 'Symmetrical archaeology', *World Archaeology*, 39(4), 589–96.

——and C. Tilley, 1987. *Social Theory and Archaeology.* Cambridge: Polity Press.

——Platt, D., and W. L. Rathje, 2004. 'The perfume of garbage: modernity and the archaeological', *MODERNISM/modernity*, 11(1), 61–83.

Shapland, A., 2009. 'Over the horizon: human–animal relations in Bronze Age Crete', unpublished Ph.D thesis, Institute of Archaeology, University College London.

——2010*a*. 'Wild nature? Human–animal relations on Neopalatial Crete', *Cambridge Archaeological Journal*, 20, 109–27.

——2010*b*. 'The Minoan lion: presence and absence on Bronze Age Crete', *World Archaeology*, 42(2), 273–89.

Shaw, M. C., 2009. 'Review article: a bull-leaping fresco from the Nile Delta and a search for patrons and artists', *American Journal of Archaeology*, 113, 471–7.

Sheller, M., 2004. 'Mobile publics: beyond the network perspective', *Society and Space*, 22, 39–52.

Shennan, S., 2002. *Genes, Memes and Human History*. London: Thames & Hudson.

Shennan, S. J., and J. R. Wilkinson, 2001. 'Ceramic style change and neutral evolution: a case study from Neolithic Europe', *American Antiquity*, 66, 577–93.

Sheringham, M., 2000. 'Attending to the everyday: Blanchot, Lefebvre, Certeau, Perec', *French Studies*, 54(2), 187–99.

——2006. *Everyday Life: Theories and Practices from Surrealism to the Present*. Oxford: Oxford University Press.

Sherratt, A., 1995. '*Fata Morgana*: illusion and reality in Greek–barbarian relations', *Cambridge Archaeological Journal*, 5(1), 139–56.

——1997. *Economy and Society in Prehistoric Europe: Changing Perspectives*. Edinburgh: Edinburgh University Press.

——and E. S. Sherratt, 1991. 'From luxuries to commodities: the nature of Mediterranean Bronze Age trade', in N. H. Gale (ed.), *Bronze Age Trade in the Mediterranean: Papers Presented at a Conference Held at Rewley House, Oxford, December 1989*, 351–86. Jonsered: SIMA vol. 90.

————1998. 'Small worlds: interaction and identity in the ancient Mediterranean', in E. H. Cline and D. Harris-Cline (eds.), *The Aegean and the Orient in the Second Millennium. Proceedings of the 50th Anniversary Symposium. Cincinnati, 18–20 April 1997*, 329–43. Liège: Aegaeum 18.

Shove, E., Watson, M., Hand, M., and J. Ingram, 2007. *The Design of Everyday Life*. Oxford: Berg.

Sillar, B., 1996. 'The dead and the drying: techniques for transforming people and things in the Andes', *Journal of Material Culture*, 1(3), 259–89.

——and M. S. Tite, 2000. 'The challenge of "technological choices" for materials science approaches in archaeology', *Archaeometry*, 42(1), 2–20.

Simandaraki, A., 2008. 'The Minoan body as a feast', in L. Hitchcock, R. Laffineur, and J. Crowley (eds.), *Dais: The Aegean Feast. Proceedings of the 12th International Aegean Conference, University of Melbourne, Centre for Classics and Archaeology, 25–29 March 2008*, 29–38. Liège: Aegaeum 29.

Sindbaek, S., 2006. 'Networks and nodal points: the emergence of towns in Early Viking Age Scandinavia', *Antiquity*, 81, 119–32.

——2007. 'The small world of the Vikings: networks in early medieval communication and exchange', *Norwegian Archaeological Review*, 40, 59–74.

Sinha, C., 2005. 'Blending out of the background: play, props and staging in the material world', *Journal of Pragmatics*, 37, 1537–54.

Skeates, R., 1995. 'Animate objects: a biography of prehistoric "axe-amulets" in the central Mediterranean region', *Proceedings of the Prehistoric Society*, 61, 279–301.

Slingerland, E., 2008. *What Science Offers the Humanities: Integrating Body and Culture.* Cambridge: Cambridge University Press.

Smith, A. T., 2003. *The Political Landscape: Constellations of Authority in Early Complex Polities.* Berkeley: University of California Press.

Smith, M., 2005. 'Networks, territories, and the cartography of ancient states', *Annals of the Association of American Geographers*, 95(4), 832–49.

Sofaer, J., 2007. *The Body as Material Culture: A Theoretical Osteoarchaeology.* Cambridge: Cambridge University Press.

Soja, E., 1996. *Thirdspace: Journeys to Los Angeles and Other Real-and-Imagined Places.* Oxford: Blackwell.

Spencer, L., 2006. 'Pottery technology and socio-economic diversity on the Early Helladic III to Middle Helladic II Greek mainland', unpublished Ph.D thesis, Institute of Archaeology, University College London.

Stafford, B.M., 2007. *Echo Objects: The Cognitive Work of Images.* Chicago: Chicago University Press.

——2011. 'Crystal and smoke: putting image back in mind', in B. M. Stafford (ed.), *A Field Guide to a New Meta-Field: Bridging the Humanities–Neurosciences Divide*, 1-63. Chicago: Chicago University Press.

Stein, G., 2002. 'From passive periphery to active agents: emerging perspectives in the archaeology of interregional interaction', *American Anthropologist*, 104(3), 903–16.

——(ed.), 2005. *The Archaeology of Colonial Encounters: Comparative Perspectives.* Santa Fe, N. Mex.: School of American Research.

Sterelny, K., 2003. *Thought in a Hostile World: The Evolution of Human Cognition.* Oxford: Blackwell.

Stiegler, B., 2009. *Technics and Time, 2: Disorientation*, trans. Stephen Baker. Stanford: Stanford University Press.

Stout, D., 2002. 'Skill and cognition in stone tool production: an ethnographic case study from Irian Jaya', *Current Anthropology*, 43(5), 693–722.

——Toth, N., Schick, K. D., and T. Chaminade, 2008. 'Neural correlates of Early Stone Age tool-making: technology, language and cognition in human evolution', *Philosophical Transactions of the Royal Society of London B*, 363, 1939–49.

Strathern, M., 1988. *The Gender of the Gift: Problems with Women and Problems with Society in Melanesia.* Berkeley: University of California Press.

Suchman, L., 2006. *Human–Machine Reconfigurations: Plans and Situated Actions*, 2nd edn., Cambridge: Cambridge University Press.

Summers, D., 2003. *Real Spaces: World Art History and the Rise of Western Modernism.* London: Phaidon.

Susi, T., 2005. 'In search of the Holy Grail: understanding artefact mediation in social interactions', in B.G. Bara, L. Barsalou, and M. Bucciarelli (eds.) *Proceedings of the 27th Annual Conference of the Cognitive Science Society*, 2110–15. Mahwah, NJ: Lawrence Erlbaum.

——and T. Ziemke, 2001. 'Social cognition, artefacts, and stigmergy: a comparative analysis of theoretical frameworks for the understanding of artefact-mediated collaborative activity', *Cognitive Systems Research*, 2(4), 273–90.

———— 2005. 'On the subject of objects: four views on object perception and tool use', *TripleC: Cognition, Communication, Co-operation*, 3(2), 6–19.

Swyngedouw, E., 2004. 'Globalisation or "glocalisation"? Networks, territories and rescaling', *Cambridge Review of International Affairs*, 17(1), 25–48.

Taylor, A. S., Harper, R., Swan, L., Izadi, S., Sellen, A., and M. Perry, 2006. 'Homes that make us smart', *Personal and Ubiquitous Computing*, Special Issue, 'At Home with IT: Pervasive Computing in the Domestic Space'.

Terrell, J., 1977. *Human Biogeography in the Solomon Islands*. Chicago: Field Museum of Natural History.

———— 2010. 'Language and material culture on the Sepik Coast of Papua New Guinea: using Social Network Analysis to simulate, graph, identify, and analyze social and cultural boundaries between communities', *Journal of Island and Coastal Archaeology*, 5(1), 3–32.

Thelen, E., and L. Smith, 1994. *A Dynamic Systems Approach to the Development of Cognition and Action*. Cambridge, Mass.: MIT Press.

Thomas, J., 1993. 'The hermeneutics of Megalithic space', in C. Tilley (ed.), *Interpretative Archaeology*, 73–97. Oxford: Berg.

———— 2004. *Archaeology and Modernity*. London: Routledge.

Thrift, N., 1996. *Spatial Formations*. London: Sage.

———— 2005. 'Beyond mediation: three new material registers and their consequences', in D. Miller (ed.), *Materiality*, 231–55. Durham, NC: Duke University Press.

———— 2006. 'Space', *Theory, Culture and Society*, 23(2–3), 139–55.

Tilley, C. (ed.), 1990. *Reading Material Culture*. Oxford: Blackwell.

———— 1994. *A Phenomenology of Landscape. Places, Paths and Monuments*. Oxford: Berg.

———— 1999. *Metaphor and Material Culture*. Oxford: Blackwell.

———— 2004. *The Materiality of Stone: Explorations in Landscape Phenomenology*. Oxford: Berg.

———— 2007. 'Materiality in materials', response to Ingold's 'Materials against materiality', *Archaeological Dialogues*, 14(1), 16–20.

———— Keane, W., Küchler, S., Rowlands, M., and P. Spyer (eds.), 2006. *Handbook of Material Culture*. London: Sage.

Tite, M. S., Maniatis, Y., Kavoussanaki, D., Panagiotaki, M., Shortland, A. J., and S. F. Kirk, 2009. 'Colour in Minoan faience', *Journal of Archaeological Science*, 36, 370–8.

Todaro, S., 2012. 'Craft production and social practice at Prepalatial Phaistos: the background to the first palace', in I. Schoep, P. Tomkins, and J. Driessen (eds.), *Back to the Beginning: Reassessing Social, Economic and Political Complexity in the Early and Middle Bronze Age on Crete. Proceedings of the Conference held in Leuven, 1–2 February 2008*, 195–235.

Toivonen, R., Kovanen, L., Kivelä, M., Onnela, J.-P., Saramäki, J., and K. Kaski, 2009. 'A comparative study of social network models: network evolution models and nodal attribute models', *Social Networks*, 31, 240–54.

Tomasello, M., 1999. *The Cultural Origins of Human Cognition*. Cambridge, Mass.: Harvard University Press.

Tomkins, P., 2007. 'Communality and competition: the social life of food and containers at Aceramic and Early Neolithic Knossos, Crete', in C. Mee and J. Renard (eds.),

Cooking Up the Past. Food and Culinary Practices in the Neolithic and Bronze Age Aegean, 174–99. Oxford: Oxbow Books.

Tomkins, P., 2012. 'Behind the horizon. Reconsidering the genesis and function of the 'First Palace' at Knossos (Final Neolithic IV-Middle Minoan IB)', in I. Schoep, P. Tomkins, and J. Driessen (eds.), *Back to the Beginning: Reassessing Social, Economic and Political Complexity in the Early and Middle Bronze Age on Crete*, 32–80. Oxford: Oxbow Books.

Trachtenberg, A., 2003. 'Things on film: shadows and voice in Wright Morris's field of vision', in B. Brown (ed.), *Things*, 431–56. Chicago: University of Chicago Press.

Trigger, B., 1989. *A History of Archaeological Thought*. Cambridge: Cambridge University Press.

Tsipopoulou, M., and E. Hallager, 2007. *The Hieroglyphic Archive at Petras, Siteias*. Danish Institute at Athens.

Turner, J. H., 1991. 'Dramaturgical theory: Erving Goffman', in J. H. Turner, *The Structure of Sociological Theory*, 5th ed., 447–71. Belmont, CA: Wadsworth.

——and A. Maryanski, 1991. 'Network analysis', in J. H. Turner, *The Structure of Sociological Theory*, 5th edn., 540–72. Belmont, Calif.: Wadsworth.

Urry, J., 2002. 'Mobility and proximity', *Sociology*, 36(2), 255–74.

——2004. 'Connections', *Society and Space*, 22, 27–37.

Valente, T. W., 2005. 'Network models and methods for studying the diffusion of innovations', in P. J. Carrington, J. Scott, and S. Wasserman (eds.), *Models and Methods in Social Network Analysis*, 98–116. Cambridge: Cambridge University Press.

Van der Leeuw, S. E., 2008. 'Agency, networks, past and future', in C. Knappett and L. Malafouris (eds.), *Material Agency: Towards a Non-Anthropocentric Perspective*, 217–47. New York: Springer.

——and C. L. Redman, 2002. 'Placing archaeology at the center of socio-natural studies', *American Antiquity*, 67(4), 597–605.

Van de Moortel, A., 2002. 'Pottery as a barometer of economic change: from the Protopalatial to the Neopalatial society in central Crete', in Y. Hamilakis (ed.), *Labyrinth Revisited: Rethinking Minoan Archaeology*, 189–211. Oxford: Oxbow Books.

Villani, M., Bonacini, S., Ferrari, D. 'and R. Serra, 2009. 'Exaptive processes: an agent based model', in D. Lane, D. Pumain, S. van der Leeuw, and G. West (eds.), *Complexity Perspectives on Innovation and Social Change*, 413–32. Berlin: Springer Verlag.

Vygotsky, L., 1978. *Mind in Society: The Development of Higher Psychological Processes*, ed. M. Cole. Cambridge, Mass.: Harvard University Press.

Walberg, G., 1976. *A Study of the Character of Palatial Middle Minoan Pottery*. Uppsala: Boreas.

Warnier, J.-P., 2001. 'A praxeological approach to subjectivation in a material world', *Journal of Material Culture*, 6(1), 5–24.

——2006. 'Inside and outside: surfaces and containers', in C. Tilley, W. Keane, S. Küchler, M. Rowlands, and P. Spyer (eds.), *Handbook of Material Culture*, 186–95. London: Sage.

——2007. *The Pot-King: The Body, Material Culture and Technologies of Power*. Leiden: Brill.

Warren, P. M., 1972. *Myrtos: An Early Bronze Age Settlement in Crete*. London: Thames & Hudson.

——2006. 'Religious processions and stone vessels', *Proceedings of the 10th International Cretological Conference, Elounda 1–6 October 2001*, Vol A3, 259–71. Heraklion: Cretan Historical Society.

Wasserman, S., and K. Faust, 1994. *Social Network Analysis: Methods and Applications*. Cambridge: Cambridge University Press.

——Scott, J., and P. J. Carrington, 2005. 'Introduction', in P. J. Carrington, J. Scott, and S. Wasserman (eds.), *Models and Methods in Social Network Analysis*, 1–7. Cambridge: Cambridge University Press.

Watts, C., 2007. 'From purification to mediation: overcoming artifactual "otherness" with and in Actor-Network Theory', *Journal of Iberian Archaeology*, 9/10, 39–54.

Watts, D. J., 1999. *Small Worlds: The Dynamics of Networks Between Order and Randomness*. Princeton: Princeton University Press.

——2002. 'A simple model of global cascades on random networks', *Proceedings of the National Academy of Sciences USA*, 99, 5766–71.

——2003. *Six Degrees: The Science of a Connected Age*. London: William Heinemann.

——2004. 'The "new" science of networks', *Annual Review of Sociology*, 30, 243–70.

——and S. H. Strogatz, 1998. 'Collective dynamics of "small-world" networks', *Nature*, 393, 440–2.

Webmoor, T., and C. Witmore, 2005. *Symmetrical Archaeology*, Metamedia, Stanford University @ http://traumwerk.stanford.edu:3455/Symmetry/home, accessed 26. Nov. 2006.

Weingarten, J., 1986. 'The sealing structures of Minoan Crete: MM II Phaistos to the destruction of the palace at Knossos', *Oxford Journal of Archaeology*, 5, 279–98.

——1990. 'Three upheavals in Minoan sealing administration: evidence for radical change', in T. G. Palaima (ed.), *Aegean Seals, Sealings and Administration*, 105–20. Liège: Aegaeum 5.

Wellman, B., 2001. 'Physical place and cyberplace: the rise of networked individualism', in L. Keeble and B. D. Loader (eds.), *Community Informatics: Shaping Computer-Mediated Social Relations*, 17–42. London: Routledge.

Wenger, E., 1998. *Communities of Practice*. Cambridge: Cambridge University Press.

Wengrow, D., 2008. 'Prehistories of commodity branding', *Current Anthropology*, 49 (1), 7–34.

Wertsch, J. V., 1998. *Mind as Action*. Oxford: Oxford University Press.

Wheatley, D. and M. Gillings, 2002. *Spatial Technology and Archaeology: The Archaeological Applications of GIS*. London: Taylor & Francis.

Wheeler, M., 2005. *Reconstructing the Cognitive World: The Next Step*. Cambridge: Mass.: MIT Press.

White, D. R., and U. C. Johansen, 2005. *Network Analysis and Ethnographic Problems: Process Models of a Turkish Nomad Clan*. Lanham, Md.: Lexington Books.

White, H., 1992. *Identity and Control: A Structural Theory of Social Action*. Princeton: Princeton University Press.

White, H. C., Boorman, S. A., and R. L. Brieger, 1976. 'Social structure from multiple networks: I. Blockmodels of roles and positions', *American Journal of Sociology*, 81 (4), 730–80.

Whitelaw, T. M., 1983. 'The settlement at Fournou Korifi Myrtos and aspects of Early Minoan social organisation', in O. Krzyszkowska and L. Nixon (eds.) *Minoan Society*, 323–45. Bristol: Bristol Classical Press.

——2004. 'Estimating the population of Neopalatial Knossos', in G. Cadogan, E. Hatzaki, and A. Vasilakis (eds.) *Knossos: Palace, City, State*, 147–58. London: British School at Athens Studies 12.

——2007. 'House, household and community at Early Minoan Fournou Korifi: methods and models for interpretation', in R. Westgate, N. Fisher, and J. Whitley (eds.), *Building Communities: House, Settlement and Society in the Aegean and Beyond*, 65–75. London: BSA Studies 15.

——Day, P. M., Kiriatzi, E., Kilikoglou, V., and D. E. Wilson, 1997. 'Ceramic traditions at EM IIB Myrtos Fournou Korifi', in R. Laffineur and P. P. Betancourt (eds.), *TEXNH: Craftsmen, Craftswomen and Craftsmanship in the Aegean Bronze Age*, 265–74. Liège: Aegaeum 16.

Wiener, M. H., 1990. 'The isles of Crete? The Minoan thalassocracy revisited', in D. A. Hardy *et al.* (eds.), *Thera and the Aegean World*, III(1), 128–60. London: The Thera Foundation.

Wilford, J., 2008. 'Out of rubble: natural disaster and the materiality of the house', *Environment and Planning D: Society and Space*, 26, 647–62.

Willey, G. R., 1953. *Prehistoric Settlement Patterns in the Viru Valley, Peru*. Washington, DC: Bureau of American Ethnology Bulletin 155.

Wills, D., 2008. *Dorsality: Thinking Back Through Technology and Politics*. Minneapolis: University of Minnesota Press.

Wirtz, K., 2009. 'Hazardous waste: the semiotics of ritual hygiene in Cuban popular religion', *JRAI* ns 15, 476–501.

Witmore, C., 2007. 'Symmetrical archaeology: excerpts of a manifesto', *World Archaeology*, 39(4), 546–62.

Wolfe, A. W., 2006. 'Network perspectives on communities', *Structure and Dynamics: eJournal of Anthropological and Related Sciences*, 1(4), Article 2. http://repositories. cdlib.org/imbs/socdyn/sdeas/vol1/iss4/art2

Wood, D., Bruner, J., and G. Ross, 1976. 'The role of tutoring in problem solving', *Journal of Child Psychology and Psychiatry*, 17, 89–100.

Woodward, I., 2007. *Understanding Material Culture*. London: Sage.

Wright, J. C. (ed.), 2004. *The Mycenaean Feast*. Princeton: American School of Classical Studies at Athens.

Zachary, W. W., 1977. 'An information flow model for conflict and fission in small groups', *Journal of Anthropological Research*, 33(4), 452–73.

Zeimbekis, M., 2004. 'The organisation of votive production and distribution in the peak sanctuaries of state society Crete: a perspective offered by the Juktas clay animal figurines', in G. Cadogan, E. Hatzaki, and A. Vasilakis (eds.), *Knossos: Palace, City, State*, 351–61. London: BSA Studies 12.

Index

Printed in the USA/Agawam, MA
October 23, 2015

625253.005